THEORIES OF
PUBLIC ORGANIZATION

■ THEORIES OF PUBLIC ORGANIZATION ■

ROBERT B. DENHARDT
University of Missouri, Columbia

Brooks/Cole Publishing Company
Monterey, California

Brooks/Cole Publishing Company
A Division of Wadsworth, Inc.
© 1984 by Wadsworth, Inc., Belmont, California 94002. All rights reserved.
No part of this book may be reproduced, stored in a retrieval system, or transcribed,
in any form or by any means—electronic, mechanical, photocopying, recording, or otherwise—
without the prior written permission of the publisher, Brooks/Cole Publishing Company,
Monterey, California 93940, a division of Wadsworth, Inc.

Printed in the United States of America

10 9 8 7 6 5 4

Library of Congress Cataloging in Publication Data

Denhardt, Robert B. [date]
    Theories of public organization.

    Bibliography: p.
    Includes index.
    1. Public administration.   I. Title.
JF1351.D46   1984   350   83-7996
ISBN 0-534-02736-9

Subject Editor: *Marquita Flemming*
Production Editor: *Richard Mason*
Manuscript Editor: *Steve Bodian*
Permissions Editor: *Carline Haga*
Interior and Cover Design: *Katherine Minerva*
Typesetting: *Instant Type, Monterey, California*

(Credits continue on page 198)

FOR MY PARENTS

PREFACE

This is a book about theory, but it is also a book about practice. It is written to introduce theories of public organization to students of public administration and to those outside the field who wish to involve themselves in organizations committed to public purposes. But, more important, this book is an attempt to develop a critique of the mainstream literature in public administration theory based on its inability to connect with the real experiences of those working in and with public organizations.

In recent years, the traditional separation of theory and practice in the field of public administration has become even more pronounced. Academicians and practitioners, who have always viewed one another with some skepticism, now seem to be on the verge of outright hostility. Such a situation is extremely unfortunate, limiting both our understanding of public organizations and our actions within public organizations. To understand more clearly the separation of theory and practice and to begin to reconcile their differences—such is the primary intent of this book.

To achieve this purpose, I first review a number of past efforts in the field, not to present a comprehensive historical review of theories of public organization but to examine representative works that embody the commitments and views of various groups and various times. Based on this review, I then consider several contemporary studies of public organizations and suggest ways in which we might better understand the real world of public administration. Several more generic organization theorists who have made sustained contributions to the field of public administration are included as well.

In my review of these works, I have discovered more consistency among the various theorists than I expected. This discovery has led me to the following conclusions, which are implicit in all that follows: (1) Although there have been many diverse theories of public organization, the mainstream work in public administration theory has centered on elaborating a so-called *rational* model of administration and a view of democratic accountability implicitly based on the politics-administration dichotomy. (2) As a theory of learning, this approach has limited itself to a positivist understanding of knowledge acquisition, failing to acknowledge or to promote alternative ways of viewing public organizations. Specifically, this approach has failed to integrate explanation, understanding, and critique in theories of public organization. (3) As a theory of organization, this approach has limited itself to instrumental concerns expressed through hierarchical structures, failing to acknowledge or to promote the search for alternative organizational designs. Specifically, this approach has failed to integrate issues of control, consensus, and communication. (4) Theories of public organization have consequently appeared to practitioners to be unrelated to their concerns, failing especially to provide a *moral* context for personal action in public organizations.

To fulfill the promise of public administration theory, we now require a shift in the way we view the field, a shift that will lead us to concern ourselves not merely with government administration but also with the broader process of managing change in pursuit of publicly defined societal values. Following such a perspective, which is elaborated in chapter 1, we are led to a broadened concern for the nature of administrative work in public organizations, one that incorporates not only the requirements of efficiency and effectiveness but also the notion of *democratic responsibility*. This shift has implications for the field of government administration and for the larger field of management as well. To the extent that large and complex organizations dominate the social and political landscape, it is appropriate to ask whether all such organizations should be governed in such a way as to seriously maintain our commitments to freedom, justice, and equality among persons. The question is not how we should view the operations of government agencies but rather how organizations of all sorts might be made more public, how they might aid in expressing the values of our society.

For nearly a century, private administration, or business administration, has stood as a model for public administration. Here I suggest that public agencies and the theories and approaches that support them may become models for reconstructing organizations of all types along more democratic lines. The tradition of public administration contains elements of organizational reform that are important for all our institutions. If democracy is to survive in our society, it must not be overridden by the false promises of hierarchy and authoritarian rule. Democratic outcomes require democratic processes.

The connection between theory and practice will be very important in accomplishing this goal. A theory that stands apart from practice and from the values and meanings implicit in practice will never enable us to do more than modify our practice incrementally. It will not permit the kind of broad commitment to the notion of democratic administration that our society requires. In my view, however, the connection between theory and practice can only occur through the process of personal learning. Only as individuals reflect on their experiences and generalize from them will they develop *theories of action.*

Consistent with this view, I have incorporated into this book an appendix on the Administrative Journal. The journal provides a way of connecting theory and practice by examining one's administrative experiences from four different perspectives. Careful use of the Administrative Journal will make the material in this text come to life for the reader. (After the introductory chapter, no case studies are included in the book. The reader is asked to develop his or her own case studies through work in the Administrative Journal.) Just reading or thinking about theories independent of practice will not substantially affect our actions. In order for truly significant learning to occur, we need to demonstrate to ourselves the relevance and meaning of theory in our everyday lives. Theory, we will find, is ultimately a very personal matter.

It is only appropriate, therefore, that I comment on my own learning. Through this work, I have come to believe more firmly that ideas do make a difference. Human action requires human thought, and, without thought, our actions are blind. But, as we recognize that thought leads to action, we must also recognize the responsibility of those who theorize. The connection between thought and action, theory and practice, demands that those who think and those who write share a *moral obligation* with those who act in public organizations. This responsibility, the responsibility of the theorist, has, for the most part, been underplayed in our field. A more thorough understanding of the vocation and the obligation of the theorist is very much needed in our discipline—and indeed in all of the social sciences.

A word of special appreciation should go to those who have been most important in my own learning about public organizations and to those who have provided help and support during my work on this project. Foremost among these I list my colleagues in the Department of Public Administration at the University of Missouri, Columbia, all of whom have been helpful in more ways than they will know. They include Stan Botner, Ed Jennings, Michael Diamond, Jay White, and Mike Sabath. I have also benefited greatly from my association with a network of other public administration theorists around the country, including such poets and prophets as Sloane Dugan, John Nalbandian, Orion White, Guy Adams, Larry Kirkhart, Michael Harmon, Naomi Lynn, Brint Milward, Charlene May, Bayard Catron, Jim Wolf, Cynthia McSwain, John Forester, and Ralph Hummel. I also want to recognize the very important contribution of some administrative practitioners who have been particularly helpful in focusing my thinking in recent months. They include Frank Bailey of the Council of State Governments, Louis Fox of the city of San Antonio, Bob Scribner of the state of Missouri, Earl Forsythe of the Federal Regional Council in Atlanta, Linda Wolf of the American Public Welfare Association, and Jan Perkins, wherever she may be. Furthermore, I also appreciate the advice and commentary of Robert Berne, New York University; Don Kettl, University of Virginia; Hugh MacNiven, University of Oklahoma; Gerald Miller, University of Kansas; and Neil Snortland, University of Arkansas.

A word of thanks must also be extended to those who have labored with me through the actual production of this project in their research or staff capacities: Diane Doran, Gayle Placial, Cindy Zoul, and especially Lil Dunbar, whose expertise amazes us all. Finally, Kathy and Michael Denhardt have sustained me and my interests, while at the same time pursuing their own. It is my hope that a good time was had by all!

Robert B. Denhardt

CONTENTS

1

LEARNING ABOUT PUBLIC ORGANIZATIONS 1

2

THE INTELLECTUAL HERITAGE: MARX, WEBER, & FREUD 20

3

THE POLITICAL HERITAGE: FROM WILSON TO WALDO 40

4

THE RATIONAL MODEL OF ORGANIZATION   69

5

ORGANIZATIONAL HUMANISM AND THE NEW PUBLIC ADMINISTRATION   91

6

THE POLICY EMPHASIS IN PUBLIC ADMINISTRATION   117

7

BEYOND RATIONAL ACTION 150

8

THE PRACTITIONER AS THEORIST 176

APPENDIX:
THE ADMINISTRATIVE JOURNAL 188

The welfare, happiness, and very lives of all of us rest in significant measure upon the performance of administrative mechanisms that surround and support us. From the central matters of food and shelter to the periphery of our intellectual activity, the quality of administration in modern society touches our daily lives. Today your life may depend upon the administration of purity controls in a pharmaceutical house, tomorrow it may depend upon the decisions of a state department of motor vehicles, next week it may rest with the administrative wisdom of an official in the Department of State. Willy-nilly, administration is everyone's concern. If we wish to survive, we had better be intelligent about it.

—*Dwight Waldo (1955, p. 70)*

Free and unfree, controlling and controlled, choosing and being chosen, inducing and unable to resist inducement, the source of authority and unable to deny it, independent and dependent, nourishing their personalities and yet depersonalized: forming purposes and being forced to change them, searching for limitations in order to make decisions, seeking the particular but concerned with the whole, finding leaders and denying their leadership, hoping to dominate the earth and being dominated by the unseen—this is the story of man and society told on these pages.

—*Chester Barnard (1948, p. 296)*

1

LEARNING ABOUT PUBLIC ORGANIZATIONS

Dwight Waldo's appraisal of the importance of public organizations in our daily lives is even more relevant today than when it was written some twenty-five years ago. During that time, public organizations at the federal, state, and local levels have grown tremendously, to the point that today over 16 million people are employed by government in this country. More important, the range and complexity of the issues addressed by government agencies has been extended far beyond what we might have envisioned even a few years ago. Because of the serious impact of public organizations on our lives, when we talk about administration, as Waldo says, we had better be intelligent.

But, as Chester Barnard points out, we must also maintain a sense of the quality of organizational life. Although we often think of the public bureaucracy as an impersonal mechanism, in fact, behind each of our encounters with public organizations lies a lengthy and complex chain of human events, understandings, and behaviors developed in the everyday lives of people just like us. Organizations are indeed the products of individual human actions, actions with special meaning and significance to those who act. The allegedly impersonal organization is the backdrop for a very personal world.

1

For this reason, public organizations may look quite different, depending on our particular perspective. As an example, we often talk about the endless maze of confusion and red tape that seems to characterize public organizations. Certain agencies, despite their alleged interest in efficiency and service, seem designed to prevent satisfactory solutions to our problems. On the one hand, the bureaucracy may seem to be so routinized as to be uncaring; on the other hand, it may seem so arbitrary as to be cruel. Consequently, it is not surprising that many Americans have a rather low opinion of public bureaucracy.

But this picture changes as we become more familiar with the bureaucracy and the people who inhabit it. These individuals are, for the most part, highly concerned and competent, working to make a living and seeking to deal effectively with the complex issues they face. For most, the old notion of the public service is not dead. Working for the government is not just another job; it is a chance to participate in solving difficult public problems. It is the "real world," in which people experience pain and pride, joy and disappointment. It is a very personal place.

In one sense, this book is concerned with what it means to be intelligent about public organizations, but it is also concerned with how our knowledge may be used to deal compassionately with human problems. We will be concerned with a fairly basic set of questions: How can we develop a better and more systematic understanding of public organizations? What do we need to know in order to make public organizations more responsive? How can we employ the knowledge that we have gained to improve the quality of our lives?

■ ———————————————————————————————— ■

THE ACQUISITION OF KNOWLEDGE

These questions have practical as well as theoretical importance. Any administrative practitioner must constantly (though not necessarily consciously) ask what knowledge can be generated and how it can be applied. What do I need to know about this organization, how can I find out, and how can I use this information? In all cases, the manager must make certain choices about the accumulation of knowledge, then make decisions and take actions based on that knowledge. Indeed, one might argue that issues of knowledge acquisition lie at the heart of administration.

Of course, people gain knowledge in many ways. Our understanding of public organizations is clearly influenced by events that occur even before we regularly encounter those organizations. Our experiences in the family teach us much about power, authority, and communication, while our experiences in church and in school present us with information about more structured organizations. By the time we begin to deal with major public organizations, either as members or as clients, we have been thoroughly socialized in terms of some basic patterns of behavior and action. (Denhardt,

1972, pp. 15–19). Nevertheless, there is still a great deal of information we must acquire and a number of different ways in which we can acquire it. We can depend on rumor or hearsay, we can investigate the organization's past practices, we can listen and learn from the advice of others in the organization, or we can let ourselves be guided by efficiency experts and organization development specialists.

Deriving Theory from Practice

In each of these ways, we are constructing our own personal approach to or theory of public organizations; we are seeking explanations or understanding that will allow us to systematically view public organizations, their members, and their clients. The body of observations and evaluations we make may be said to constitute implicit theories of public organizations, in the sense that, although they may be rarely articulated or even consciously considered, they constitute a set of propositions about the way in which public organizations work. Most important, these theories do not exist apart from practice; they are integrally related to the way we act as members or clients of public agencies. Our every action occurs within the framework of the theories we hold, or, more precisely, as an expression of our theoretical positions. In the field of action, theory and practice are one.

This statement seems simple enough, but exactly the opposite characterization, that theory and practice are disconnected, is in fact the one more frequently heard in contemporary discussions of public administration. Administrative practitioners often complain that theorists, from the Founding Fathers to present-day academics, live and work in ivory towers so distant from the world of practice that their principles and pronouncements hardly correspond to life in the real world. Meanwhile, academicians, even those most concerned with the relevance of administrative studies, complain that practitioners in public agencies are so concerned with the nuts and bolts of administration that they fail to maintain a theoretical overview. The gulf between theory and practice seems too great to bridge.

Far more than a contest between academicians and practitioners is at stake here; rather, as we will see, the theory-practice issue is central to the question of developing an intelligent and compassionate approach to public organizations. For this reason, a central aim of this book will be to develop an understanding of public organizations that will enable us to integrate theory and practice, reflection and action. To that end, subsequent chapters will present an overview of those theories of the individual, the organization, and society that have been proposed as guidelines for explaining the actions of public organizations, and it will be specifically asked how those theories and the arguments on which they have been built inform our own processes of theory building—processes that lead to our implicit theories of administration. In the course of reviewing these works, the relationship between theory and practice will be critically examined, and this relationship will ultimately be reconstructed around the concept of personal action.

Different Approaches: Case 1

We have indicated that both academicians and practitioners have sought to solve the problem of knowledge acquisition in public administration. In order to understand in a practical manner the issues they have raised, we will examine two cases that illustrate some of the central topics in public administration theory. In each case, you might begin by asking how you as an observer would characterize the various actors and how you would analyze their relationships with one another. What kind of information (complete or incomplete, objective or subjective, etc.) do you have available? (Typically, students reviewing cases such as these comment that they need more information, that the case did not tell them enough. But, of course, those involved would say the same thing; it just seems that there is never enough information.) Does your asking for more information suggest that you hold a certain view of organizations that would be made more complete with the addition of this information? If your questions reflect a set of assumptions about life in public organizations, how would you characterize those assumptions?

You might then consider the case from the standpoint of those involved. Try to understand exactly what was taking place from their point of view. Specifically, you might try to reconstruct their analysis of the situation. On what knowledge or understanding of organizational life did they act? What information did they have? What information did they lack? How would they have characterized their general approach to life in public organizations? What expectations about human behavior did they hold? How did they see the primary tasks of their organization? What was their understanding of the role of government agencies and those working in such agencies? What was the relationship between their frame of reference and their behavior?

Our first case illustrates the relationship between the way we view organizational life and the way we act in public organizations.

Ken Welch was a summer intern in the management services division of a large federal installation. During his three-month assignment, Ken was to undertake a variety of projects related to the management concerns in the various laboratories at the center. The management services division was a part of the department of personnel, but, since personnel in the division often acted as troubleshooters for top management, the unit enjoyed considerable prestige within the department and, correspondingly, received special attention from its director.

After a period of about two weeks, in which Ken was given a general introduction to the work of the division, the department, and the center, Rick Arnold, one of the permanent analysts, asked Ken to help him with a study of the recruitment process in one of the computer laboratories. Since this was exactly the kind of project Ken had hoped would grow out of his summer experience, he jumped at the opportunity to become involved. He was especially pleased that Rick, who was clearly one of the favorites of the division's chief and who was jokingly but respectfully known as Superanalyst, had asked for his help. In addition to gaining some experience himself, Ken would have the opportunity to watch a high-powered management analyst at work. Moreover, since it was clear that Rick had the ear of the division's chief, there were possibilities for at least observing some of the interactions at that level, perhaps even participating in meetings at the highest levels of the center's management. All in all, it was an attractive assignment, one on which Ken immediately began to work.

As it turned out, however, Ken could not do all that much. Since Rick was the principal analyst, he clearly wanted to take the lead in this project, something that seemed perfectly appropriate to Ken. But, since Rick had several other ongoing projects, there were considerable periods in which Ken found himself with little to do on the recruitment project. He was therefore more than happy to help out when Eddie Barth, one of the older members of the staff, asked if Ken would help him put together some organizational charts requested by top management. Eddie was one of a small group of technicians who had formed one of the two units brought together several years before to form the management services division. Ken soon discovered that the construction of an organizational chart, especially in the hands of these technicians, became a highly specialized process, involving not only endless approvals but also complicated problems of graphic design and reproduction far beyond what might be imagined. Ken was certainly less interested in this work than in the more human problems he encountered in the recruitment project, but Eddie had always been cordial and seemed to be happy to have some help. So Ken drew charts.

After a couple of weeks of working on the two projects, Ken began to receive signals that all was not well with his work. Another intern in the office overheard a conversation in the halls about the overly energetic interns that had been hired. One of the secretaries commented that she hoped Ken could "stand the heat." Since Ken felt neither overly energetic nor under any heat, these comments were curious. Maybe they were talking about someone else, he thought.

A few days later, however, Ken was asked to come to Jim Pierson's office. Jim, another of the older members of the staff, who, Ken thought, had even headed the technical unit, had remained rather distant, though not unpleasant, during Ken's first weeks at the center. While others had been quite friendly, inviting Ken to parties and asking him to join the personnel department's softball team, Jim had seemed somewhat aloof. But then Ken and Jim had very little contact on the job, so maybe, Ken reasoned, it was not so strange after all. Ken saw the meeting as a friendly gesture on Jim's part and looked forward to getting better acquainted. Any hopes of a friendly conversation, however, were immediately dispelled: as soon as Ken arrived, Jim began a lecture on how to manage one's time, specifically pointing out that taking on too many projects meant that none would be well done. Although there were no specifics, Jim was clearly referring to the two projects on which Ken had been working.

Ken was stunned by the meeting. No one had in any way questioned the quality of his work; there were no time conflicts between the two projects, and, even if there had been, Ken wondered, why would Jim take it on himself to deliver such a reprimand. Later that afternoon, Ken shared his conversation with the other intern, who commented that Jim had always felt angered that, when the two units were brought together, he was not made director. Ken hinted at the controversy the next day in a conversation with Rick but received only a casual remark about the "out-of-date" members of the division. Ken began to feel that he was a pawn in some sort of office power struggle and immediately resolved to try to get out of the middle. As soon as he had an opportunity to see the division chief, he explained the whole situation, including his feeling that no real problems existed and that he was being used. The chief listened carefully but offered no real suggestions. He said he would keep an eye on the situation.

Later in the week, at a beer-drinking session after a softball game, the director of the department of personnel asked how the internship was going. In the ensuing conversation, Ken told him what had happened. The director launched into a long discourse on the difficulties he had experienced in reorganizing units within his department. But he also pointed out how the combination of the two units into the division had decreased his span of control and made the operation of the department considerably easier. It was clear that he preferred the more analytical approach to management services represented by the chief and by Superanalyst. In part, he said that the reorganization had buried one of his main problems, or, Ken thought later, maybe he said it would do so soon.

This case illustrates a wide range of issues confronting those who wish to know more about public organizations. What motivates people working in public organizations? How can we explain faulty patterns of communication in public agencies? How can we best understand the relationship between bureaucracies and bureaucrats? How can we cope with, or perhaps even direct, organizational change?

But, even more important for our purposes, this case indicates the central role of the acquisition of knowledge as the basis for our actions. Each of the persons involved here was faced with the problem of accumulating knowledge about the specific circumstances; then they had to determine how that information fit into (or required them to modify) their own frame of reference, their own implicit theories about how people and organizations behave. Each of these persons had to resolve three basic questions about their understanding of public organizations: (1) What knowledge is needed as a basis for action? (2) What are the best possible sources of that knowledge? and (3) How can that knowledge be applied to the situation at hand? Only after resolving these questions (at least implicitly) were they able to act.

Take Ken Welch, the central character in this case, as an example. Among the many categories that Ken might have used to help him understand what was happening in this situation, Ken chose to emphasize those relating to power and authority. His concern (perhaps even obsession) with power and authority provided a special lens through which he viewed the world, a lens that highlighted some events and filtered out others. After obtaining a certain amount of information, Ken concluded that he was a "pawn" in "an office power struggle" and tried to work things out by appealing to those who had authority in the organization. If, on the other hand, Ken had focused on other topics—for example, the breakdowns in communication that often occur in complex organizations despite attempts at cooperation—he would have acted quite differently, probably trying to discover the cause of the confusion and seeking to work out a more effective relationship with his fellow workers. In any case, it is clear that Ken's own perspective on organizational life, his own implicit theory of organization, was crucial in directing his actions.

Different Approaches: Case 2

Let us examine another case, one that illustrates again the connection between the theories people hold and the actions they take, but one that also illustrates several other themes that are central to the study of public organizations.

John Taylor and Carol Langley worked for a local community development agency. Following a rather massive reorganization of the agency in which a number of new programs were taken on, John was asked to supervise a new housing loan program, and Carol was asked to assist him. The program was designed to provide low-interest loans to assist persons in rehabilitating housing in certain parts of the city. Although John and Carol had experience in related areas, neither was familiar with this particular program. To make matters worse, seminars to provide help in establishing such programs had been held some months earlier. John and Carol were simply given a manual and told to begin.

The program involved a number of new activities and took considerable time to set up. For example, it was necessary to train new housing inspectors to coordinate their inspection activities with those provided by the city, and relationships had to be established with the many agencies that would provide information about the applicants being processed.

John soon began receiving considerable pressure to complete the processing of the first group of applications within a very brief period of time. For one thing, the first group of applicants consisted of some forty persons who had originally applied for other programs but had been turned down. Since their applications had been on file in the agency for as long as a year, they were quite anxious to have their applications processed quickly. Initial visits and phone calls from several of the applicants made John quite aware of their feelings. In addition, however, John was aware that this particular loan program would have a significant impact on the community and that, consequently, his doing an efficient job under these difficult circumstances would be important to the agency and in turn important to his own future in government service.

Carol recognized the necessity to do the work as quickly as possible, but she also felt a special obligation to the applicants themselves. She took seriously the agency director's comment that the agency could use this opportunity to help "educate" the applicants about the procedures involved in such projects. She felt that it was very important to check periodically with the applicants to let them know what was happening, for example, with the inspections, cost estimates, loan amounts, financial information, and terms and conditions of the loans. Unlike John, who spent most of his time in the office, she talked frequently with the applicants, many of whom she knew personally from her previous position in the agency.

For each applicant, John and Carol were to accumulate a complete file of information about financial status and about the rehabilitation project the applicant had in mind. This file was to be received and signed by the applicant, then forwarded to the federal regional office of HUD for its action on the loan.

John felt the process could be completed more quickly if Carol would simply get the applicants to sign a blank set of forms that could be kept at the office. When information was received regarding a loan, the appropriate items could be entered on the signed forms, bypassing the time involved reviewing each form with the applicant. Also, this procedure would eliminate the often lengthy process of coordinating several office visits to discuss the material.

When John asked Carol to obtain the signed forms, she refused. Not only was she concerned that the applicants see and understand the materials before signing, she was afraid that getting people to sign blank forms might be illegal. When she talked with John's supervisor about the request, she was told that the procedure was not illegal and had even been used before by persons in the regional office.

John and Carol obviously had different orientations toward the role of public administration in modern society. Similarly, they had different understandings of how one might be effective as an administrator. Consequently, when they encountered this particular situation, they immediately fit the given circumstances into their administrative frame of reference, and this framework became the basis for their actions. John seemed to be most concerned with the efficient completion of the task he had been presented; Carol seemed more concerned that she be immediately responsive to members of the client group and help them understand the loan process.

As we will see, the issues that seem to separate John and Carol are not unusual; indeed, they lie at the heart of public administration theory. On the one hand, government agencies are urged to attain the greatest possible efficiency in their delivery of services, to cut through red tape whenever possible. On the other hand, since public agencies should presumably operate in the public interest, they must be responsive to the needs and desires of those with whom they work. Moreover, one might argue that public agencies bear a special responsibility to help educate citizens to deal more effectively with social problems on their own.

This case also provides an interesting commentary on another issue that we will encounter in our study of public organizations: where we stand considerably influences what we see. Specifically, a person's actions often look quite different from the inside than from the outside. We might, for example, characterize John's behavior as self-serving, concerned only with impressing those who might influence his impending promotion; more charitably, however, we might characterize John as highly concerned for the clients of the agency, anxious to help them receive their loan approvals as quickly as possible in order to ease their financial difficulties. John himself might describe his actions in either of these ways, or he might speak of the situation in completely different terms—for example, he might say that he felt tremendous pressure to get the job done both from those inside and from those outside the organization and that, consequently, he experienced this entire situation, especially the conflict with Carol, as a source of personal anguish. Although we can rather readily describe the behavior of individuals in organizations, it is much more difficult to assess the meaning their activities have for them. Yet, in seeking intelligence and compassion in our understanding of public organizations, both are necessary.

■ _____ ■

FORMAL THEORIES OF PUBLIC ORGANIZATION

We mentioned earlier the number of sources from which we derive our understanding of public organizations. Whether we consciously attempt to develop our perspectives or not, they do develop, and we are guided by them. If we wish to sharpen our abilities to respond with greater intelligence and compassion to those situations we face as members or clients of public organizations, we need to consider more carefully the implicit theories we hold. One way to do that, of course, is to compare our own implicit theories of public organization with those more explicit theories developed by theorists and practitioners, in an attempt to better understand the organizational world in which we live. We can compare formal theories of public organization with our own perspectives, then make the adjustments or refinements that would enable us to understand more clearly our own actions and the actions of others.

Why Study Formal Theories?

There are clearly certain advantages to examining formal theories. Although those who construct such theories entertain essentially the same questions as others seeking a better understanding of organizational life, they do so with considerably more care, rigor, and sophistication. Not that they are any brighter or more perceptive than others—they simply have more time to devote to the effort. Because formal theories are more carefully developed, they reflect both a wider range of topics than we might ordinarily consider and an agenda emphasizing those items that seem most important. For this reason, formal theories provide a benchmark against which we may measure our own approaches to organizational life. In seeking to improve our own understanding, we would be well advised to study the way in which other theorists and practitioners have attempted to construct their own theories. By doing so, we get an idea of the range of questions that we should consider, an overview of the issues that have been debated back and forth (and among which we will inevitably have to choose), and a sense of where we stand with respect to the central questions facing those in public organizations.

Of course, theorists differ with respect to what constitutes an appropriate theoretical base for understanding public organizations; however, at a very broad level, most agree that the purpose of theory generally is to provide a more coherent and integrated understanding of our world than we might otherwise hold. Theory seeks to move beyond a simple observation of facts or a blind adherence to certain values to provide more general interpretations. It does not simply draw together facts, it draws from them; it does not simply recognize values, it reorders them. In this way, theories add a symbolic dimension to our experience. A theory is not simply an arrangement of facts or values but a thoughtful reconstruction of the way we see ourselves and the world around us. It is a way of making sense of a situation. Theories may then be evaluated in terms of their capacity to aid us in seeing our world more clearly and in acting more effectively in that world.

As we have already seen, administrative practitioners have to make choices about the kind of knowledge they need, the ways in which it can be successfully acquired, and the ways in which it may be applied. Theorists must do the same—they must ask what kinds of knowledge they wish to produce, how they can assure that their results are complete and accurate, and how the newly acquired knowledge can be applied. Theorists must make certain choices about what to study and how to study it. And, having made those choices, theorists and their theories are bound by them.

For this reason, we should maintain some skepticism concerning theories of public organizations (and concerning other theories as well). We must realize that theories of public organization, like public organizations themselves, are the results of human activity, particular constructions that may be more or less appropriate for various purposes. All theories emphasize certain things and deemphasize others; they are therefore reflective of the broader commitments of a given culture. For this reason, as we consider various theories, we will see life reflected, but we should realize that this reflection is imperfect, filtered as it is through the lens of the general culture and the specific choices made by the theorist. Consequently, theories may sometimes conceal reality, at other times project it.

The Role of Models

This fact can be illustrated by a consideration of the roles of models in transmitting knowledge. Public administration theorists often speak of their work as the task of developing models of organization or models of administration. In this sense, the term *model* does not mean an ideal form of organization or type of administration but rather a representation of real life (in this case, a verbal representation). One organization theorist, for example, has compared models of organizations to the models of molecular structures found in physics, with the balls being various offices and the connecting rods being lines of authority (Weiss, 1956, p. 2). In any case, the models developed by theorists share some of the same characteristics of other models.

Consider for a moment a particular model automobile. This model car is intended to represent a real, full-sized car. It has the same general shape as the larger car; it has bumpers and windows; and it even has wheels that roll. In these respects, the model car reflects reality rather well. But, in one sense, the model car is drastically different—it has a rubberband motor instead of a gasoline combustion engine. In this respect, the model car distorts rather than reflects reality. Yet this distortion was intentional. The model maker wished to illustrate the fact that the automobile moves along the ground and felt that it was more important to illustrate this aspect of the full-sized car's performance than to accurately portray the device by which it is propelled. The resulting model is then both a reflection and a distortion of reality. For the model to be meaningful to us, we must recognize which is which.

In investigating theories of public organization, therefore, we should always seek to be aware of the choices theorists have made in constructing their theories and the distortions to which these choices may have led. In terms of language, we should always inquire into what is said, what is left unsaid, and what should be said next. This last point is particularly important, for, as earlier discussion showed, theory invites action. Thus, we should not only ask how theories express who we and our organizations are but also who we and our organizations might become.

■ _____ ■

BUILDING THEORIES OF PUBLIC ORGANIZATION

Let us now turn to the choices that theorists have had to make with respect to building theories of public organization. Specifically, it will be argued here that the choices theorists have made have left our understanding of life in public organizations incomplete but that, although a comprehensive and integrated theory of public organization has not yet been developed, a number of very important themes appropriate to that study have been explored in great detail. Moreover, the possibility now exists that these themes can be brought together to finally fulfill the promise of public administration theory—to help make sense of our involvement with public organizations and in turn to improve the overall quality of the public service.

Although this argument will be developed throughout the book, it is appropriate at this point to review some of the ways in which the issue of theory building in public administration has been viewed in the past and to outline some of the ways in which a more integrated approach might be developed. With respect to the scope of public administration theory, at least three orientations can be identified. First, public administration has been viewed as a part of the governmental process and therefore akin to other studies in political science. In this view, a theory of public organization is simply a part of a larger political theory. Second, public organizations have been viewed as much the same as private organizations. In this view, a theory of public organization is simply a part of a larger theory of organizations. Third, it has been argued that public administration is a professional field, much like law or medicine, that draws on various theoretical perspectives to produce practical impacts. In this view, a theory of public organizations is both unattainable and undesirable.

Public Administration and Government

The view that public administration is distinguished by its relationship to the governmental process was held by many early writers in the field and continues to attract numerous followers. From this perspective, the public bureaucracy is recognized not only as being an arm of government but also as playing a significant role in the governmental process. Public organizations are said to affect the development and implementation of public policy in various ways and consequently to affect the "authoritative allocation of values" in society (Easton, 1965, p. 50). But, if this is the case, then such organizations must be subject to the same criteria of evaluation as other actors in the political process. Terms such as *freedom, equality, justice, responsiveness,* and so on are as appropriately applied to the public bureaucracy as to the chief executive, the legislature, or the judiciary. Therefore, according to this view, the body of theory most appropriate to inform the operations of the bureaucracy is political theory, and the most important recommendations theorists might make are those that would guide the formulation and implementation of public policy.

This view of public organizations as central to the political process was held by many early theorists, especially those from the discipline of political science. (Curiously, the relationship between the subfields of public administration and political theory is marked by considerable ambivalence.

Though often seen as the practical and philosophical extremes of the discipline, public administration and political theory share an important heritage based on their concern for effective democratic governance.) Although the roots of public administration in political theory have often been neglected, usually in favor of more immediate technical concerns, some theorists have maintained an interest in the political theory of public organizations, an interest that we will later see especially marked in the "new public administration" and in certain aspects of the recent emphasis on public policy.

Public Administration and Private Organizations

In contrast to this position, others have argued that the behavior of individuals within organizations and the behavior of organizations themselves is much the same, regardless of the type of organization being studied. This generic approach to organizational analysis has also attracted many followers and has indeed created an interdisciplinary study drawing from work in business administration, public administration, organizational sociology, industrial psychology, and various other fields. Proponents of this view argue that the basic concerns of management are the same whether one is the manager of a private corporation or a public agency. That is, in either case, the manager must deal with issues of power and authority, with issues of communications, and so forth. If this is the case, we should expect that lessons learned in one setting would be easily transferable to the other. More important, lessons learned in either setting would contribute to a general theory of organizations. For example, both research on the motivation of assembly-line workers in the automobile industry and research on the effects of new incentive patterns in the public sector would contribute to a more general explanation of employee motivation.

Typically associated with the view that a generic study of administration should be undertaken is the view that the chief concern of such a study should be efficiency. In part, this view grows out of the early relationship between science and business, which clearly emphasized the use of scientific principles to increase the productivity of the organization. But this concern was soon voiced as well in the public sector; indeed, in an article which is often cited as inaugurating the field of public administration, Woodrow Wilson (1887) argued that such a study might permit the same gains in efficiency as those being made in the private sector. In any case, this viewpoint, proposing a generic study of organizations based around an interest in making organizations more efficient, remains an important, perhaps even a dominant, one among students of public administration.

Public Administration as a Profession

Finally, there is the view that public administration is best viewed as a profession, like law or medicine, drawing from many theoretical perspectives. Dwight Waldo (1975, pp. 223–224) has been especially vocal in promoting this viewpoint, drawing an analogy with the field of medicine: "There is no single, unified theory of illness or health, theories and the technologies based on them constantly change, there are vast unknowns, there is bitter controversy over medical questions of vital importance, the element of 'art' remains large and important. 'Health' proves, on close scrutiny, to be as undefinable as 'good administration'." Yet, in spite of the apparent lack of coherence in theory, medical schools purport to train professionals in the field of medicine and do so by drawing on the theoretical perspectives of many different disciplines. Similarly, one might argue that education for careers in public administration should follow a comparable strategy, with our being less concerned with the disciplinary background of certain ideas and techniques than with their applicability to problems administrators actually face. Given that no single discipline can currently provide the kind of knowledge needed by administrators in the public sector, we might hope that all disciplines would contribute what they can.

Unfortunately, this view of public administration as a profession, perhaps even more than the other views presented here, precludes the possibility of a comprehensive and integrated theory of public organizations as well as the possibility that theory will fully match the interests and concerns of practitioners. To say that public administrators must merely draw from theoretical perspectives developed within the context of such traditional academic disciplines as organizational analysis or political science is to say that public administrators must depend for guidance on theories not directly suited to their interests. From the standpoint of the administrator, political theory remains incomplete, for it leaves out essential concerns of management; similarly, organizational analysis is incomplete, for it leaves out a concern for democratic responsibility. In any case, the administrator is left with the theoretical problem of reconciling the two perspectives, a task that even the most talented theorists have not yet been able to accomplish.

Recall the differences between the perspectives on public administration held by John Taylor and Carol Langley. John was clearly more interested in efficiency than Carol, Carol more interested in democratic responsibility than John. As they each presented their point of view, they found it to be in conflict with that of their fellow worker. One question posed by the case is whether the two viewpoints can be reconciled so that a concern for efficiency can be meshed with a concern for democratic responsibility. (Incidentally, in the actual situation on which this case was based, John and Carol were able to reconcile their differences. To fully understand how they were able to do so might entail a theoretical advance of great importance.)

Focusing on Complex Organizations

Before the scope of theories of public organization can be examined further, it is important to note two other tendencies in public administration theory that have limited the range of questions entertained by the field. First, most, though certainly not all, public administration theorists have focused their work primarily on large and complex organizations. Thus, for example, definitions of the term *organization* have revolved around features most clearly associated with traditional bureaucratic structures. Organizations are said to be groups of people brought together to accomplish some purpose; they are seen as directing the activities of many individuals so that some particular goal can be achieved. In addition, the direction of these activities occurs through a series of authority relationships in which superiors and subordinates interact. Characteristically, in these relationships, authority flows primarily from the top down. Bureaucratic organizations are also defined by their structure, hierarchy, which results from dividing labor and clarifying authority relationships (so that each person only has one boss).

Although most definitions of *organization* developed by persons studying large and complex organizations involve some combination of these elements, it is possible to define *organization* in a more open-ended fashion. For example, Barnard (1948, p. 73) describes an organization as "a system of consciously coordinated activities or forces of two or more persons." Note that Barnard's definition not only expands the range of groups we might consider organizations, it also suggests that we focus on coordinated activities rather than formal mechanisms. Although most of the theories reviewed in this book concentrate on large and complex organizations, the wide range of public agencies suggests that we remain open to a less restrictive definition of our subject matter. Moreover, we should be aware that, by taking attributes of large bureaucratic structures as defining characteristics of public organizations, we may unconsciously commit ourselves to a continuation of such structures. If public administration practitioners and theorists choose to study only bureaucratic organizations, they are far less likely to consider alternative modes of organization. Indeed, they may tend to try to fit other organizations to this model. (As we will see later, there is a great advantage to being more flexible on this issue.)

Equating Public and Government Administration

Second, most, though again not all, public administration theorists have largely equated public administration with government administration—that is, with carrying out the mandates of government. Students of public administration have concentrated on those agencies formally a part of government: departments, boards, and commissions at the local, state, and federal level. Paul Appleby (1945, ch. 1) has argued that since "government is different" from private enterprise, so public administration is different from business administration. Certainly there are reasons for thinking that the field of public administration can be differentiated from other similar fields, but is this simply because it is attached to government? When those in public agencies are asked what they see as distinctive about their work, they tend to clearly distinguish their perception of their own work from their perception of work in private industry. For example, they note that government agencies are typically more interested in service than in production or profit. Consequently, they argue that the purposes of government agencies are considerably more ambiguous than those of private industry and are usually stated in terms of service rather than of profit or production. With goals that are more difficult to measure, they argue, government agencies are inherently limited in the degree of efficiency they can attain. Moreover, practitioners point out that the decision-making process in public agencies is pluralistic, and that not only need agency personnel be attentive to other factors in the environment but also their ability to act may be effectively preempted by decisions made elsewhere in the government system. The requirement that government agencies be responsive to the interests of the citizenry places obvious, though certainly proper, restrictions on the decision-making process. Finally, practitioners note that their actions occur much more in the public eye than those of their counterparts in industry. As the old saying goes, public administrators live in a goldfish bowl, their every movement scrutinized by an often critical public.

For many administrators in this country, these opportunities and constraints do indeed set the world of public administration apart. However, there are signs that these features are not simply the result of the fact that government is involved. One could certainly argue that less democratic political systems can be more precise in their objectives, less pluralistic in their decision-making processes, and more careless about openness or accountability. It is quite possible to conceive of totalitarian systems in which administrative activities would appear to have none of these distinguishing characteristics. In addition, many so-called private enterprises are today being increasingly thrust into the public arena and are finding it necessary to modify traditional management practices. Many private and quasi-public organizations are more and more oriented toward service objectives. They carry out their efforts with increasing concern for the impact of uncertain environmental factors, and their operations are subjected to careful scrutiny by both government and the public.

This development suggests not that government and business are becoming more and more alike (although they may be) but that the degree of democratization to which an organization is committed determines the publicness of its management processes. Those organizations that are committed to following an open, public process in the formation and execution of policy will indeed encounter the special opportunities and constraints that we associate with public organizations.

■ _____ ■

REDEFINING THE FIELD

It will be argued here that a theory of public organization may indeed be obtained through a redefinition of the field. To move beyond the restrictions of past definitions, an alternative should have the following characteristics: it should clarify the perspectives of earlier approaches to the field—the political, the generic, and the professional; it should identify public administration as a process rather than as something that occurs within a particular type of structure (i.e., hierarchy); and it should emphasize the public nature of that process rather than its connection to formal systems of government. Such an alternative will be outlined later; first, a definition of the field will be developed on which such an alternative can be built.

Democratic political theory, as typically described, is concerned with the way in which public institutions promote societal values that have been defined and applied with a high degree of citizen involvement and with a high degree of responsiveness to the needs and interests of the citizenry. Democratic theory thus focuses on such issues as freedom, justice, and equality. Theories of organization, in contrast, are concerned with how individuals can manage change processes to their own or to corporate advantage, especially in large systems. Such theories focus on issues of power and authority, leadership and motivation, and the dynamics of groups in action.

Bringing these two perspectives together, this book will argue that public administration is concerned with managing change processes in pursuit of publicly defined societal values. Such a definition of the field suggests that public administration is more than simply the conjunction of several other approaches to study and practice, that it contains an essential and indeed distinctive coherence of subject matter. This being the case, our new definition would permit theories *of* public administration rather than theories *related to* public administration. To the extent that we are able to define our subject matter in a distinctive way, we will be able to focus on the development of a coherent and integrated theory of public organization. Moreover, to the extent that our definition corresponds to practice, it will be of considerably greater relevance to those active in the field than other theories that have thus far been proposed. Indeed, it will recognize the awkward complexity that characterizes the work of the public manager.

This view of the public manager suggests an individual sensitive to the impact of interpersonal and structural relationships on the development of stable or changing patterns of organizations, someone able to recognize and respond to the subtleties of organizational change processes. It also acknowledges that the public manager stands in a special relationship to the design and implementation of societal values, a relationship that provides an ethical basis for public management. "The manager lives in the nexus of a political and an administrative world and therefore is neither an independent actor nor solely an instrument of the political system. In this singular position, the manager accepts, interprets, and influences the values which guide the application of skills and knowledge" (Denhardt and Nalbandian, 1980).

As we examine various approaches to understanding life in public organizations, our definition of public administration—i.e., managing change processes in pursuit of publicly defined societal values—should become clearer.

However, it is important to recognize that such a definition only permits, but does not ensure, the development of a comprehensive theory of public organization. To achieve such a theory and to sort out its implications for administrative practice will require the examination and reconciliation of many diverse viewpoints. As such, the development of a theory of public organization constitutes a major and difficult task not only for theorists but for practitioners as well.

CONCLUSION

With these considerations in mind, we may now turn to some of the forces that have shaped our understanding of the role of public organizations in modern society. As we have seen, all of us construct implicit theories that guide our involvement in public organizations. One way to focus our own theories more clearly and to improve their effectiveness as guides to action is to study more formal theories of public administration. By doing so, we are able to test our personal theories by comparing them with those of others and to consider more carefully how our theories might assist us as members or clients of public organizations.

The next several chapters will examine how theorists and practitioners in public administration have sought to develop more formal perspectives on public management. The purpose will be, not to present merely a historical overview of the development of public administration theory, but rather to examine those ideas that might be of greatest relevance to the eventual construction of a comprehensive and integrated theory of public organizations. Although the contributions of such disciplines as political science and organizational analysis will be noted, attention will focus on the works of those theorists who have consciously emphasized the study of public organizations and, in doing so, have formed the basis for the modern study of public administration.

Our discussion will begin with a consideration of the broad significance of the study of public organizations for individuals in modern society. As discussion in this chapter has made clear, building a theory of public organizations is not simply a matter of accumulating sets of techniques that can be applied to particular situations. To speak of the meaningfulness of our experiences or the impact those experiences have on the values of society is to begin a much more complex study, one that suggests that we be attentive not only to empirical questions related to the management of change in complex systems but also to the larger social, political, and ethical context within which public organizations exist.

REFERENCES

Appleby, Paul. *Big Democracy.* New York: Knopf, 1945.
Barnard, Chester. *The Functions of the Executive.* Cambridge, Mass.: Harvard University Press, 1948.

Denhardt, Robert B. "Learning About Bureaucracy." *Personnel Administration,* May-June 1972, pp. 15–19.

Denhardt, Robert B., and Nalbandian, John. "Teaching Public Administration as a Vocation." Paper presented at the annual meeting of the American Society for Public Administration, 1980.

Easton, David. *A Framework for Political Analysis.* Engelwood Cliffs, N.J.: Prentice-Hall, 1965.

Waldo, Dwight. *The Study of Public Administration.* New York: Doubleday, 1955.

Waldo, Dwight. "Education in the Seventies." In *American Public Administration,* edited by Frederick C. Mosher, pp. 181–232. University: University of Alabama Press, 1975.

Weiss, Robert S. *Processes of Organization.* Ann Arbor: University of Michigan Press, 1956.

Wilson, Woodrow. "The Study of Administration." *Political Science Quarterly,* June 2, 1887, pp. 197–232.

2

THE INTELLECTUAL HERITAGE: MARX, WEBER, AND FREUD

Theorists of public organization, like other social theorists, must address themselves to a particular tradition of discourse, one that at least in part defines the nature of their work. The questions considered by earlier writers must be either accepted, reformulated, or shown to be irrelevant; the omissions made by earlier theorists must be pointed out and corrected. Under all circumstances, theories must be adapted to the changing social and cultural circumstances of the times. Only in this way can theories claim to improve our understanding of life, in public organizations or elsewhere.

Obviously, theorists focusing on public organizations must take into account previous works in public administration theory. But they also must relate their work to the larger cultural and intellectual tradition of which that work is a part. If for no other reason than to justify that their study is an important one that addresses central human concerns, theorists of public organization must resist the temptation to take a very narrow or mechanical view of their topic. Like other social theorists, they must ask how their work fits with other cultural and intellectual efforts of their time and how it addresses the broadest questions regarding the human condition. To fail to do so may itself ensure that their studies have little relevance for the general advancement of humanity.

This chapter, therefore, will examine the works of three theorists—Karl Marx, Max Weber, and Sigmund Freud—whose works have defined the intellectual orientation of the Western world in this century and have presented the most articulate and influential statements of the quality of life in modern industrial society. Taken together, the efforts of these three theorists have substantially influenced the direction of social theory over the past several decades, and, although their work did not directly influence the early development of the field of public administration, they established an agenda to which all social theorists today must address themselves. Thus, before more explicit theories of public organization are examined, the basic orientations of these thinkers and the ways in which they have influenced the development of modern social theory will be reviewed. Moreover, an attempt will be made to integrate their works into a critical standard by which specific works on organizational life might later be evaluated.

KARL MARX

Karl Marx (1818–1883) is, of course, best known for providing the theoretical basis for the expansion of socialism and communism in the twentieth century; in addition, his work provides an important and quite fundamental statement of the conditions of social life in modern industrial society. Marx expresses an intense concern for the restrictions that modern institutions place on the development of human capabilities. Whether or not one agrees with the revolutionary implications of his analysis, the challenge it presents to social and organizational life cannot be ignored.

Marx and Hegel

Marx's efforts are based in large part on Hegel's view of history as the unfolding of reason and of the freedom that reason implies. According to this view, existing circumstances, seen as passing phases in the evolution of freedom, must be removed in order to ensure the continued extension of reason and freedom. The present is compelling, however, in the sense that it occupies our attention, thereby diverting us from the task of expanding freedom. For this reason, the present is more important for what it conceals than for what it reveals. The task of social theory becomes one of unmasking the false appearances generated in the present order to permit expanded freedom in the future. It is through the act of critique that we exceed the limits of the present and permit the possibilities of the future.

To demonstrate the way ideas would play themselves out in the development of reason, Hegel employed a dialectical approach that sees ideas as being produced in a continuous process of conflict and conciliation. In its classical exposition (though one from which Hegel often departed), the dialectic involves an original idea, a *thesis*, countered by its opposite, the *anti-thesis*, or antithesis. From the interaction of thesis and antithesis occurs a *synthesis*, not merely a compromise between the two opposing ideas but an advancement beyond them. The synthesis in turn becomes a new thesis, is opposed by an antithesis, and so on. Accordingly, the development of ideas occurs through a process in which conflict is central.

Marx's specific contribution was to connect Hegel's understanding of dialectical processes to the historical analysis of forms of economic organization, or "forces of production." Marx (in Tucker, 1978, p. 699) saw history as largely a consequence of contending economic patterns that result in conflicts between economic classes: "All history is the history of class struggles." For example, the dialectical relationship between the ancient slave societies and the emergence of feudalism eventually gave way to the development of capitalism. Later, in Marx's view, the contention of capitalism and socialism will lead to communism.

Division of Labor and the Accumulation of Capital

According to Marx, all systems of production involve establishing a set of social relationships for the distribution and exchange of goods and services, although some are clearly more "developed" than others. When the tasks of production start being divided among various workers and specialization begins, the possibility of class relationships emerges. Here a minority group, a controlling group, is able to accumulate profits from the surplus production of the mass of workers. In their position of control, they both dominate and exploit the workers. Such an accumulation of profits is, of course, dependent on the notion of private property. Where all property is held in common, economic and political relationships are characterized by a more communal spirit; but, where property is held by individuals, small groups, or corporate structures, there is no longer any spirit of communalism. The modern corporation is not required to demonstrate its contribution to society; it exists to make a profit.

In this way, the consciousness of any age reflects the basic forces of production that lie at its heart. Each individual and each society develops its own understanding of the world, but this understanding is conditioned by the social and economic circumstances that characterize the particular epoch. Moreover, those who control the means of production also have substantial influence over the dissemination of knowledge through society and, by virtue of this influence, may be said to direct the consciousness of the society. Only those ideas consistent with the interests and perspectives of the dominant class will be articulated in the society. Of course, many members of the society may come to adopt a consciousness or a view of the world that is in fact contradictory to their own best interests. Workers may come to believe that their work should contribute to the accumulation of private property by others, whom they may see as more fortunate and even more deserving. To the extent that the consciousness of a social group is at odds with the interests that group would express, if free to do so, that consciousness may be described as false, a deception.

Transition to Socialism

Marx held that within capitalist societies there exist inherent tendencies that will eventually lead to the transition to a socialist society. Capitalism, for example, is based on an unstable relationship between two classes, the owners, or *bourgeoisie,* and the workers, or *proletariat.* The instability of this relationship will lead to an economic crisis, at which point the workers, recognizing their condition of alienation, will begin a revolutionary struggle to overthrow the existing system. Their struggle will culminate in the establishment of a communist state.

Specifically, as increasing centralization occurs, the groundwork is laid for the abolition of private property and the common ownership of the means of production. In this phase, all workers are owners and receive from the state an amount equivalent to their contribution. But this "dictatorship of the proletariat" is itself incomplete, for persons are still viewed in terms of their partial contribution to the completion of certain productive tasks (Marx, in Tucker, 1978, p. 538). The workers are in a position of control, but they are still workers in the sense of being objectified, alienated, and dependent. Only with the eventual abolition of the division of labor is alienation transcended; at that point, we are not defined by the partial contribution we make to a product that exists apart from us but rather as autonomous beings able to direct our energies and intentions toward whatever tasks we find important.

Industrial Organization and Individual Development

Marx's work has obvious flaws as a prediction of historical developments in this century. In capitalist countries, the growth of the welfare state has more or less moderated the economic crises that have occurred, and, in socialist countries, a considerable degree of repression has continued. However, Marx's analysis of the impact of modern industrial organization on individual development remains one of the most important and influential statements on this topic. In the dialectical movement of economic processes in modern society, the forces of production seem to require an increasingly complex and oppressive mode of organization epitomized in bureaucratic capitalism. In this situation, the individual suffers increasing alienation and depersonalization; we lose touch both with ourselves and with others.

This important argument grows from Marx's basic understanding of the intimate connection between the human condition and the process of production. Marx saw the individual as possessing certain natural capacities, "natural powers, vital powers," comparable to instincts. At the same time, however, the individual is a "suffering, conditioned, and limited creature" dependent on outside forces for sustenance (Marx, in Tucker, 1978, p. 115). Since the objects of our instincts lie outside, we must engage in an attempt to control the outside world in such a way that it serves our interests. "The first historical act is thus the production of the means to satisfy [our] needs" (Marx, in Tucker, 1978, p. 156). Thus, in the most basic sense, people are defined by the work they do.

Growth of Alienation

Marx's discussion of alienation begins with the view that, under capitalism, the accumulation of wealth by the owners occurs only with a corresponding impoverishment of the workers. Those who own land and capital are interested in personal profit and provide workers with only those wages necessary to continue their production. The individual worker's contribution to the productive process is expropriated by those in a position of dominance to increase their own gain. The struggle between the capitalist and the worker over wages and profits is, of course, one in which the owners of capital have a distinct advantage.

Under bureaucratic capitalism, the individual's work is assimilated into the production of standard units, which no longer bear the stamp of the individual. Unlike the craftsperson, who can point with pride to the product of his or her labor and consider it a unique contribution, the assembly-line worker only treats a passing object in a certain routine way. In this process, the quality of the work is no longer important, only the quantity matters, and, to that quantified production, the individual's labor merely adds a twist here or a turn there.

Under these conditions, we no longer see the product of our labor as an expression of our own creativity, our own personality; rather, we view the product as simply an object existing apart from us, and we come to view the work process itself in an objective fashion. In doing so, we become alienated or estranged from our work. "The fact that labor is *external* to the worker, i.e., it does not belong to his essential being; that, in his work, therefore, he does not affirm himself but denies himself, does not feel content but unhappy, does not develop freely his physical and mental energy but mortifies his body and ruins his mind. The worker therefore only feels himself outside his work, and in his work feels outside himself. He is at home when he is not working, and when he is working he is not at home" (Marx, in Tucker, 1978, p. 74).

But, even more important, if we are defined by the work we do, yet that work is taken from us and made into an object, then we are separated from our own sense of self. We are not only alienated from the specific work processes in which we engage, we are alienated from our basic character as human beings. No longer do we work to satisfy our most basic human need to produce. Instead, we see work as something to be avoided wherever possible. We work only because we have to, because we need the money or because we are forced to work. Our labor is involuntary. We come to treat work as something we do in order to supply other satisfactions. Work is no longer an end in itself but only a means to an end.

We are alienated from our work and from our basic nature, but we are also alienated from one another. As our work becomes increasingly detached and objectified, as we come to view our work in instrumental terms, we also recognize others as mere objects in our instrumental world. As this orientation affects more and more interactions, those interactions become devoid of human qualities and better described in the language of the machine, the chief metaphor of industrial processes. As we see ourselves as objects in a system of production, we see others in the same way, and the distance between ourselves and others increases. In sum, bureaucratic capitalism creates conditions in which our alienation from our work, ourselves, and others is inevitable.

That we continue to submit to such a situation is in part the result of our domination by others, those who control the means of production and who appropriate and objectify our labor for their personal profit. For very practical reasons, the slave must submit to the master, the worker to the manager. But our submission may be even more subtle. Our condition of confinement and alienation is accompanied by a particular form of social justification that portrays the existing situation as the way things are supposed to be, as a natural order in which some are to lead and others to serve, some are to be rich and others poor. To the extent that we become captive to this ideology or consciousness, we do not question the circumstances under which we live. Although we may occasionally complain about working conditions or the amount of our pay, we may fail to address the underlying condition of domination and exploitation that is the basis of our suffering.

Social Theory as an Impetus to Action

Yet we do suffer. And occasionally our suffering is so clearly revealed to us that we are compelled to act. The task of social theory, Marx suggested, is to reveal to us how our understanding of our situation has been clouded by ideology and other forms of mystification, to illustrate the conditions of domination that chain us, and to point the way toward freedom. In this view, the critical function of social theory is paramount. Present conditions are examined in light of larger historical processes and of the individual's potential for greater autonomy and responsibility in the future. Critique leads us to action.

This last point is of particular importance. The critical social theory that

Marx devised in an attempt to help us understand the limits of personal freedom in a complex bureaucratic society also demands that we take action to alter our situation. The connection between reflection and action, between theory and practice, is very close. A theoretical knowledge of the true conditions under which we live reveals so much that we are compelled to act to improve our circumstances. Knowledge of the limits that society has placed on us is so striking that we must respond. Theory and practice become one, a connection described by Marx with the Greek term *praxis*. Through *praxis*, we engage in critical reflection on our own situation and that of our society to reveal the basis of social domination and the suffering it promotes; then, recognizing the reality of our situation (moving beyond our false consciousness), we are compelled to act to increase our sense of autonomy and responsibility, both for ourselves and for our society.

MAX WEBER

The German sociologist Max Weber (1864-1920), although best known to students of public administration for his analysis of rational bureaucracy, has had a broad impact on the social sciences. Weber envisioned a sociology that would combine a concern for objectivity with an understanding of the meaning of human action for those involved—a combination extremely difficult to achieve. Indeed, Weber struggled with this issue through many of his works, and his interpreters have taken widely differing positions based on their understanding of this issue. In any case, of the three writers whose work is examined in this chapter, Weber has clearly had the most direct impact on theories of public organization, although even his influence was felt fairly late in the development of the field. For this reason, his work and its extensions will be studied in some detail.

Capitalism and the Protestant Ethic

Weber's most famous book, *The Protestant Ethic and the Spirit of Capitalism* (1930), examines the relationship between social thought and economic action, specifically with reference to Calvinist protestantism and capitalist economic life. In contrast to Marx's emphasis on the relationship between economic conditions and patterns of social change, Weber acknowledged that change could be propelled by other forces—for example, tradition or belief. Importantly, these forces were not necessarily tied to the class position of the individual; indeed, it might be argued that they cut across class relationships. Therefore, according to Weber, the interests expressed in changing societies are not merely economic; they relate as well to the world of ideas and ideals.

As an example, Weber argued that the belief in predestination was so discomforting to followers of Calvin that they sought a sort of loophole in their destiny, a way of assuring that they would be among the elect who enter the state of grace. The loophole they developed was earthly success, and they diligently sought to extend their holdings. The result, according to Weber, was an accumulation of capital and an entrenchment of the capitalist system unparalleled elsewhere. In this case, a system of belief propelled an economic system rather than vice versa.

Although Weber, as a social scientist, did not endorse one economic system or another, he was careful to point out that, from the perspective of technical rationality (i.e., formal efficiency), the capitalist dependence on private ownership, managerial control of the means of production, and reliance on competitive pricing in the marketplace was clearly at an advantage. Especially in contrast to socialist systems of planning, Weber saw capitalism as maintaining the capacity to calculate in formal terms the most rational (i.e., efficient) organization of the productive mechanism. Not that Weber glossed over the possible detrimental effects of such a system, especially with respect to individual creativity and personal development— capitalism and the type of rationality it represented were mixed blessings, capable of tremendous material advances but at odds with a concern for individual prerogative.

Rationalization of Social Theory, the Notion of the "Ideal Type"

There is an interesting connection between Weber's work on the Protestant ethic and his later work on rational bureaucracy. Weber contrasted the ascetic approach to life that seemed to characterize the modern age, and that he seemed to prefer himself, with the mystical spirit he saw elsewhere. To the ascetic, experiences were generally seen as means to an end; for example, the Calvinist worked in order to assure his salvation. The mystic instead seemed to appreciate experiences as ends in themselves. The question of whether human action, including human labor, is best seen in instrumental terms, as a means to an end, lies at the heart of Weber's analysis of the rationalization of society.

But, to understand Weber's formulation of this question, we must first understand his approach to the development of social theory. Although Weber was interested in establishing the scientific legitimacy of an objective social science, he was also well acquainted with the special considerations that differentiate the work of the social scientist from that of the natural scientist. He felt that objectivity in the social sciences can be achieved through procedures designed to eliminate personal prejudice in the research process. Although science can tell us what is, it cannot, in his view, tell us what ought to be; although science can assess the likelihood that given actions will move us efficiently toward our objectives, it cannot say what those objectives should be. These questions need to be addressed in quite a different forum and must be carefully eliminated from research.

But Weber also recognized that values do play a part in social science, with respect both to the way in which the values of individual social actors influence social relationships and to the way in which the social scientist selects those topics that are of greatest interest or significance. Clearly, all actors bring to their interactions with others preferences and concerns that affect their behavior; it is futile to attempt to understand action without reference to the meanings held by the actors involved. The social scientist, then, unlike the natural scientist, must be constantly aware of the way in which cultural values manifest themselves in the activities of individuals. Moreover, since the social scientist is also a social actor, the scientist's own values influence both the topic to be studied and the boundaries of the study itself. In large measure, the social scientist makes these decisions based on an estimation of the cultural significance of the particular subject to be investigated. Those topics of importance to a particular society are those that will most likely be given attention by social scientists. Sociology, according to Weber, is "a science concerning itself with the interpretive understanding of social action and thereby with a causal explanation of its course and consequences" (Giddens, 1947, p. 328). The sociologist is interested in how interacting subjects constitute structures of meaning that in turn guide future action.

This issue has important implications for the conduct of social science, for, while the social scientist seeks objective explanations of the phenomenon under investigation, those explanations need not be of the same order as those of the natural scientist. Indeed, what distinguishes the search for explanation in the social realm is not the comprehensiveness of one's theoretical perspective but rather the capacity of explanations to help one understand the uniqueness of human undertakings. We seek to understand those aspects of our lives that strike us as somehow out of the ordinary. Even if we seek general theoretical frameworks, we do so in order to understand what is unique.

This point leads directly to Weber's notion of the "ideal type" as a way of formulating social understanding. Through the elaboration of ideal types, according to Weber, social scientists can provide an objective analysis of the impact of social events on individuals and societies. The ideal type is not ideal in a normative sense; it does not suggest that a particular social configuration is desirable and should be pursued. Rather, the ideal type is an abstraction and elaboration of a particular set of elements whose combination imparts a special cultural significance. As such, the ideal type is more than just a description of a set of events; indeed, it may never have existed in an empirical sense. Yet it is of conceptual importance in that it contains an explanation and interpretation of a significant component of social reality. Importantly, however, the ideal type grows out of an interest in specific and definable problems. According to Anthony Giddens (1947, p. 337), "the creation of ideal types is in no sense an end in itself; the utility of a given ideal type can be assessed only in relation to a concrete problem or range of problems, and the only purpose of constructing it is to facilitate the analysis of empirical questions."

Ideal-Type Bureaucracy

Most familiar to students of public administration, of course, is Weber's analysis of the ideal-type bureaucracy, a discussion that occurs in the context of a larger examination of patterns of social domination. Weber argued that every system of authority must establish and secure a belief in its legitimacy but that this may be done in many different ways. Variations will occur with respect to the kind of legitimacy claimed, the kind of obedience sought, the kind of administrative staff supporting the authority, and the way in which authority is exercised. Specifically, Weber identified three "pure types" of legitimate authority: (1) legal authority, based on a belief in the legality of certain patterns or rules and in the right of those in positions of legal authority to issue commands; (2) traditional authority, based on a belief in the importance of enduring traditions and those who rule within such traditions; and (3) charismatic authority, based on an emotional attachment or devotion to a specific individual.

Legal authority, which depends on the establishment of legal norms within a group and the agreement of members of the group to be bound by the legal system, is exercised through a bureaucratic administrative staff. Weber's discussion of the pure type of legal authority with the employment of a bureaucratic administrative staff outlines the central characteristics of bureaucratic organization. In this form, officials operate according to the following criteria:

1. They are personally free and are subject to authority only with respect to their impersonal official obligations.

2. They are organized in a clearly defined hierarchy of offices.

3. Each office has a clearly defined sphere of competence, in the legal sense.

4. The office is filled by a free contractual relationship. Thus, in principle, there is free selection.

5. Candidates are selected on the basis of technical qualifications. In the most rational case, these qualifications are tested by examination, guaranteed by diplomas certifying technical training, or both. Candidates are appointed, not elected.

6. They are remunerated by fixed salaries in money, for the most part with a right to pensions. Only under certain circumstances does the employing authority, especially in private organizations, have a right to terminate the appointment, but in addition to this criterion, the responsibility of the position and the requirements of the incumbent's social status may be taken into account.

7. The office is treated as the sole, or at least the primary, occupation of the incumbent.

8. The office constitutes a career. Promotion is based on seniority, achievement, or both and depends on the judgment of superiors.

9. Officials work entirely separated from ownership of the means of administration and without appropriation of their positions.

10. They are subject to strict and systematic discipline and control in the conduct of the office (Weber, 1947, p. 328).

Weber pointed out that bureaucratic organization may be applied equally well in a number of different settings. Although the term *bureaucracy* is most often applied to government agencies, this form of organization is also found in business organizations, voluntary associations, even religious institutions. Bureaucratic organization is so attractive because it appears to be the most efficient approach to controlling the work of large numbers of people in pursuit of given objectives. Weber (1947, pp. 333–334) put it this way: "Experience tends universally to show that the purely bureaucratic type of administration . . . is, from a purely technical point of view, capable of attaining the highest degree of efficiency and is in this sense formally the most rational known means of carrying out imperative control over human beings." Because bureaucratic organization provides exacting structures of authority within which commands may be transmitted, it allows a degree of "calculability of results" for those in positions of authority (p. 337).

Expansion of Bureaucracy

Given the complexity of modern society, Weber saw the expansion of bureaucratic systems to all spheres of human activity as the single most important development in the modern world. Businesses, governments, churches, all seem to organize around the same principles, which emphasize the exercise of authority through hierarchical structures. This development, according to Weber, though stimulated by the rise of capitalist systems, is not restricted to such systems. Indeed, Weber noted that socialist systems may require an even higher degree of bureaucratization than capitalist systems in order to provide a stable economic life. "Bureaucratic administration is, other things being equal, always, from a formal, technical point of view, the most rational type. For the needs of mass administration today, it is completely indispensable. The choice is only that between bureaucracy and dilettantism in the field of administration" (Weber, 1947, p. 337).

It is difficult to determine whether Weber's analysis of bureaucratic administration constitutes an endorsement of this mode of organization or whether his presentation is more a warning of the inevitable consequences of increasing bureaucratization. Herbert Marcuse (1968, pp. 223–224) has argued the former—that Weber's critical analysis ultimately turns into "apologetics" that are quite favorable to the extension of capitalist domination through bureaucratic mechanisms. Marcuse sees in Weber a melding of formal and substantive rationality, in the sense that the technical requirements of continued capitalist expansion come to displace a concern for some larger concept of reason—for example, that associated with notions of freedom, justice, and equality. Most important is Marcuse's argument that Weber sees the increasing rationalization of modern life as the "fate" of modern man, thus implying its inevitability. Such a viewpoint strikes Marcuse as excessively deterministic, failing to recognize that conditions that have been socially and historically constructed can be reconstructed through reasoned and aggressive human action. For Weber to argue that the inevitable future of mankind lies in our submission to rigid, disciplined, bureaucratic orders hardly provides the impetus for efforts to work out a more satisfactory relationship between the individual and the organization.

Weber, however, was not unmindful of the negative consequences of bureaucratic organization, either the complaints of red tape and inefficiency or the more enduring sociological consequences of extended formalistic impersonality. Weber's formulation may be read as an ideal type pointing out those features of the social landscape that uniquely influence the development of society, both positively and negatively. In this respect, at least according to some analysts, Weber was entertaining essentially the same question that occupied Marx: the increasing limitation of the human spirit under conditions of rapidly expanding bureaucratic regulation. Wolfgang J. Mommsen (1974, pp. 56–57), an observer more sympathetic to Weber, makes the following comparison between Marx and Weber:

> Max Weber was just as concerned as Marx was with the inhuman consequences of modern industrial capitalism. Yet he did not conceive them primarily in terms of the objectively (or possibly only subjectively) depressed social condition of the working classes and of their deprivation of the means of production; rather, he had in mind the inhuman tendencies of the social institutions created by capitalism. Capitalism depended more or less on formal rationality in all spheres of social life. It was, moreover, driven by irresistible forces to create conditions which would allow a maximum of productivity and a maximum degree of efficiency. For this very reason, it was pushing all forms of individually-oriented social conduct more and more in the background. To put it in other words, the further advance of capitalism was inevitably tied up with the rise of ever more efficient bureaucracies and an ever greater degree of formal rational organization on all levels of social interaction. Weber envisaged that this process was likely to eventually result in the emergence of a "new iron cage of serfdom," in which all forms of value-oriented social conduct would be suffocated by the almighty bureaucratic structures and by the tightly-knit networks of formal-rational laws and regulations, against which the individual would no longer stand any chance at all.

The only possible escape, in Weber's work, from the pattern of increasing social regulation lies in his hope that charismatic leaders might emerge in positions to control the otherwise enduring systems of bureaucratic administration. The charismatic leader is one to whom followers have an emotional attachment, one with a certain presence or ability to inspire followers to greater endeavors. But charismatic leadership is not simply inspirational, it is creative as well. Such leadership provides a spark that permits societies to grow and to develop. Indeed, it was Weber's dream that, through the direct democratic choice of charismatic leaders, societies might finally be able to transcend the limitations of bureaucratic regulation.

■   ■

SIGMUND FREUD

Sigmund Freud (1856–1939) was the first person to employ the notion of the unconscious in the pursuit of a more healthy mental attitude. But Freud did much more: he developed an understanding of the life of groups, organizations, and societies. We will focus here on this more global interpretation of Freud's work; however, to comprehend this work, we must start with some basic concepts of individual psychotherapy.

Psychotherapy and Personality Theory

The relationship between the therapist and the patient is initiated because the patient vaguely recognizes some personal problem. But neither the therapist nor the patient knows exactly what the problem is, much less its source or its likely cure. However, they can use certain clues to begin to recover and discuss a portion of the patient's life history that has formerly been concealed. Other clues may emerge as the therapist develops an interpretation of the symbols provided in the patient's dreams or in free association. Still other clues may reveal themselves in the patient's personal peculiarities, behaviors such as forgetfulness or slips of the tongue. These clues may be taken as symptomatic of certain conditions lying beneath the surface of the patient's personality.

To begin to reconstruct these conditions based on the clues provided by the patient requires some understanding of the way in which symptoms are related to the underlying conditions they reflect. In other words, a theory of personality development is necessary. Freud's attempt to develop such a theory begins with the supposition that the individual seeks certain pleasures or gratifications but that relatively few of these wishes can be fulfilled. When the wishes of the individual are denied, they are repressed into the unconscious, where they remain hidden and unrecognizable but capable of great influence over the individual's development.

More formally, the *id* is the source of psychic energy, that aspect of our being that seeks to reduce tension by means of the pleasure principle; the *ego* serves to mediate between the individual and the objective world, obeying as it does the reality principle; finally, the *superego* comprises the internal representation of the values and ideals of the society, including matters of right and wrong. In the contending of these forces, the ego plays a mediating role, checking the primitive and impulsive tendencies of the id but also preventing the personality from being overwhelmed by moralistic considerations.

There are various ways in which the ego may respond to the object choices of the instincts (meaning by this both the specific thing required to satisfy a need and all the behaviors that might go into securing that object). In addition to the central mechanism of repression, the ego may engage in displacement (varying the object choice by substituting a new choice for the original), projection (externalizing an internal wish or desire), reaction formation (replacing an object choice with its opposite), and fixation or regression (stopping development at a particular stage or in fact regressing to an earlier stage).

The repression of wishes that cannot be fulfilled creates the greatest discomfort for the patient. To quote Freud (1955, p. 27): "We have come to the conclusion, from working with hysterical patients and other neurotics, that they have not fully succeeded in repressing the idea to which the incompatible wish is attached. They have, indeed, driven it out of consciousness and out of memory and apparently saved themselves a great amount of psychic pain, but, in the unconscious, the suppressed wish still exists, only waiting for its chance to become active, and finally succeeds in sending into consciousness, instead of the repressed idea, a disguised and unrecognizable surrogate-creation, to which the same painful sensations associate themselves."

The role of the therapist is to trace the symptoms revealed in the outer world back to the repressions they represent in the inner world, then to work with the patient toward a more satisfactory resolution than that provided by the mechanism of repression. This resolution can occur in a number of ways. The patient may come to recognize either that the wish should have been accepted from the beginning and actions taken to seek its fulfillment or that the wish was in fact inappropriate and should have been released more easily. Or the energy of the wish may be redirected toward a more creative end. The interpretation provided by the therapist, therefore, is designed to restore a part of the repressed history of the individual in such a fashion that the patient takes corrective action.

Understanding the Behavior and Impact of Group Psychology

Though concentrating initially on the therapeutic role of psycho-analysis, Freud later began to examine more closely the implications of his work for understanding social groups and even entire cultural systems. In his work on group psychology, Freud discussed the "unconscious life of the group," those patterns or relationships that lie beneath the surface of a group's existence but influence the work of that group in direct but often unexplainable ways. He began by noting that the behavior of the group is often quite at odds with the behavior one might expect from a collection of rational adults, appearing to be based more on childlike impulses. Some primitive or instinctual force seems to drive the group beyond the normal bounds of logic or explanation. The "mind" of the group is erratic, impulsive, chaotic, and confused. "A group is extraordinarily credulous and open to influence, it has no critical faculty, and the improbable does not exist for it," Freud (1955, p. 28) wrote. "It thinks in images, which call one another up by association . . . and whose agreement with reality is never checked by a reasonable function. The feelings of the group are always very simple and very exaggerated. So that a group knows neither doubt nor uncertainty" (1955, p. 28).

Nowhere is the confusion of the group more apparent than in the relationship between the group and its leader. Members of groups are highly desirous of leadership, hoping to find someone who can assist them in achieving the fulfillment of their desires; the leader is seen as one who can actualize the fantasy of the group. But leaders and groups operate in an environment that is not theirs to control, so the leader will inevitably be forced by the realities of his or her own situation to come up with either less or more than the group desires. Moreover, leaders often have their own ideas about the direction the work of the group should take, and these ideas may not be at all consistent with the desires of the group's members. In either case, the leader inevitably fails in the eyes of the group and thus (at least symbolically) earns their hatred. Leaders must then live with the special guilt that the group assigns them, being at once the object of the group's envy and the object of its scorn. According to A. K. Rice (1965, p. 11), whose seminars on group relations have recently become quite popular: "Followers depend on their leaders to identify their goal, to devise ways of reaching it, and to lead toward it. A leader who fails or even falters, as inevitably he sometimes must, deprives his followers of satisfaction and hence earns their hatred . . . . This inevitable and mutual dependence increases the need of both leaders and followers to defend themselves against the destructive power of their potential hostility to each other."

Freud himself illustrated the relationship between the leader and the group through the "scientific myth" of the primal horde. This myth imagines a time when a father ruled over several brothers, who simultaneously respected and feared their father. When their fear and hatred of their father became unbearable, they banded together to murder him, an act that led to extraordinary guilt on their part. After living for a while in a fatherless, leaderless world, one of the brothers emerged as the leader, but only after assuming responsibility for the murder of the father and correspondingly assuming a massive burden of guilt.

Of course, this myth contains an analogy to the individual's struggle to overcome the influence of the father figure, the reality-enforcing authority in his or her life. But we can also speculate that social groups and social organizations develop in the same way. As groups form in an attempt to control a part of the world around them, whether the natural or the social world, they inevitably do damage to that world, for which they must assume a certain amount of guilt. But as the leader of the group begins to speak for and be identified with the group, the group members can shift their own guilt to the leader. Then, recognizing the evil of the leader and the guilt the leader bears, the group can only recoil against him or her, thus creating an inevitable tension between the leader and the group. As this tension is repressed into the unconscious mind of the group, it creates patterns that are inexplicable on the surface but nonetheless control the group's behavior.

Groups and organizations, in this view, appear as much more significant to the personal and psychological development of the individual than it might first appear. Individuals use groups and organizations not only to accomplish established ends but also to serve as direct sources of need gratification, to provide a sense of security, a defense against the vagaries of an uncertain world. "Many of the organizations we invent, the controls we accept in everyday life, are not so much constructive attempts to solve our problems as defenses against our own lightly buried primitive impulses" (Rice, 1965, p. 84). This point is extremely important, for it suggests that complex organizations can never be viewed apart from their role in the development of the individual. The organization is not simply an instrument or a technique to be used by an individual or group and then passed on to someone else; rather, the group, the organization, is itself integral to the development of the person, a direct purveyor of influence and values, of hopes and aspirations, dreams and desires. The individual's relationship to the group, the organization, and ultimately the society itself is critical to an understanding of the human condition.

Individual Autonomy and Cultural Constraints

Freud was well aware of this, and in *Civilization and Its Discontents* (1961), he directed his critical insights toward an examination of the impact of civilization on the possibilities for human satisfaction. At its base, civilization implies constraint, the requirement that individuals give up a part of their own autonomy and submit to the restrictions of the group. Although we recognize that we can never be completely happy living a social life, we are attracted to the sense of security and solidarity that the culture seems to provide. This creates a basic tension between the efforts of individuals to achieve some expression of their individuality and the efforts of the culture to achieve compliance and order. Freud (1961, p. 43) indicated the pervasiveness of this tension: "A good part of the struggles of mankind center round the single task of finding an expedient accommodation—one, that is, that will bring happiness—between this claim of the individual [for autonomy] and the cultural claims of the group."

As long as we live and work together, we cannot escape the ambivalence of our relationship with our culture. Again, we find the juxtapositions of love and hate, attraction and repulsion, which Freud discussed in terms of an instinct toward life and an instinct toward death and destruction. We seek life through civilization and the unity and continuity it represents; but we must also abide our instinct toward death. Freud (1961, p. 69) remarked that our "inclination to aggression is an original, self-sustaining instinctual disposition in man, and . . . it constitutes the greatest impediment to civilization." We are left with the conclusion that civilization represents a massive struggle between the life instinct, Eros, and the death instinct, Thanatos, a struggle that can only lead to guilt and repression on the part of the individual.

As Marx put it, we are "suffering, conditioned, and limited creature[s]," dependent on the outside world for the satisfaction of our desires (Tucker, 1978, p. 115). But, as Freud pointed out, our culture, it seems, can only thwart those desires, limiting our freedom and our independence. Consequently, we face an increasingly restrictive social world, one that provides the outward symbols of status and reward but at the same time prevents expressions of our individuality. For us to grow as individuals requires that we act creatively to mold the world to our desires and, ultimately, that we transcend the limitations of that world. But the creative expression of the individual personality is exactly what our organizational society seems to fear most.

WHAT CAN WE LEARN?

How might we be guided in our study of public organizations by the insights of Marx, Weber, and Freud? Certainly, any commentary their works might provide would be indirect, for the study of public organizations was hardly the central task of any of the three. However, from their collective work may be derived certain insights that will enable us to develop a more comprehensive understanding of the role of public organizations in our lives. In the work of Marx, Weber, and Freud, we begin to see some common themes that may guide our own study of life in public organizations, hints at a view of public organizations that puts our involvement in such organizations into perspective.

Clearly, all three theorists see the primary task of modern man as one of finding an effective relationship between the individual and the society. More specifically, given the complexity and the consequent rationalization of society, Marx, Weber, and Freud depict the individual as engaged in a struggle with the forces of organization in society, especially those forces represented by large and complex bureaucracies, both public and private. The study of public organizations in this book involves a similar analysis, although different terms may be used to describe the relationship between the individual and the organization—terms such as *management styles* or *client relationships.* We too must try to place in perspective the crucial relationship of the individual and the society.

The central message of Marx, Weber, and Freud for our study may be that, more than anything else today, we need a perspective for understanding the world and our place in it, a perspective cognizant of, yet not bound by, the impact of complex organizations on our lives. Maybe Marx, Weber, and Freud all intended to argue exactly this—that our personal and collective survival depends on our developing both a basic intelligence and a sense of compassion as we live and work in a society of large and complex organizations.

Controlling our Environment

Why would we want to develop such a perspective? What purposes might be served by our acquiring such knowledge? One reason might be to control our physical or our social environment to our own advantage. For example, we seek knowledge of energy sources in order to provide heat, to protect ourselves against one of the threats that our environment presents. We seek knowledge of weather conditions and drainage patterns in low-lying areas in order to protect ourselves against another of the threats. Similarly, if we know how people will react to certain situations that we can change, we can begin to alter their behavior. For example, if we know that an individual's motivation to work is affected by enhanced prestige, we can behave in such a way as to produce a result. In this case, we seek knowledge to explain causal relationships, to predict outcomes, and to control behavior.

Seeking knowledge for purposes of control means that we are most interested in *instrumental* statements—statements that suggest the proper means toward a given end. If our objective is to achieve greater production, we want to know what steps we can take to lead to that result. This knowledge, of course, does little to tell us which objectives we should be seeking, unless those objectives are conceived simply as means themselves toward some larger objective; but such knowledge can be used effectively in moving toward already established goals or objectives.

Interpreting the Intentions of Others

Control, however, is not the only purpose served by knowledge. We may also seek knowledge in order to understand or interpret the intentions of others. In this view, we comprehend the actions of individuals as having specific meanings to those individuals and as being based on those meanings—that is, we find that all action occurs within the framework of the intentions of individual actors. To understand what is happening in any situation, we must not only observe the behavior of the individual but also understand the motives or intentions that support that individual's action. Some theorists use the term *behavior* to refer to what can be observed from the outside and the term *action* to refer to what is intended by the individual. In such a formulation, it is clear that an individual's behavior as viewed by others can be far different from what he or she intends. Recall our discussion of John and Carol in chapter 1, in which we noted that our perspective significantly affects our perceptions.

If we wish to understand the intentions of others, the meanings that they attach to certain activities, we must do more than describe their behavior. We must interpret their actions, that is, we must seek to understand their intentions in acting. We seek *interpretive* statements, those that allow us to comment on the meaning and signficance people place on their actions. We ask, What was the point? What was he or she trying to do? Through the act of interpretation, we achieve understanding. Interpretation allows us to reconstruct the individual's own outlook on the world; to understand a person is to know the meaning or the significance he or she attaches to events.

Freeing Ourselves from Limiting Perspectives

But we may seek knowledge for still another purpose—to free ourselves from patterns of thought and action that we have come to accept, even to depend on, yet that do not reflect our true needs or interests. Knowledge of this type allows us to exceed the limitations that "reality" imposes on us and to see the opportunities that the future presents. In this view, our lives are seen to be dependent on the acceptance of a particular view of the world, a "reality" that we take to be natural and unchanging but that is in fact the result of a social process by which we have come to believe in its truth. Now, if this process has been biased in some way, so that we focus on one set of events or interpretations instead of another, we may be restricted in the range of possible actions that appear open to us. Particularly where a certain definition of reality has been imposed on us by those in positions of control, that is, where we simply assume the dominant view (the view of the dominant), we will indeed be misled. We will see our possibilities as quite limited when, in fact, they may be quite broad. We may be so taken in by our beliefs that we no longer recognize them as beliefs or no longer recognize their source and are therefore subjected to the most extreme form of control—control that is not even recognized by those being controlled.

Critical knowledge allows us to broaden our perspectives, to see more accurately the conditions that constrain us, and in turn to explore possibilities for more completely and more fully expressing our own potential. As Freud instructs us, such knowledge permits a more complete self-understanding, the basis for self-transformation; as Marx instructs us, such knowledge permits a clearer comprehension of social conditions and opens the possibility of social change. In either case, the knowledge we acquire through critical self-reflection not only permits but indeed compels action in the direction of greater autonomy and responsibility.

There are therefore various reasons we might wish to acquire knowledge and various uses we might make of instrumental, interpretive, and critical studies. In later chapters, we will find that each of these three approaches is reflected in an approach to practical and to scientific understanding and that these approaches direct our attention in different ways. For now, the lesson that we learn from Marx, Weber, and Freud is that appearances mask realities no less than realities mask appearances. What seems to be objective reality may be an illusion that, when penetrated, may reveal conditions that we find extremely limiting, both to ourselves and to our society. More important, we learn that modern societies encourage us to view the world in instrumental terms and that to resist such a view is very difficult—but at the same time very important. Under these conditions, what guidance would we wish from theories of public organization?

■ —— ■

REFERENCES

Freud, Sigmund. *The Origin and Development of Psychoanalysis.* Chicago: Regnerry, 1955.

Freud, Sigmund. *Civilization and Its Discontents.* New York: Norton, 1961.

Giddens, Anthony. *Capitalism and Modern Social Theory.* Cambridge, England: Cambridge University Press, 1947.

Marcuse, Herbert. "Industrialism and Capitalism in the Work of Max Weber." In *Negations: Essays in Critical Theory,* translated by Jeremy J. Shapiro, pp. 201–226. Boston: Beacon Press, 1968.

Mommsen, Wolfgang J. *The Age of Bureaucracy.* New York: Harper & Row, 1974.

Rice, A. K. *Learning for Leadership.* London: Tavistock, 1965.

Tucker, Robert C., ed. *The Marx-Engels Reader.* New York: Norton, 1978.

Weber, Max. *The Protestant Ethic and the Spirit of Capitalism.* London: Allen & Unwin, 1930.

Weber, Max. *The Theory of Social and Economic Organization.* New York: Oxford University Press, 1947.

3

THE POLITICAL HERITAGE: FROM WILSON TO WALDO

If public organizations are by definition committed to the pursuit of publicly defined societal values, their members carry a special burden that others do not—always to act in keeping with democratic norms. Whether they assist in the development of public purposes or facilitate their achievement, members must always be attentive to those values that give public organizations their distinctive character. Public administrators, in this view, must help to assure that the central political commitments of the society are extended, and, in part, they must do this by the example of their own work. For these reasons, the study of public administration must embrace not only social theory but also political theory, an understanding of the ways in which public organizations contribute to the growth of a democratic society.

Curiously enough, although such a political theory of public organizations would seem to be the single most important topic for students of public organizations to consider, concerns other than those we normally associate with democratic political theory have historically been given precedence. Issues of freedom and justice, equality and participation, have often taken a back seat to issues of efficiency, technique, and control. Even so, a political theory of public organizations has been constructed, perhaps as much by default as by design.

This was the significant message in Dwight Waldo's perceptive work, *The Administrative State* (1948). In this book, Waldo proposed to trace the development of the field of public administration in the first part of this century from the perspective of political theory and the history of ideas. "Looking closely at the literature of public administration through the lens of Political Theory," he later reflected, "it seemed to me plainly true that, paradoxically, it had a matrix of political theory: paradoxically because those producing the literature frequently, characteristically, presumed or stated that they were getting away from mere pleasant cloudgazing and were addressing themselves directly to the world of facts and the hard, important business of how modern government does and should perform its functions" (1965, p. 6). As viewed by Waldo, the early writers commented on such highly theoretical questions as the good life, criteria for public action, and who should rule. They were confronted with questions that had important theoretical implications, and their answers constituted a form of political theory, a political theory of public organizations. Indeed, as Waldo argued, that political theory is perhaps the most important of our age, for its specifies the commitments we are willing to make in the conduct of public affairs in an organizational society.

The early writings on public administration not only constituted a political theory of public organizations but also set a tone for later work in the field of public administration. By virtue of what was included or excluded by the early writers, public administration and its relationship to the larger political system were defined. For this reason, an examination of the works of the early writers and their influence on administrative theory and practice will provide us with a better sense of the central metaphors that continue to guide our understanding of public organizations.

■ ⎯⎯⎯⎯⎯⎯⎯⎯⎯⎯⎯⎯⎯⎯⎯⎯⎯⎯⎯⎯⎯⎯⎯⎯⎯⎯⎯⎯⎯⎯ ■

BEGINNINGS OF PUBLIC ADMINISTRATION THEORY

Even before the formal study of public administration emerged around the turn of the century, many theorists and practitioners had commented on the role of administrative agencies in performing the work of the state. Most noteworthy in the early days of the country's history were the viewpoints expressed by Alexander Hamilton and Thomas Jefferson. Hamilton's administrative theory, as expressed in the Federalist papers and later exemplified in his own career as a member of the executive branch, argued on behalf of a strong national government with considerable power residing in the executive. Leonard White (1948, p. 510) describes this position as growing directly from certain elitist tendencies among the Federalists generally: "The Federalist preference for the executive branch was a faithful reflection of their distrust of the people. An intelligent perception of sound public policy, in their view, could come only from well-educated men of affairs, men with trained minds and broad experience—in short from the upper classes."

But Hamilton also preferred executive prerogative on the grounds of administrative principle. In this view, action, to be effective, must have clear direction, and such direction can come from only one source, a unified executive. Whereas dissent and discussion are important in legislative deliberations, the executive branch cannot function effectively without unity of command, one final arbitrator whose decisions will be accepted by all. Moreover, a single executive can be held responsible for his or her actions; a single center of power means a single center of responsibility. This preference for a strong national executive did not preclude Hamilton from envisioning some decentralization at the state and local levels; however, it did clearly indicate a certain structure of administration at the national level (Ostrom, 1973, pp. 81–88).

In contrast, Jefferson saw the problem of administration and organization as directly connected to the problem of extending the notion of democracy. Lynton Caldwell (1944, pp. 23–30) points out two fundamental principles central to Jefferson's administrative theory: "government must be decentralized to the extent that each citizen may personally participate in the administration of public affairs and . . . government must serve to school the people in political wisdom and must train a self-reliant citizenry." In contrast to the wide discretion of the executive proposed by Hamilton, Jefferson argued on behalf of strict legal and constitutional limits on the power of the executive branch, limits that would ensure the responsibility of officials. Although it is certainly possible to describe the Jeffersonians as confirming rather than denying the Federalist view of the national administrative system in practice, it is also true that Jefferson's views set a tone or spirit that was to significantly influence the development of public organizations over the years. Indeed, one might argue that the essentials of the Hamiltonian and Jeffersonian views underlie important conflicts in public administration theory today.

Extending Democracy

Although there were certainly important developments in public administration over the next century or so, the detailed and self-conscious study of public administration did not emerge until the late 1800s, and when it did, it was very clearly a reflection of the particular character of the political system at that time. During this period, the Jeffersonian commitment to democracy was quite strong, perhaps even stronger than the Founding Fathers (certainly Hamilton) had intended. As a consequence, a highly decentralized view of government had developed. Local governments, including cities, counties, and special districts, had considerable autonomy in their operations. The various branches of government were also separated from one another—for example, through elected rather than appointed judgeships—and were consequently able to act with some independence. Although attractive for many reasons, such a view also led to problems. Too often, autonomy became arrogance, insulation became isolation, and independence became caprice. Lubricated by the remaining influence of the spoils system, government was not only dispersed but disorganized and sometimes even downright dishonest.

Early students of public administration were basically reformers bent on restoring a sense of decency to public government. But, in a larger sense, they saw their mission as extending democracy, as demonstrating that democracy could be maintained under modern conditions. These writers, either explicitly or implicitly, were political theorists, engaged in the theoretical task of outlining a workable democratic system. For this reason, many early statements make reference to the importance of normative issues in the study of public administration. For example, Leonard D. White (1948, p. 10), whose *Introduction to the Study of Public Administration* was for many years the standard textbook in the field, remarked that "the study of public administration . . . needs to be related to the broad generalizations of political theory concerned with such matters as justice, liberty, obedience, and the role of the state in human affairs." At the same time, these writers were practical people concerned with establishing specific mechanisms that would enable them to respond to the increasingly urbanized technological society in which they found themselves. To engage in a more formal study of the growing administrative operations of government might be one way in which this objective could be met.

Wilson's "Businesslike" Approach

The general tenor of such a study of public administration was set in an essay by Woodrow Wilson (1887). Wilson argued that students of politics prior to that time had been largely preoccupied with constitutional questions and had ignored the active operations of government agencies. But, especially with the growth of government, these operations were becoming both visible and troublesome. For this reason, Wilson argued, "It is getting harder to run a constitution than to frame one" (p. 200). As part of the new study of public administration that he endorsed, Wilson suggested that stable principles of administrative management, "businesslike" principles, should be permitted to guide the operations of public agencies. "The field of administration is a field of business" (p. 209). In order to achieve some measure of efficiency in the operations of government, Wilson suggested that we look to the private sector for models of administrative management.

This latter supposition arose in large part from the experience of business organizations during this period and from the general thrust of research into scientific management in business. The study of business administration had developed somewhat earlier in a society of rapidly expanding business characterized by extreme managerial prerogatives and vast social influence. Moreover, in keeping with the emerging scientism of the age, business fully embraced technology, applying it not only to machines but to human beings as well. It is not accidental that early business organizations were built like machines; the machine is the epitome of efficiency and was therefore considered the appropriate model for human organizations as well as for production. These features easily carried over into the public sector.

From the field of business, Wilson drew the lesson that administrative efficiency as well as administrative responsibility would be enhanced through the establishment of single centers of power controlling basically hierarchical structures. In Wilson's view, and in the view of many others who wrote in the early period, governmental power needed to take on a more integrated and centralized structure. According to Wilson, the responsibility for public action should be located in a single authority in order to assure trustworthiness and efficient operations. Wilson saw no real problem with the possible inconsistency of this view with democratic norms of decentralization and public participation. To the contrary, he wrote, "there is no danger in power, if only it be not irresponsible; . . . if it be centered in heads of the service and in heads of branches of the service, it is easily watched and brought to book" (pp. 213–214).

One might, of course, question whether the traditional business interest in productive efficiency achieved through hierarchical organization was so easily transferable to the public sector, distinguished as it is by more ambiguous purposes, by more pluralistic decision-making processes, and by the necessity of public oversight. Yet Wilson's view was clear: in pursuit of democracy, government must follow the model of business, even where it appears nondemocratic. As Waldo (1948, p. 200) was to later summarize the developing orthodoxy of the period following Wilson's work: "The means and measurements of efficiency, it was felt and strongly stated, were the same for all administration: democracy, if it were to survive, could not afford to ignore the lessons of centralization, hierarchy, and discipline."

For administrative agencies to work efficiently and in a businesslike manner, it was necessary to insulate them from the vagaries of the political process. This view was the basis for Wilson's well-known distinction between politics and administration: "Administration lies outside the proper sphere of politics. Administrative questions are not political questions. Although politics sets the tasks for administration, it should not be suffered to manipulate its offices" (1887, p. 210). In the realm of politics, issues were to be debated, and decisions about the direction of public policy were to be made; in the realm of administration, policies were to be implemented by a neutral and professional bureaucracy. Through this distinction, Wilson felt, we could achieve a proper balance between democratic responsiveness and administrative competence.

In Wilson's work, we find two prominent themes that have served as a focus for the study of public administration throughout most of its history: the supposed distinction between politics (or policy) and administration and the search for scientific principles of administrative management that would assist in attaining organizational efficiency. As we will see, even today these isues continue to be central to the mainstream or orthodox interpretation of public administration.

■ _____ ■

POLITICS-ADMINISTRATION

An examination of early trends in the study of public administration reveals two interesting, though somewhat contradictory, streams of thought. There is the view that public administration is made distinctive by its relationship to the governmental process and that this relationship requires that special attention be paid to such normative concerns as justice, freedom, and responsibility. There is also the view that, after decisions are made in a democratic manner, their implementation depends on the same managerial techniques employed in private industry. The eventual ascendancy of the latter viewpoint is represented by the politics-administration dichotomy, whose symbolic importance cannot be overemphasized.

As is often the case, however, the symbol somewhat exceeds the reality. Many who have commented on the earliest writings in public administration have placed far too much emphasis on the politics-administration dichotomy as a key to the early theoretical writings. For example, Howard McCurdy (1977, p. 19) describes the old politics-administration dichotomy as "the holy writ of American public administration." True enough, the politics-administration dichotomy was mentioned by a number of early writers, yet it was hardly "holy writ." Moreover, the dichotomy was never as sharply drawn as many later commentators like to believe.

Especially at the local level, where the council-manager form of government assigned the policy role to the council and the administrative role to the city manager, a fairly sharp distinction seemed to be proposed. Yet, even here, areas of responsibility often overlapped. Surprisingly, the interaction of politics and administration actually characterizes two formal works usually cited as advocating a strict politics-administration dichotomy, Frank Goodnow's *Policy and Administration* (1900) and W. F. Willoughby's *The Government of Modern States* (1935), both of which take a more carefully reasoned position than is generally attributed to them. In fact, Goodnow's argument can be read as fundamentally opposed to the separation of governmental functions into the executive, the legislative, and the judicial branches.

Reconciling Theory and Reality

Goodnow's book is first of all a critique of the formalist view of government, which holds that the study of the Constitution or other legal requirements is sufficient to understand the operations of government actors. To the contrary, he argues, the strict separation of powers contained in the United States Constitution has been violated many times and for good reason. Therefore, it is appropriate to rethink the formal theory of separation of powers so that our theory might more closely match our practice. Specifically, the theory of assigning to the legislature the role of making policy and to the executive the role of carrying it out is not reflected in the actual practice of government.

True enough, as Goodnow points out, it is possible to distinguish, for analytical purposes, those operations of the state that are essential to the "expression of its will" and those necessary to the "execution of that will" (p. 15). Politics is concerned with the expression of the will of the state in policies; administration is concerned with the execution of that will. But, "while the two primary functions of government are susceptible of differentiation, the organs of government to which the discharge of these functions is entrusted cannot be clearly defined" (p. 16). Although one organ of government, the legislature, is primarily concerned with expressing the will of the state, it is not the only organ of government to do so, nor does that activity preclude its acting as well to affect the execution of that will. Similarly, agents of the government charged with executing the will of the state often have enough discretionary power that they may be said to express the will of the state.

Goodnow's comments on the relationship between central and local government responsibilities are also instructive. He notes that legislative centralization is often accompanied by administrative decentralization. In such cases, the local administrative agency may "change the will of the state as expressed by the body representing the state as a whole and so adapt it to what are believed to be the needs of the local community" (p. 50). Although Goodnow specifically recommends somewhat greater administrative centralization (accompanied by greater legislative autonomy for local governments), his analysis of this point is again in direct contrast to a strict separation of politics and administration. His point is clear: the formal legal bases for the division of governmental responsibilities, both horizontally and vertically, are substantially altered by governmental practice.

Extending the Branches of Government

Many of the same comments apply to W. F. Willoughby's examination of the various functions of government. Although, in an earlier book (Willoughby and Willoughby, 1891, p. 42) he commented that "the duties of the executive are to enforce and apply the laws of the nation after they are made by the legislature and interpreted by the courts," by the time of his 1919 text (revised 1935), Willoughby recognizes certain difficulties in this position. Here he contends that there are not just three branches of government, as generally conceived, but instead five classes of governmental powers: the legislative, judicial, executive, electorate, and administrative branches. In addition to the three traditional branches, Willoughby argues that the electorate should be recognized because the source of authority in a democracy shifts from the ruler to the people. In addition, the electorate has its own "definite and distinguishable functions" (1919, p. 217). Similarly, the administrative branch should be recognized, since there exists a "difference between the function of seeing that laws are enforced and that of actually doing things the law[s] call for" (p. 219). To Willoughby, "the executive function is essentially political, [and] the administrative function is concerned with putting into effect . . . policies as determined by the other organs" (p. 220). While arguing against the traditional separation of powers, Willoughby does recognize a distinction between policy-making and policy-executing activities, although that distinction is not absolute.

"A Seamless Web of Discretion and Action"

A similar acknowledgment of the difficulty of separating politics and administration, though one with quite a different tone, is found in Luther Gulick's essay "Politics, Administration, and the 'New Deal'" (1933). Gulick bases his argument on the range of discretion held by administrators in carrying out legislative mandates. To Gulick, "every act [of the public employee] is a seamless web of discretion and action" (p. 61). Although the amount of discretion varies within agencies, discretion is exercised from the top of the organization to the bottom. Even those who deal directly with the public must exercise considerable discretion on occasion, although Gulick notes that this situation occurs more often in "badly organized and poorly directed administrative units" (p. 62). In any case, Gulick sees the necessity of administrative flexibility as being increasingly important.

Beyond the era of spoils politics, in which efforts to distance administration from the corruption and inefficiency of politics were appropriate, Gulick feels that the government in the future will assume important new roles. The national government will become a super holding company, "devising and imposing a consistent master plan of national life" (p. 66). Such a highly organized society would provide little opportunity for citizen involvement. According to Gulick, "the success of the operation of democracy must not be made to depend upon extended or continuous political activity by citizens nor upon unusual knowledge or intelligence to deal with complicated questions" (p. 58). Apparently, in the organized, administered world of the future, the politics-administration dichotomy will be resolved by giving administrators power once held by citizens.

The Interaction of Policy and Administration

A more persuasive practical and theoretical understanding of politics and administration is presented in Leonard White's classic text *The Study of Public Administration* (1939). While acknowledging that a certain separation of policy and administration is implicit in his definition of public administration, White also recognizes the interaction between the two spheres. He finds particularly noteworthy an increasing trend toward "executive initiative in public policy," which occurs both as administrators exercise discretion in carrying out vague or general legislation and as the advice and counsel of permanent civil servants is sought in the development of policy recommendations. Importantly, White points out the special advantage of employing administrative personnel in policy formulation: their impartiality and technical skill may equip them to make especially good recommendations. At one point, White even comments that bureaucrats may be in the best position to make policy: "Administration may be the best-equipped branch of government to make genuinely public policy free from overwhelming favoritism to one particular pressure group" (p. 13). Although this point is not elaborated, and specific mechanisms for enhancing the policy potential of the bureaucracy are not explored, White does open the possibility that "democratic administration" might parallel "democratic policy," presumably overlapping with one another in many instances.

Administrators as Significant Policy Actors

In any case, the emerging orthodoxy—that administrators are fully implicated in the policy process—was summarized in the late forties in a series of lectures by Paul H. Appleby. Appleby (1949) begins by noting the tendency of many academicians and practitioners to view policy and administration as separate activities and in turn to see administrators as having little or no policymaking role. To the contrary, Appleby argues administrators are significant policy actors who influence the policymaking process in several ways, most importantly in the exercise of administrative discretion: "Administrators are continually laying down rules for the future, and administrators are continually determining what the law is, what it means in terms of action" (p. 7). In addition, administrators also influence policy through recommendations to the legislature. As a result, according to Appleby, "public administration is policymaking" (p. 170). What is perhaps most distinctive about Appleby's formulation, however, is his philosophical tone—for administrators to be involved in making policy is perfectly appropriate in a democratic society, where "there is always more of politics" (p. 27). Such involvement is to be expected in a democratic society, but it does raise again the need to examine the relationship between administrative action and democratic governance.

■   ■

THE LINGERING INFLUENCE OF POLITICS-ADMINISTRATION

A reading of Goodnow's and Willoughby's original formulations of the distinction between politics and administration indicates that their treatment is far less rigid than many, even now, have assumed. Both in fact argue against the formal legal view that government operations follow the constitutional separation of powers into the executive, the legislative, and the judicial branches. In contrast, Goodnow and Willoughby argue that the relationship between such governmental functions as policymaking and policy execution is much more complex than was previously realized. They are indeed preoccupied with the relationship between politics and administration, but they are not preoccupied with the distinction between politics and administration. The role of the bureaucracy throughout the policymaking process was soon not only recognized but emphasized. One might well wonder, then, how the politics-administration dichotomy gained its remarkable symbolic power and, even more to the point, how it continues to guide the study of public administration.

Limiting the Field

In my view, there are three reasons for the continuing influence of politics-administration. The first two derive from an interesting and very important shift in administrative studies that occurred with Willoughby's 1927 text *Principles of Public Administration*. Where earlier studies had termed administration a function that ocurs within various governmental settings, including the legislature and the judiciary, Willoughby defines the study of public administration as concerned with the "operations of the administrative branch only" (p. 1). This distinction is extremely important in at least two ways. First, attaching administration to a particular institution, a particular branch of government, does in fact imply a politics-administration dichotomy, at least to the extent of saying that administration can be studied apart from the political process. Second, as Marshall Dimock (1936) soon pointed out, such an approach confirms an interpretation of administrative studies as only concerned with improving the managerial efficiency of highly structured organizations.

Despite, or perhaps because of, these features—features that will be examined more closely a little later in this chapter—the shift from a process or functional definition of public administration to an institutional view was soon confirmed. A very influential text by Simon, Smithburg, and Thompson (1950, p. 7) contains the following statement: "By public administration is meant, in common usage, the activities of the executive branches of national, state, and local governments; independent boards and commissions set up by Congress and state legislatures; government corporations; and certain other agencies of a specialized character." Subsequent texts did not focus so distinctly on the executive branch but did make it clear that government employees or government agencies were their primary concern. For most purposes, public administration came to be government administration, mainly the operations of the executive branch.

Beginning with Willoughby's institutional definition of public administration, we find a confirmation of the politics-administration dichotomy without a discussion of it. All the academic and practical discussions of the issue during the first half of the twentieth century pointed out the interdependence of policy and administration. Many writings indeed were serious and sustained attacks on the supposed dichotomy. As a theoretical matter, the politics-administration dichotomy was soon dead (although it is perhaps more accurate to say that it had never been alive). As a practical matter, however, because Willoughby and later writers wished to direct their works to the practical problems of a specific audience—administrative personnel—the politics-administration dichotomy lived on in an institutional definition of public administration. And, to the extent that public administration is still defined in institutional terms, the dichotomy survives.

Adopting Business Management Techniques

However, the desire to appeal to a particular audience is not the only reason that politics-administration continues to influence the field. As Dimock commented (1936, p. 7), Willoughby's institutional definition of the field had the effect of confirming the earlier view of Wilson and others that the administration of government exactly parallels the management of organizational affairs in any sphere and has efficiency as its primary concern. In turn, it was felt that the field of public administration might learn much from the field of business management. Willoughby himself adopted just such a perspective in his 1927 text, using a business analogy in which legislators operated as "the board of directors of the government as an operating organization" (p. 2). Such a view was certainly consistent with Wilson's earlier comments concerning the parallel between government administration and private management, but even more directly followed Frederick A. Cleveland's argument that "the institutions of democracy are cast on practically the same lines as are the institutions of private business. . . . Practically the same organization was adopted, the citizen taking the place of the stockholder" (1913, p. 452).

As we will see in the following section, just such a view, that public and private administration are essentially similar, was adopted throughout the twenties and thirties by those writers who concentrated on questions of organization and management. Clearly, the interest in structural issues, scientific management, and organizational efficiency that characterized public administration theory during this period was only possible given an institutional definition of public administration and the assumption that politics (or values) would not enter in. Only the emergence of the view that administration could be studied apart from politics made possible the adoption of the techniques and approaches of business management.

The Role of Public Organizations in a Democracy

A third major reason for the continued symbolic importance of politics and administration for the study of public administration is that the relationship (not distinction) between politics and administration is indeed important to students and practitioners in the field of public administration. In fact, ultimately the whole issue of whether there is something special about public administration, whether, as Appleby (1945, ch. 1) wrote, "government is different," may ultimately rest on this issue. More to the point, the relationship between politics and administration has come to symbolize the question of the proper role of public organizations in a democratic society. Specifically, is there or should there be any difference in the administration of affairs in a democratic, as opposed to an authoritarian, society? Certainly, Frederick Cleveland (1920, p. 15) expressed the prevailing view that "the difference between an autocracy and a democracy lies not in the administrative organization but in the absence or presence of a controlling electorate or representative body outside of the administration with power to determine the will of the membership and to enforce the will on the administration." In this view, the requirements of democratic government are satisfied by legislative direction and review of a neutral and competent civil service organized according to the best principles of business. As we will see, however, the best principles of business management are themselves not always consistent with the norms of democracy; indeed, they are often directly at odds with democratic norms.

Dwight Waldo has been foremost among those questioning whether democracy can survive nondemocratic public organizations. He too notes that the affirmative view began with the separation of democratic political concerns from those of efficient administration. Reviewing the development of public administration theory into the early fifties, Waldo (1952, p. 7) writes: "Both private and public administration were in an important . . . sense false to the ideal of democracy. They were false by reason of their insistence that democracy, however good and desirable, is nevertheless something peripheral to administration." Most early writers handled the relationship between political democracy and public organizations by strictly separating the two, assuming that autocracy in public organizations may be required to effectively achieve a democratic society. In contrast, an opposing perspective concerning the relationship between politics and administration, democracy and bureaucracy, might maintain that, whether or not politics and administration are separated, the administration of affairs in a democracy must always adhere to democratic norms and principles. However, before this viewpoint is developed, the principles of business management that have influenced theories of public organization need to be more clearly and specifically examined.

SCIENTIFIC APPROACHES TO MANAGEMENT

If politics could be separated from administration, it was only logical to assume that the same lessons learned by students of management in the private sector could be applied to administration in the public sector. Thus, in addition to initiating a lengthy consideration of the relationship between politics and administration, Wilson's early essay implied a generic approach to management, which would consider the study of management to be the same, regardless of its setting. In turn, students of public administration would come to adopt essentially the same agenda as that of students of business—to seek scientific principles of administrative management that would assist in attaining organizational efficiency. Again, a tone was set for much of the research into public organizations that immediately followed, a tone still reflected in theories of public organization.

Scientific Principles

The cornerstone of the emerging study of management was the attempt to derive scientific principles that would guide the actions of practicing managers as they sought to design or to modify organizational structures. The emphasis on science was paramount, though in the beginning somewhat more symbolic than real. Students of management, like social scientists in general, were somewhat awed by science, especially as they witnessed the incredible impact of science and technology in industrial processes. Physics, chemistry, and, to a lesser extent, biology stood as models for the kind of scholarly activity that would lead to individual and societal benefits. But, as students of management sought to emulate the natural sciences, their work became almost a parody of "real" science.

In part, the problem lay in the fact that social scientists had not yet clearly resolved the issue of what it meant to be scientific with respect to understanding social life. To many, being scientific simply meant being rigorous and precise in gathering and interpreting data; to others, indeed to an increasingly dominant group, being scientific meant adhering to a particular philosophical and epistemological viewpoint. The early writers on public administration can certainly be accused of being naive and unsophisticated in their understanding of science, but their later critics were not without fault themselves. Specifically, the particular interpretation of science that came to dominate the study of management through the middle of this century was itself limited in its comprehension of organizational life. But, in any case, the interest in developing a science of administration was and continues to be a particular preoccupation of students of public administration.

Taylor's "One Best Way"

The naiveté of the early management scientists is reflected in the very influential work of Frederick W. Taylor. Specifically, Taylor (1923, p. 7) felt that "the best management is a true science, resting upon clearly defined laws, rules, and principles." At the base of this science is the careful study of the behavior of individual workers in order that their efficiency might be substantially improved; but, beyond this, scientific management implies the extension of these scientific principles to all realms of productive activity. Taylor's science was therefore both a technique (or mechanism for production) and a philosophy of social life. At the technical level, Taylor argued that the best craftspersons of any period knew how tasks could best be performed; their folk wisdom, derived largely from experience, permitted them to develop the most efficient work processes. For any particular task, there was "one best way" of performing, a way that could be discovered (through scientific research) and applied by others. What Taylor proposed to do was to investigate the various components of work in a thorough and rigorous (i.e., scientific) fashion, then make his results known so that all workers could use what had previously been the method of only a few. By engaging in detailed studies of the time and motion required for even the most mundane tasks, Taylor sought to demonstrate that management could vastly improve the efficiency of the productive process.

As an example, in order to demonstrate that "every single act of every workman can be reduced to a science," Taylor examined the "science of shoveling" (p. 64). This investigation was based on the premise that, for any top-notch shoveler, a certain shovel load would result in the biggest day's work. To discover this "one best way" to shovel, Taylor designed a very careful experiment in which the weight of the load was varied for several "first-class shovelers" who had agreed to the experiment. It was discovered that these workers would shovel the greatest tonnage per day with a shovel load of about twenty-one pounds.

Obviously, scientific management recommends to managers a view of workers as machines to be tuned to their peak efficiency, but it also more positively recommends a new role for managers themselves. Managers were now needed to design and to conduct experiments, to discover the most efficient techniques available, to plan work processes that would take advantage of these techniques, and to train and supervise workers using these techniques. Managers, whose job it was to make the organization more efficient, were required in increasing numbers and thus gained a new place in production.

Science Defined

An attempt should be made at this point to clarify the approach to science implied in scientific management. Taylor himself provided the following explanation of this use of the term *science* in testimony before a Congressional committee:

> A very serious objection has been made to the use of the word "science" in this connection. I am much amused to find that this objection comes chiefly from the professors of this country. They resent the use of the word *science* for anything quite so trivial as the ordinary, everyday affairs of life. I think the proper answer to this criticism is to quote the definition recently given by a (well-recognized) professor . . . as "classified or organized knowledge of any kind." And, surely, the gathering in of knowledge which has existed but which was in an unclassified condition in the minds of workmen and

then the reducing of this knowledge to laws and rules and formulae . . . represents the organization and classification of knowledge, even though it may not meet with the approval of some people to have it called science [pp. 41–42].

Such a definition of *science* obviously lacks the rigor and sophistication of the definitions used in the natural or social sciences. It provides the basis for careful examination of work processes and the systematic organization of that data, but it hardly contributes to a broader theoretical understanding of organizational life. Moreover, it remains loose enough that it can embrace not only descriptions but also recommendations about the way organizations should be run, recommendations that then appear to have the endorsement of science.

The philosophical implications of Taylor's work are of great significance for students of public administration. Although we may be amused by the crudities of Taylor's science, we cannot dismiss the impetus Taylor gave to the idea of applying a rigid scientism to the study of organizations, an approach that was soon to prevail in management science. Moreover, scientific principles were first applied at the level of production but then extended "upward and outward" to higher levels of the organization, perhaps to society generally. "There is an urge to extend the objective, positivist approach to an ever-enlarging complex of phenomena; indeed, having embarked upon this course, extension a further step seems always logically and practically imperative" (Waldo, 1948, p. 57).

Science Applied to Public Administration

One realm into which the concern for scientific principles moved was the new field of public administration. Since its beginnings, public administrationists, like other social scientists, held forth the possibility of achieving a scientific study of its subject matter. Throughout most of the early writing on public administration, the term *science*—or other terms, such as *principles*, which came to stand for science—were used in an extremely loose and ill-defined way. Not until Herbert Simon's *Administrative Behavior* (1957) was there an explicit formulation of science based on a carefully reasoned epistemology. Nonetheless, the reverence for and pursuit of a scientific approach was unquestioned.

An important transition in the literature on public organizations, however, prepared the way for Simon's work. Again, the damage seems to have been done by Willoughby. In the preface to his aptly titled *Principles of Public Administration* (1927, p. ix), Willoughby writes: "Objection may be raised to the designation of administration as a science. Whether this objection is valid or not, the position is here taken that, in administration, there are certain fundamental principles of general application analogous to those characterizing any science which must be observed if the end of administration, efficiency in operation, is to be secured, and that these principles are to be determined and their significance made known only by the rigid application of the scientific method to their investigation." In this view, science can produce principles, guides to action, explanations to aid the administrator in improving organizational efficiency.

Early Formulations: Leonard White

The earliest attempts to formulate principles focused mainly on organizational structure and dealt with issues such as the division of labor and the chain of command. Such an approach came under serious attack, but, importantly, the central elements of Willoughby's formulation remained intact: (1) the scientific method can be employed in the study of administration; (2) science can produce guides to action; and (3) those guidelines will improve organizational efficiency, the main criterion for judging the work of organizations. Few argued that science, or any particular interpretation of science, was inappropriate to the study of human organizations; few questioned whether the results of scientific investigation could be applied in practice; and few saw anything other than efficiency (for example, democracy) as the goal of public organizations. What eventually occurred was a reconceptualization of the "principles" approach into one more acceptable as legitimate social science.

A first step in this transition was taken by Leonard D. White in an essay entitled, "The Meaning of Principles in Public Administration" (1936). Describing the term *principle* as it is used in public administration as a "magic word" with supposedly "occult powers," White suggests that the term may no longer be appropriate to developing a scientific study (p. 13). For instance, physical scientists no longer use the term; one does not seek principles of chemistry or physics. Moreover, the ambiguity accompanying the use of the term in public administration restricts the development both of statements indicating causal relationships and of statements that might be appropriate guides to administrative action. One way to bring these two purposes together is to think of principles in terms of hypothesis and verification, "to restrict the use of the term to mean a hypothesis or proposition so adequately tested by observation and/or experiment that it may intelligently be put forward as a guide to action or as a means of understanding" (p. 18). (A hypothesis is a formal statement of a relationship subject to verification.)

Early Formulations: Edwin O. Stene

Clearly, this interpretation more closely aligned the study of public administration with other efforts to develop the scientific study of human behavior. Another step was taken by Edwin O. Stene a few years later in an essay entitled, "An Approach to a Science of Administration" (1940). Stene argued that what had been termed *principles* in the literature of public administration amounted to little more than speculation or opinion and, as such, hardly constituted the science of public administration sought by so many. In contrast, Stene proposed to "determine causal relationships" as the basis for a science of administration (p. 425). Through a series of preliminary definitions, axioms, and propositions, Stene sought a rational basis for empirical research upon which a science of administration could be built. In this way, a science of administration could be achieved. For example, one hypothesis stated: "Coordination of activities within an organization tends to vary directly with the degree to which essential and recurring functions have become part of the organization routine" (p. 1129). (We might note the striking similarity to James Thompson's discussion of securing the "technical core" of organizations some twenty-five years later [Thompson, 1967]).

Stene clearly moved the study of public administration toward a more formal, scientific approach, but, in important ways, he also continued existing trends. For example, a scientific effort was sought to provide guides to action in pursuit of organizational efficiency. What was left out was also important—the question of democracy only entered as a device for assuring full dissemination of important information: "The principles involved suggest the importance of certain democratic processes within administration, such as consultation with the minor officials in charge of activities which will be affected by a contemplated decision" (Stene, 1940, p. 1137).

Waldo's Warning

Although terminology and approaches varied, there was little doubt that a scientific understanding of organizations could provide guides for action leading to greater efficiency. But, in the process, other concerns were increasingly dismissed. By the late 1940s, political science was moving away from its earlier concerns for moral philosophy and political economy and toward what was taken to be a true science of politics. But, as Waldo described it, when the new science of politics merged with the progressive ideology of administrative efficiency, the results were somewhat disturbing. "So far did [political scientists writing on public administration] advance from the old belief that the problem of good government is the problem of moral men that they arrived at the opposite position: that morality is irrelevant, that proper institutions and expert personnel are determining" (Waldo, 1948, p. 23). In retrospect, Waldo's warning was, if anything, too tentative, although it hardly seemed so at the time. The new science of administrative efficiency that the early writers sought served not to extend democratic institutions but to restrict them, not to relieve us of moral responsibility but merely to veil us from it.

■ _____ ■

ADMINISTRATIVE MANAGEMENT AND
ORGANIZATIONAL STRUCTURE

When students of public administration looked toward the study of business management for advice, they discovered not only scientific management but also a strong interest on the part of scholars and practitioners in issues of administrative management. Especially important were writings on organizational structure. The problem that occupied many writers on business management was how organizations, particularly large and complex organizations, might best be designed to permit efficient operations. The assumption seemed to be that a set of principles of organizational design could be developed that would be applicable to all such organizations, public or private. Not surprisingly, the hierarchical model of the military and the Catholic Church came immediately to mind.

In the early thirties, former General Motors executives James Mooney and Alan C. Reiley (1939) offered their advice on the abstract principles by which organizations should be structured. In their view, four principles were involved. The first, coordination through unity of command, emphasized the importance of strong executive leadership exercised through a hierarchical chain of command. In such a structure, in which each person would have only one boss and each boss would supervise a limited number of subordinates, no confusion would exist as to whose orders to obey. Second, Mooney and Reiley discussed the "scalar" principle, the vertical division of labor among various organizational levels. For example, in military terms, the difference between a general and a private reflects the scalar principle. Third, the functional principle, that various functions of the organization could be grouped, referred to the horizontal division of labor. Again, in military terms, the difference between infantry and artillery would represent the functional principle. Fourth, Mooney and Reiley discussed the relationship between line and staff: line offices represent the direct chain of command, the structure through which authority flows, and staff offices such as personnel or finance should be available to advise the chief executive but should exercise no direct authority over line offices. The line represents authority; the staff represents ideas and advice.

Centralization and Integration

Mooney and Reiley's concerns for organizational structure were paralleled in the field of public administration in several important works. First among these was White's *Introduction to the Study of Public Administration* (1926), which examined several important trends in the theory and practice of public organization. Two issues seemed paramount, centralization and integration: the increasing centralization from local to state to national government and the increasing concentration of administrative power in a single executive at whichever level. The first concern, the move to centralization at the national level, seemed to White to be based on the greater level of administrative competency available at that level as well as on the need to provide uniform services and uniform treatment for citizens. The trend toward "the principle of administrative supervision and unified leadership" seemed to gain its major thrust from the emerging scientific study of management, especially as voiced in various university "bureaus" active in the reorganization movement (p. 475). Despite these trends, White was quick to point out the potential dangers of centralization in a democratic society. The more highly centralized an administrative machine becomes, the more the machine itself tends to become an independent center of authority, and the more likely it is to attempt to interfere in the processes by which democracies seek to control their public officials.

White (1926) advanced three arguments against increased centralization: (1) certain matters may indeed be handled better at the local level and should remain there; (2) administrative officials at the center may act in an arbitrary and capricious manner; and, (3) most important, centralization will not permit citizens to gain experience in assuming their civic responsibility. "If administration is to be the work of a highly centralized bureaucracy, it is impossible to expect a sense of personal responsibility for good government," which is best acquired through involvement with local agencies (p. 96).

The second major issue, integration, White described as the tendency to pull together many agencies of government into one massive unit controlled by a single executive. White noted that this tendency is based on the presumption that responsible government will best be achieved by locating executive power in a single office, by permitting the occupant of that office to exercise considerable administrative power over subordinates, and by holding that person responsible for the outcome. Under such a plan, its advocates claim, the multiplication of overlapping services, the independence and lack of coordination among agencies, and the absence of constraints or safeguards can be overcome. Those who oppose such moves toward greater integration, however, hold that the centralization of power opens the possibility for political abuse while limiting the opportunities for political control. White's own position seems to steer a path between these two, concentrating on those mechanisms of accountability and control that would permit a chief executive to effectively oversee the operations of responsible public agencies.

Toward Greater Efficiency: W. F. Willoughby

For White, the issues of centralization and integration are clearly bounded by a concern for maintaining democratic responsibility. Willoughby and Gulick, in contrast, focus more strictly on the development of principles to guide the actions of administrators seeking greater efficiency. In their work, concerns for democratic responsibility, though not absent, take a back seat to concerns for structure, control, and efficiency.

Willoughby, for example, begins with a picture of the legislature as directing, supervising, and controlling the work of the administrative branch of government. The legislature serves as a board of directors, overseeing the operations of the administration. But this can be done in various ways, including detailed, advance specification of what is to be done and how it is to be done or more general grants of discretion accompanied by detailed reporting requirements. Of these, Willoughby feels good management principles require the latter, which leads to the question of who will be responsible for the execution of policies: Should responsibility be vested in several administrative officers or in the chief executive? Willoughby responds that, without question, administrative authority should be vested in the chief executive, who should be given appropriate duties and powers to carry out the work assigned. This step is the first in making the administrative branch a "single, integrated piece of administrative machinery;" to do otherwise would be to fail to conform to "correct principles in respect to the exercise of administrative authority" (1927, pp. 37, 51).

According to Willoughby, the next step in creating the administrative system prescribed by the principles of administrative management is to integrate the various departments and activities within the executive branch so that groups with similar missions and frequent working relations are grouped closely together. Such a technique ensures simplicity, avoids conflicts of jurisdiction, and permits far greater economy and efficiency in government. But the task of grouping organizational units together requires that "the principle of grouping . . . shall be the correct one. . . . As regards what this principle should be, there can be no doubt; it should be that of bringing together under separate departments all those services, and those services only, which have the same general function in respect to the work to be undertaken by them" (p. 86). The tenor of Willoughby's work is apparent: by following scientific principles of administrative management, the administrative branch can operate much more efficiently. And the principles to be followed are essentially those of private or business organization—unity of command, hierarchical authority, and division of labor. In this discussion, the issue of citizen involvement simply does not arise.

Toward Greater Efficiency: Luther Gulick

Much the same is true of Gulick's well-known essay "Notes on the Theory of Organization" (1937a), occasioned by the work of the President's Committee on Administrative Management in 1937. Gulick saw the problem of government organization, like the problem of organization generally, as one concerned with "the structure of coordination imposed upon the work-division units of an enterprise" (p. 3). In other words, the problem is one of achieving a satisfactory division of labor, then developing appropriate means of coordination and control. For example, in describing the creation of new agencies designed to carry out new programs, Gulick suggested four steps: (1) to define the job to be carried out, (2) to select a director, (3) to determine the nature and number of units required, and (4) to establish a structure of authority through which the director can coordinate and control the activities of the units (p. 7). The tension in organizational design is between the necessity for specialization and the division of labor, on the one hand, and coordination through a structure of authority, on the other. "Division of work and integrated organization are the bootstraps by which mankind lifts itself in the process of civilization" (p. 44).

A division of labor is required by the very nature of work processes—people differ in their knowlege and skills and because of the limits of space and time, one person cannot do everything to accomplish the tasks of a modern organization. But work can be divided in a number of different ways. For this reason, Gulick proposes a set of "principles of departmentalization" that might be used by anyone seeking to analyze the work of a unit and arrive at an appropriate division of labor (pp. 21–29). Specifically, Gulick suggests that work may be divided on the basis of:

1. Purpose. One may organize on the basis of the major purpose being served by the agency, such as providing education or controlling crime. Although this approach has advantages in providing a focus for public attention, it has disadvantages in that governmental purposes are difficult to divide neatly. Moreover, various specialists within the agency will tend to pursue different and conflicting approaches.

2. Process. One may organize on the basis of the major process employed by the unit, such as engineering, law, medicine, etc. Here a legal department would have all the lawyers, an engineering department all the engineers, and so forth. This way of organizing will emphasize technical skills but may occasionally obscure the major purpose sought by the organization.

3. Persons or things. One may also organize on the basis of the persons or things dealt with by the unit—for example, the Veterans Administration deals with all problems of veterans, including medical, legal, and other problems. Although this approach has the advantage of providing simple and direct contact with the consumer, it does tend to minimize the advantages of specialization. Moreover, when the government as a whole is considered, it is clear that each citizen does not fall neatly into one category or another. (For example, some veterans are also criminals.)

4. Place. Finally, one may organize according to the geographic location of those being served by the agency. This procedure has advantages in its ease of coordinating services within a particular area and in its flexibility in adapting general rules to local conditions; however, management may become too parochial and short sighted, thus neglecting the importance of uniform treatment.

Coordinating the Division of Labor

Whatever the basis for the division of labor, the various divisions need to be coordinated. Like most of his contemporaries, Gulick saw the need for a single directing authority who would supervise the work of the organization. The principle of unity of command decreed that no one worker should be subject to orders from more than one person. But, beyond that, Gulick (1937a, p. 13) felt that a general movement was needed toward a greater concentration of power in the administrative areas and especially in the chief executive. "In periods of change, government must strengthen those agencies which deal with administrative management, that is, with coordination, with planning, wth personnel, with fiscal control, and with research. These services constitute the brain and will of any enterprise."

Interesting in this regard is Gulick's discussion of the notion of government as a holding company. Earlier we noted Gulick's own use of the holding company analogy in describing the increasing range of functions to be exercised by government as part of the New Deal. Here, however, Gulick seems to have recognized that such an analogy might imply a rather loose coordination in which each agency would be an independent subsidiary with considerable autonomy. This implication, of course, was far from Gulick's intention, which was to emphasize the need for coordination at the center.

For this reason, after criticizing the holding company analogy, Gulick turns the discussion quickly to the importance of freeing the executive from the need to perform trivial tasks and from excessive legislative interference in order that he or she concentrate on the effective coordination of the enterprise. The work of the chief executive is not the actual work of the agency but those activities required in effectively coordinating the work of others. In perhaps the most memorable, though probably least important, part of his essay, Gulick (1937a, p. 13) identifies the work of the chief executive with the acronym POSDCORB—planning, organizing, staffing, directing, coordinating, reporting, and budgeting.

Again, it is important to recall that, although Gulick was writing on the theory of organization, not the theory of public organization, his purpose was to lay the groundwork for the more effective and efficient management of government agencies. For this reason, Gulick was obligated to mention, in passing, issues such as democratic responsibility. However, his treatment of these issues once again confirms that his primary interest was in extending the power of administrative management. For example, he notes that "democracy is a way of government in which the common man is the final judge of what is good for him" and, in the very next sentence, prescribes efficiency as "one of the things that is good for him" (p. 11). Citizens apparently may choose, as long as their choice is efficient administrative management.

Autocracy—The Price of Democracy?

In Willoughby and Gulick, much more than in White, we see the emergence of the administrative management viewpoint in public administration theory. Here theory is reduced to a set of general guides for designing administrative structures. The problems of public organizations are seen as essentially the same as those of private organizations and, consequently, the solution is much the same: the creation of hierarchical structures of authority overlaid on a careful division of labor and coordinated through a single directing authority. Agencies are to be governed by the principles of administrative management, principles far different from those of democratic government. But the potential conflict between the two, which has already been noted, was minimized, if it was considered at all. As Waldo (1948, p. 75) later remarked, "'Autocracy' at work is the unavoidable price for 'Democracy' after hours."

But is this point overstated? Weren't these writers simply prescribing solutions to the immediate problems of managers in the public sector? I think not. Whether by intention or not, the implications of the administrative management movement far exceeded a concentration on the minutiae of administration. Instead, a particular philosophy seemed to unite these writers, a philosophy that grew in part from the experience of a rapidly expanding federal government assuming many new functions and in part from a transposition of business values into the public sector. The expansion of government is probably best viewed by raising the issues of change: How can those in government cope with rapidly changing social conditions, and how can they alter and expand institutional structures to deal with the problems those conditions portend? The solution sought by government generally was greater centralization and a rapid expansion of government activity; the solution sought by writers on administrative management was to seek clear lines of administrative responsibility and control. The philosophy implicit in this viewpoint was a shift from dealing with problems through politics to dealing with problems through management. Through the executive's planning, organizing, staffing, and directing, a new design for society was to be achieved. Such an integrated approach would lead to more rational and controlled plans and decisions made for (not by) citizens. Not incidentally, it would also lead to what Gulick (1927, p. 58) once described as "a peak of eminence for top administrators." But this philosophy had one other aspect, the adoption of certain business values, most notably the criterion of efficiency.

■ _____ ■

EFFICIENCY: THE KEY MEASURE OF SUCCESS

The separation of politics and administration and an accompanying view of public administration as essentially the same as private administration made possible the transfer of theories of administrative management to the study of public organizations. Nowhere was this transfer of approaches and values more clear, though perhaps less understood, than in the adoption of the criterion of efficiency as the key measure for the success of public organizations. It is important to recall that the early writers on public administration were part of a culture undergoing a technological transformation, a culture awed by the impressive gains of science and industry. New ideas and inventions coupled with new techniques for their production and distribution were changing society overnight. As the resulting goods were valued, so were the instruments and processes that made them possible.

The leading metaphor for the development of science and technology became the machine, a precise, mechanical, rational, and efficient model for getting things done. Not surprisingly, when attention turned to the human organizational processes by which industry might be guided, the same metaphor was used. It seemed only appropriate to seek models of organization that would reflect the chief attributes of the machine, models that would prize efficiency above all else.

But the efficiency criterion was given impetus in our society, not only by its association with a popular view of mechanized technology; it was encouraged as well by its clear association with the values of business in a capitalist society. The goal of capital accumulation provided a clear standard by which to judge one's success or failure in the marketplace; the profit-and-loss statement provided the basis for exacting calculations of economic gains or losses; and the profit motive provided the inducement to make it all work. Efficiency, therefore, was more than a cultural value born of science and technology, it was a very personal concern. To play off Weber's discussion of the Protestant ethic: to the extent that a business culture implied that whoever was most efficient would be most successful, few values, if any, were more personal or more important.

Early Acceptance

It is hardly surprising, then, that the early writers on public administration accepted the criterion of efficiency in the evaluation of the work of public organizations. Theories of public organization were simply theories that would make organizations more efficient. For example, White (1926, p. 2) wrote, "The objective of public administration is the most efficient utilization of the resources at the disposal of officials and employees." And Luther Gulick (1937b, p. 192) concurred: "In the science of administration, whether public or private, the basic 'good' is efficiency." Efficiency was clearly the objective and the criterion of public administration.

Questions were raised concerning the pursuit of efficiency, but they were fairly readily dismissed. Marshall Dimock (1936) challenged the unquestioning acceptance of efficiency, especially in its more mechanical application. Dimock painted a picture of management as far more intuitive and compassionate. Whereas mechanical efficiency is "coldly calculating and inhuman," Dimock held, "successful administration is warm and vibrant. It is human" (p. 120). In his view, the need for a more sensitive understanding of management in human terms is especially important in considering public administration. For those in government, "the fulfillment of communal wants is the ultimate test of all their activities." Public administration, in this view, is "more than a lifeless pawn. It plans, it contrives, it philosophizes, it educates, it builds for the community as a whole" (p. 133).

More explicitly, the criterion of efficiency might conflict with other criteria that we might use to assess the work of public organizations—for example, measures of justice and participation. This potential conflict was, of course, recognized by several writers, some of whom attempted to broaden the notion of efficiency to accommodate it to more general social concerns. But, for advocates of administrative management such as Gulick, there could be no doubt which was the final word. "There are, for example, highly inefficient arrangements like citizens boards and small local governments which *may* be necessary in a democracy," . . . but these "interferences with efficiency" should not be taken to eliminate efficiency in any way as "the fundamental value upon which the science of administration may be erected" (1937, p. 193).

Efficiency as a Value

Gulick's language here is interesting. Unlike other writers, both before and after, who see efficiency as a neutral concept, an impartial and objective measure of a society's performance, Gulick acknowledges that efficiency is a value, one that may conflict with other values and that should be given precedence in such an event. In contrast, Dwight Waldo (1948) holds that efficiency itself cannot be a value, that it must always be defined in terms of the particular purpose being served. What is efficient for one purpose may be quite inefficient for another. "For the purpose of killing a bear, for example, a large-bore rifle is more efficient than a bag of meal, but, for the purpose of keeping a bear alive, the reverse is true" (p. 202). To place efficiency in a preeminent position is to fail to consider the substance of what is being done—in reality, a much more important consideration.

From Woodrow Wilson's early essay (cited in chapter 1), two important themes in the study of public administration emerge: the tension between politics and administration and the search for scientific principles of administrative management that would improve the efficiency of government organizations. As we have already seen, the politics-administration dichotomy was quickly denounced by scholars and practitioners alike, although there is considerable doubt that it ever carried the strength attributed to it. Similarly, the search for principles of administrative management was attacked as both unreasonable and unscientific. But other elements of earlier theories were retained. The early writers on public administration did conclude that the problems of public organizations are essentially the same as those of private organizations, subject to solution through the scientific principles of administrative management. Similarly, they saw democracy as best preserved through the efficient operation of government agencies and efficiency in turn as best produced through sound business management. In these ways, preserving the essence of the politics-administration dichotomy and the study of administrative management, the early writers on public administration set a tone for the study of public organizations for the next several decades.

■   ■

DEMOCRATIC ADMINISTRATION

But two points remain to be considered in this chapter: that the viewpoint being expressed by the early writers constitutes a somewhat more embracing prescription than is usually recognized, a political philosophy that the administrative state urges on its citizens; and that, although the administrative management approach came to dominate early writing on public administration (and indeed continues to dominate the field) other viewpoints, minority opinions, were also being expressed. Both these points may be illustrated though Waldo's book, *The Administrative State* (1948), and a subsequent essay entitled, "Development of a Theory of Democratic Administration." As mentioned earlier, Waldo argued that the early writers commented on political theory, perhaps without even realizing it, but his own work was explicitly and unabashedly theoretical in content, applying a philosophical understanding of democratic theory to the study of public organizations.

Administrative Theory and Democratic Governance

Although many writers attempted to limit the focus of public administration to immediate technical matters, Waldo argued that the attempt was futile. Inevitably, questions of value arise, questions of the relationship between administrative practices and democratic theory. Sometimes such questions are addressed explicitly; more often, they are addressed by default. Yet the result is the same either way—a political theory of public organizations. Once such a theory is formulated, the next obvious step is to ask how it relates to larger questions of democratic governance.

The orthodox view of public administration that we have described—that administration is disconnected from the political process and relies on scientific principles of administrative management—is just such a political theory. Indeed, Waldo proposes a rendition of that theory in *The Administrative State*. But, unlike many of Waldo's later works, which appear to chronicle the field more than advance it, *The Administrative State* contains a strong message: that an uncritical acceptance of an administrative outlook constitutes a rejection of democratic theory and that this is a societal problem, not simply a problem of administrative management. Waldo (1948, p. 57) notes the messianic tendencies of management thought, especially scientific management, the tendency "to extend the objective, positivist approach to an ever-enlarging complex of phenomena." As we have seen, this same expansion of power and responsibility appears in public administration theorists interested in administrative management. They too seem to think inevitable the creation of a new guardian class of public managers, directing society through centralized administrative structures. But in neither case is the extension of ideology, the accumulation of power, overt; rather, the philosophy of managerial domination moves at the margin, subtly, incrementally.

Of course, this very possibility was feared by Marx, Weber, and Freud—that bureaucratic thought would extend itself through society, rationalizing greater and greater sectors of group life, until little room remained for individual choice and democratic responsibility. Certainly, one does not have to be a Marxist or a Weberian or a Freudian to recognize the intrusion of complex organizations into our personal and political life or to decry the excessive control and objectification that this intrusion implies. The extension of bureaucratic thought undermines a sense of autonomy and responsibility, both for the individual and for the society as a whole. In this way, the orthodox view of public administration carries with it a social and a political theory, but a negative one, an antipolitical theory, an attempt to turn the problems of politics into problems of administration.

Toward a Democratic Administration

Was there, and is there, an alternative? Perhaps. Among the early writers were several who would have accepted David M. Levitan's argument (1943, p. 359) that "a democratic state must not only be based on democratic principles but also democratically administered, the democratic philosophy permeating its administrative machinery." Others followed the work of Mary Parker Follett (Metcalf and Urwick, 1940, p. 9), who believed that dynamic administration must be grounded on "a recognition of the motivating desires of the individual and of the group."

Despite the obstacles that Waldo saw to restricting the development of democratic administration—specifically the authoritarian bias of organizational thought, with its emphasis on hierarchy, control, and discipline—he held forth some hope for a democratic alternative, one that would comprise a "substantial abandonment of the authority-submission, superordinate-subordinate thought patterns which tend to dominate our administrative theory." His final call was plaintive: "In rare moments of optimism, one permits himself the luxury of a dream of a society of the future in which education and general culture are consonant with a working world in which all participate both as "leaders" and "followers" according to "rules of the game" known to all. Such a society would be postbureaucratic" (1952, p. 103).

The early writers on public administration were hardly postbureaucratic. Indeed, they could almost be described as prebureaucratic. Yet they set an important course for the development of theories of public organization up to the present. The ghost of theories past still haunts the study of public administration, with its tales of politics-administration, scientific principles, and administrative efficiency. It remains to be seen when, if ever, we will develop and pursue new directions.

REFERENCES

Appleby, Paul. *Big Democracy.* New York: Knopf, 1945.

Appleby, Paul. *Policy and Administration.* University: University of Alabama Press, 1949.

Caldwell, Lynton. *Administrative Theories of Hamilton and Jefferson.* Chicago: University of Chicago Press, 1944.

Cleveland, Frederick A. *Organized Democracy.* New York: Longman, Green, 1913.

Cleveland, Frederick A. *The Budget and Responsible Government.* New York: Macmillan, 1920.

Dimock, Marshall E. "The Meaning and Scope of Public Administration" and "Criteria and Objectives of Public Administration." In *The Frontiers of Public Administration,* edited by John M. Gaus, Leonard D. White, and Marshall E. Dimock, pp. 1–12 and 116–134. Chicago: University of Chicago Press, 1936.

Goodnow, Frank. *Policy and Administration.* New York: Macmillan, 1900.

Gulick, Luther. "Politics, Administration, and the New Deal." *Annals of the American Academy of Political and Social Science,* September 1933, *169,* pp. 545–66.

Gulick, Luther. "Notes on the Theory of Organization." In *Papers on the Science of Administration,* edited by Luther Gulick and L. Urwick, pp. 1–46. New York: Institute of Public Administration, 1937a.

Gulick, Luther. "Science, Values, and Public Administration." In *Papers on the Science of Administration,* edited by Luther Gulick and L. Urwick, pp. 189–195. New York: Institute of Public Administration, 1937b.

Levitan, David M. "Political Ends and Administrative Means." *Public Administration Review,* Autumn 1943, pp. 353–359.

McCurdy, Howard. *Public Administration: A Synthesis.* Menlo Park, Calif.: Cummings, 1977.

Metcalf, Henry C., and Urwick, L., eds. *Dynamic Administration: Collected Papers of Mary Parker Follett.* New York: Harper & Row, 1940.

Mooney, James, and Reiley, Alan C. *The Principles of Organization.* New York: Harper & Row, 1939.

Ostrom, Vincent. *The Intellectual Crisis in American Public Administration.* University: University of Alabama Press, 1973.

Simon, Herbert A. *Administrative Behavior.* New York: Macmillan, 1957.

Simon, Herbert A., Smithburg, Donald W., and Thompson, Victor A. *Public Administration.* New York: Knopf, 1950.

Stene, Edwin O. "An Approach to a Science of Administration." *American Political Science Review,* December 1940, *34,* pp. 1124–1126.

Taylor, Frederick. *Scientific Management.* New York: Harper & Row, 1923.

Thompson, James. *Organizations in Action.* New York: McGraw-Hill, 1967.

Waldo, Dwight. *The Administrative State.* New York: Ronald Press, 1948.

Waldo, Dwight. "The Development of a Theory of Public Administration." *American Political Science Review,* March 1952, *46,* pp. 81–103.

Waldo, Dwight. "Administrative State Revisited." *Public Administration Review,* March 1965, *25,* pp. 5–30.

White, Leonard D. "The Meaning of Principles in Public Administration." In *The Frontiers of Public Administration,* edited by John M. Gaus, Leonard D. White, and Marshall E. Dimock, pp. 13–25. Chicago: University of Chicago Press, 1936.

White, Leonard D. *The Federalist.* New York: Macmillan, 1948a.

White, Leonard D. *Introduction to the Study of Administration.* New York: Macmillan, 1948b.

Willoughby, W. F. *Principles of Public Administration.* Baltimore: Johns Hopkins Press, 1927.

Willoughby, W. F. *The Government of Modern States.* New York: Appleton-Century-Crofts, 1936.

Willoughby, W. F., and Willoughby, W. W. *Government and Administration of the United States.* Baltimore, Md.: Johns Hopkins University Press, 1891.

Wilson, Woodrow. "The Study of Administration." *Political Science Quarterly,* June 1887, 2, pp. 197–222.

4

THE RATIONAL MODEL OF ORGANIZATION

Even at the height of its prominence, the theory of public administration described by Willoughby, White, Gulick, and others was being undermined by several important developments in the social sciences. First, in political science, as well as in many other disciplines, there was increasing concern that research efforts should contribute to a true science of human behavior, a theoretically coherent body of knowledge produced in much the same manner as knowledge in the natural sciences. Second, a movement had emerged, based on the recognition of commonalities between public and private management, to develop a generic approach to the study of administration. Neither of these trends originated within public administration itself, and, indeed, public administration proved somewhat resistant to both. Yet, in the end, these two forces were to have a critical impact on the study of public organizations for the next quarter century, up to the present. Most important, these new points of view would effectively displace the older, political conceptions of public organizations, to the point that, when politics was raised again as an issue, in the late sixties and early seventies, it would, curiously, be found under the banner of the "new public administration."

∎ _____ ∎

A SCIENCE OF HUMAN BEHAVIOR

The first and by far the major trend sweeping political science and most related disciplines was a concern for developing a science of human behavior. In keeping with the general scientism of the period, many political scientists felt that their earlier studies of government institutions and political movements lacked the rigor (and therefore, presumably, the dignity) of work in such "real" sciences as physics and chemistry. To correct this situation, they argued on behalf of an approach to science based on the philosophical perspective of logical positivism. This approach held that regularities in human behavior, as in the behavior of physical objects, could be determined by the careful and objective observation of exhibited (or manifest) behavior and that scientific theories could be logically derived from such observations. Just as one could observe the behavior of molecular structures, then develop theories concerning physical life, so, it was argued, could one observe the behavior of human beings "from the outside," then develop theories concerning social life.

The role of human values, however, proved to be a major problem. Whereas molecules have neither values nor apparent intentions in their behavior and do not seem to react to the fact that they are being observed, human beings do. In other words, the new science of human behavior was confronted with the possibility that human values would intrude on the study of behavior. But the response came that facts and values should be considered logically distinct. According to this view, the facts of administrative life, even the fact that certain administrators display certain values, could be observed without the observation either contaminating or being contaminated by personal values. In this way, the integrity (meaning "objectivity") of the research process could be maintained.

In order to further assure objectivity, a particular approach to scientific research was prescribed. A problem would be developed, hypotheses would be generated concerning the relationships among relevant variables, and a research design would be constructed and executed that would test these relationships. The findings would then be incorporated into the larger body of theoretical knowledge in the field. For example, if we were concerned with the relationship between decentralized decision making and job satisfaction, we might develop hypotheses about this relationship— for example, that greater worker participation would lead to higher levels of satisfaction—then attempt to test these hypotheses through a controlled experiment or through a field study. In any case, scientific research was to be rigorously disciplined, so that scientists could have confidence that the explanation derived was the correct one (and that all other explanations were impossible); and it was to be empirical, meaning that it was to be based on the observations of objective reality rather than on subjective belief. Ideally, any scientist performing exactly the same experiment under exactly the same conditions would arrive at exactly the same result, thus confirming the objectivity of the study—and of the method itself.

■   ■

THE GENERIC APPROACH TO ADMINISTRATION

The second major development that was to alter the course of public administration theory in the postwar period and beyond followed in part from the first. Scientists seeking to locate regularities in human behavior argued that those regularities were independent of their context—for example, that the exercise of power is essentially the same, regardless of whether it occurs in the family, the workplace, or the nation-state. Similarly, students of organizations began to suggest that organizational behavior is much the same, whether it takes place in public or private organizations. To a certain extent, this argument was, and is, compelling. Surely, basic administrative processes, such as leadership and authority, motivation and decision making, are quite similar whether one serves as executive in General Motors or as undersecretary in the State Department. Therefore, it was not surprising that a major text on public administration in this period suggested, "In actual administration, there is often a greater difference between small and large organizations than there is between public and private ones" (Simon, Smithburg, and Thompson, 1950, p. 8).

Thus, a generic study of management or administration emerged, one variously called organization theory or organizational analysis but one that soon came to be recognized as the newest social science discipline. Originally an amalgam of findings from various subparts of political science, business administration, sociology, and social psychology, organizational analysis soon took on its own identity. From business came an interest in efficiency and decision making; from sociology came both the systems and structural-functional approaches; and from social psychology came a cognitive or behavioristic orientation. Generic schools of administration were formed; journals such as the *Administrative Science Quarterly* were created; and scholars from various university departments discovered their common interests. Consequently, public administrationists within departments of political science often found that they had more in common with organizational analysts in business schools than with their departmental colleagues in comparative government, international relations, or political theory.

In this way, public administrationists, adopting the outlook of the behavioral sciences, began to emphasize fact rather than value, means rather than ends. And, by joining the move toward a generic study of administration, the field fractured its traditional and long-standing ties to the study of political values. These trends were seen in both a rejection of previous allegedly nonscientific work in public administration and in the establishment of an alternative, the rational model of administration. In each case, the work of Herbert A. Simon loomed large.

■ _____ ■

THE PROVERBS OF ADMINISTRATION

Although interest had been growing for some years in developing a more scientific approach to the study of public administration, the two most formidable calls to action did not come until the late 1940s. In 1946, Herbert A. Simon, a recent graduate of the University of Chicago doctoral program in political science, published an article entitled, "The Proverbs of Administration," in which he sharply criticized previous work in administrative theory, then outlined several requirements for a scientifically based theory of administration. Simon's article was subsequently reprinted as a chapter in his book *Administrative Behavior: A Study of Decision-Making Processes in Administrative Organization* (2nd ed., 1957), which appeared the following year. In *Administrative Behavior,* an outgrowth of his doctoral dissertation, Simon presented in its now classic form the rational model of administration, a model that has had an enormous impact on the study of organizations. Also in 1947, Robert A. Dahl, who had recently completed his doctoral work at Yale University, published "The Science of Public Administration," an alternative critique of earlier work in the field. Dahl's work was also implicitly critical of Simon's approach and precipitated a brief exchange, one that foreshadowed discussions about public organizations for many years thereafter.

Simon's Critique of Previous Theories

Simon's critique was by far the most biting, describing the principles of administration of Gulick, Urwick, and others as "proverbs," sharing a particular defect of other proverbs—that they were often in contradiction to one another. Simon focused his attack on four of the principles: specialization; unity of command; span of control; and organization by purpose, process, clientele, and place. Although Simon (1946, p. 62) agreed that these ideas were acceptable as "criteria for describing and diagnosing administrative situations," he felt that, when they were treated as inviolable principles, they were often in contradiction. He then proceeded to treat them as principles and to demonstrate the contradictions—for example, that maintaining a short span of control might prohibit a small number of organizational levels or that unity of command would prevent an organization from taking advantage of specialized leadership.

In summarizing his position, Simon (1946, p.63) wrote: "Administrative description suffers currently from superficiality, oversimplification, lack of realism. It has confined itself too closely to the mechanism of authority and has failed to bring within its orbit the other, equally important modes of influence on organizational behavior. It has refused to undertake the tiresome task of studying the actual allocation of decision-making functions. It has been satisfied to speak of 'authority,' 'centralization,' 'span of control,' 'function,' without seeking operational definitions of these terms."

Actually, Simon's conclusions were far less a departure from the main-

stream of work in the field than his harsh language implied. (In the introduction to the second edition of *Administrative Behavior,* Simon (1957a, p.xiv),
perhaps gathering momentum, commented, "We talk about organization in
terms not unlike those used by a Ubangi medicine man to discuss disease. At
best, we live by homely proverbs; . . . at worst, we live by pompous inani-
ties.") Simon did correctly recognize the preoccupation of earlier theorists
with questions of the allocation of functions and the structure of authority,
and he did properly call for an expansion of the range of topics to be
investigated. But he did not question the interest of the field in arriving at
sound bases on which administrators could make informed judgments
about organizational design. Nor did he question the central concern of the
field with efficiency. Indeed, Simon (1957a, p.38) made this the very basis
for administrative theory: "The theory of administration is concerned with
how an organization should be constructed and operated in order to
accomplish its work efficiently."

With respect to the task of building a theory of public organizations,
Simon's efforts were far more important for what they implied than for
what they explicitly stated. First, in keeping with the viewpoint of logical
positivism, Simon suggested the possibility of separating facts and values in
the study of administrative behavior, then undertaking a rigorous program
of experimental research designed to produce a comprehensive theory of
administration. Second, Simon moved very quickly away from his own
affiliation with political science and public administration, favoring instead
a generic approach. Obviously, to the extent that public administration
moved in this direction—and it moved in this direction to a considerable
extent—more and more concern would be focused on means rather than
ends, on administrative techniques rather than political principles. Interestingly enough, this argument was central to Dahl's critique.

Dahl: Efficiency and the Nonrational Quality of Human Behavior

If Simon's critique of pre-World War II public administration theory was
the more biting, Dahl's was in many respects the more radical and, in the
long run, the more telling. Dahl, like Simon, acknowledged the desire of
students of public administration to develop a true science but noted several
major difficulties that had been encountered in this effort. Dahl (1947) first
noted that the positivist interpretation of science suggested that social
sciences, including the study of organizations, could and should be value
free. Dahl contended, however, that the field of public administration, while
claiming to be value free, was actually based on a preference for particular
values, most notably, the value of efficiency. As we have just seen, earlier
students of administration, including Simon himself, held efficiency to be a
neutral criterion by which administrative actions could be judged. What
Dahl suggested was simply that efficiency itself was a value and as such had
to compete with other values, such as individual responsibility or democratic morality.

In such competition, according to Dahl, efficiency did not always fare so well. For example, how should one reconcile the need for citizen involvement in administrative decision making with the efficient operation of an agency? Or how should the study of administration evaluate the German prison camps of World War II, most of which were apparently highly efficient? Or how should we go about developing a theory of personal responsibility, one that seemed inherently to conflict with the demand for total efficiency? In these and many other cases, it was apparent that students of public administration were involved with ends as well as means and therefore needed to make their values more explicit. To continue to adhere to the doctrine of efficiency yet to disguise this doctrine as scientific fact was not only misleading but morally dangerous.

Here Dahl was clearly interested in the field of *public* administration rather than administration in general. The most serious valuational conflicts he found occurred when the value of efficiency collided with the values of democracy, especially those related to democratic morality. Of course, one might also argue that the criterion of efficiency in private enterprise sometimes runs counter to the social responsibility of business; however, Dahl was interested only in the public sector, finally arguing that the field of public administration is distinguished by its involvement with ethical questions and political values.

Dahl's second point was that the study of public administration must be based on the study of human behavior. Here Dahl simply acknowledged that most major problems of public administration revolve around human beings and that human beings, consequently, cannot be ignored in the study of public organizations. But Dahl (1947, p. 4) took his analysis a step further to suggest that capitalism has urged on us "an attempt to organize the production process along rational lines" and that such an approach had been accepted by many theorists of organization, theorists who saw the creation of rational, logical structures as most desirable. But, Dahl wrote, to adhere to such a rationalistic model ignores the fact that human beings do not always act in rational ways or even perform most efficiently in the context of rational structures. Thus, "we cannot achieve a science [of administration] by creating in a mechanized 'administrative man' a modern descendant of the eighteenth century's rational man, whose only existence is in books on public administration and whose only activity is strict obedience to 'universal laws of the science of administration'" (p. 7).

Not surprisingly, Herbert Simon (1947), who had just developed such a concept, wrote an immediate rebuttal to Dahl's article. The basis of Simon's response was an obscure and confusing comparison of pure and applied science, one designed to remove pure science from the worship of efficiency that Dahl criticized. This argument, however, was rather ineffective, especially in light of Simon's own dictum equating the theory of administration with the pursuit of efficiency. Repeatedly, Simon denied that his pure science of administration was "prescribing for public policy;" yet he failed to acknowledge the policy implications of a preoccupation with efficiency—

that, in a sense, efficiency is a policy (p. 202). In this particular exchange, therefore, Simon may have come in second. But his rational model of administration, which was just being presented to the public administration community, was to more than compensate by becoming the standard for work in administration for many years to come.

■   ■

HERBERT SIMON, THE RATIONAL MODEL OF ADMINISTRATION

As we have mentioned, the rational model of administration has held a prominent place in the literature on public organizations for the past quarter century. Terms such as *inducements-contributions,* the *zone of acceptance,* and *satisficing* are a standard part of the vocabulary of students of public administration today. If for no other reason, these terms demand attention because of their frequent use by administrative theorists and practitioners. But, more important, these terms, and the broader ideas they represent, have had an important, though not altogether positive, impact on the way in which we think about public organizations. To the extent that the rational model of administration is viewed as a model for human behavior in organizational settings, the guidance it provides should be carefully considered.

The rational model of administration was given its earliest and most forceful presentation in the literature on public organizations in Simon's *Administrative Behavior.* The model was then elaborated by Simon in a series of essays entitled *Models of Man* (1957), and in two jointly authored works, a textbook entitled *Public Administration* (1950), written with Donald W. Smithburg and Victor A. Thompson, and a detailed review of the literature in organization theory entitled *Organizations* (1958), written with James G. March. Beginning in the early fifties, Simon's work turned increasingly toward the social psychology of decision making, then to information technology and the processes of cognitive development. Consequently, although Simon's own efforts in the field of public administration have been somewhat limited in more recent times, the influence of his work remains quite substantial, and his occasional efforts in public administration today still have considerable influence.

This section will outline the rational model of administration as presented by Simon, drawing primarily on his early work, especially *Administrative Behavior.* The following section will examine two related topics: the process of human decision making (as viewed by Simon and later writers) and the closed system-open system dispute (which developed at least in part in reaction to Simon's work and culminated in a synthesis by James D. Thompson).

The Positivist Perspective

In *Administrative Behavior,* Simon undertakes the task of laying out a comprehensive theory of administrative organization based on a positivist view of knowledge acquisition and an instrumental interpretation of organizational life. Fully embracing the positivist perspective, Simon argues that the role of the scientist is the examination of "factual" propositions, those based on the observation of manifest behavior or those logically inferred from such observations. The objectivity of the scientist is paramount, and, for this reason, the scientist must take care to establish a factual basis for any conclusions that might be drawn. To prevent subjectivity from creeping into the research process, the scientist must purge theories of any intimations of human values. Neither the values of the scientist nor those of the actor being observed should enter into research and theory building.

That this is even possible, argues Simon, is because facts and values can be logically separated. "Factual propositions are statements about the observable world and the way in which it operates" (1957a, p. 45). Statements of value, on the other hand, speak to the issue of how things should be; they express preferences for desired events. In contrast to the rather elusive nature of values, factual statements are precise. Propositions of fact, according to Simon, may be "tested to determine whether they are true or false— whether what they say about the world actually occurs or whether it does not" (pp. 45–46).

Simon does note, however, that the words *good* and *bad* are often a part of discussions of administration but that the use of such terms does not compromise the neutrality of the scientific approach that he advocates. Rather, in terms of organization, good things are those that enhance the organization's capacity to attain its goals; bad things are those that do not. Whatever increases efficiency is good; whatever does not is bad. And, of course, says Simon, this stance is only what one would expect of a theory of administration, which sees efficiency as its primary aim.

The Concept of Rationality

At the basis of administrative organization is the concept of rationality. Organizations are created in order to enhance human rationality and to structure human behavior so that it may approximate abstract rationality. Simon begins by arguing that individual human beings are limited in their capacity to respond to the complex problems we face. "The capacity of the human mind for formulating and solving complex problems is very small in comparison with the size of the problems whose solution is required for objectively rational behavior in the real world—or even for a reasonable approximation to such objective rationality" (1957b, p. 198). Since individuals are limited in the degree of rationality they can attain, they find it necessary to join together in groups and organizations to deal effectively with the world around them. In organizations, we find a way of molding human behavior to rational patterns of obtaining our objectives. Thus, "the rational individual is, and must be, an organized and institutionalized individual" (1957a, p. 102).

Obviously, to speak of rationality in this way is to give the concept a far more limited and technical meaning than it holds in other contexts. In contrast to a long philosophical tradition that holds human reason to be concerned with such grand issues as justice, equality, and freedom—the essence of building human societies—Simon's view is essentially concerned with the relation between means and ends. The key to achieving rational behavior, according to one philosopher (Horkheimer, 1974, p. 50), is to "calculate probabilities and thereby coordinate the right means with a given end." To say, therefore (in the language of the rational model), that a particular organization is rational is not to say that it serves politically or morally reasonable purposes such as those alluded to by Dahl but simply to say that it operates to maximize efficiency. In such a view, rationality is equated with efficiency. To behave in a rational manner is to behave in such a way that one contributes to the accomplishment of the organization's objectives. Or, to put it the other way around, to be rational, the individual must follow the design of the organization's leaders, its "controlling group."

In the abstract, of course, it is not very difficult to lay out a rational system for obtaining a given objective, and that is essentially what the controlling group does. The problem comes when one tries to insert human beings, with human feelings, human interests, and human concerns, into the system. If we describe as rational those activities that are consistent with the efficient accomplishment of given objectives, it is clear that following the rules and carrying out one's prescribed function is the only rational path to follow. So Simon (1957a, p. 246) writes, "The stenographer's rationality is exercised in translating a piece of copy, whatever its content, into a typewritten manuscript. Her employer's rationality is exercised in determining the content of the copy."

Individual Behavior

As a later chapter makes clear, this extraordinarily limited concept of rationality obscures a number of very important questions, not the least of which is the moral responsibility of the individual. Yet it permits a very precise and well-constructed formulation of the way rational (or nearly rational) persons act in organizational settings. Simon departs most dramatically from his predecessors by focusing on the behavior of individuals in complex organizations and by asking how individuals might be brought to approximate more closely the rationality of the system. Simon argues that this can only be accomplished where individuals begin to make choices that are guided by the interests of the organization. The key to individual behavior is the decision to act. The organization is seen, therefore, as a decision-making system, defined to include "attention-directing or intelligence processes that determine the occasion of decisions, processes for discovering and designing possible courses of action, and processes for evaluating alternatives and choosing among them" (Simon, 1965, pp. 35–36).

This formulation presents two somewhat distinct problems: "One of these is concerned with the decisions of people to join, remain in, or leave organizations. The other is concerned with their behavior while they are members of organizations (Simon, 1957b, p. 167). Each is approached through a rational calculus of individual costs and benefits. For example, with respect to the decision to remain a member of the organization, Simon writes, "It may be postulated that each participant will remain in the organization, if the satisfaction (or utility) he derives . . . is greater than the satisfaction he could obtain if he withdrew. The zero-point in such a 'satisfaction function' is defined, therefore, in terms of the opportunity cost of participation" (p. 173). As long as the organization provides greater benefits than people think possible elsewhere, they will continue in the organization.

A similar kind of calculation occurs with respect to the behavior of individuals choosing to contribute their activities to the organization. Since it is in the interest of the rational system to induce members to contribute to organizationally correct behaviors, those decreed from above, this question is bound up with the issue of authority. Simon (1957, p. 133; 1957 b, pp. 74-75) argues that each individual member establishes an "area of acceptance within which the subordinate is willing to accept the decisions made for him by his superior." (Earlier, Chester Barnard (1938, p. 168) had discussed a similar "zone of indifference.") Orders that fall within this zone are followed; and those that fall outside the zone are not.

But, obviously, it is in the interest of the organization to have the zone of acceptance widely expanded; the greater the range of orders that the individual will accept, the greater the likelihood that the individual will become an efficient part of the administrative system. Therefore, the next step is to consider ways in which the zone might be expanded. Of course, such an expansion would probably occur in response to greater inducements: more money or more status might lead to more activity.

"Administrative Man"

But, beyond this, the values of the organization may simply come to displace those of the individual. The organization substitutes for the individual's own judgment an organization decision-making process (Simon, 1957a, ch. 10). To the extent that this occurs, the classical utility-seeking "economic man" is replaced by a more modern and more institutionalized "administrative man":

> Administrative man accepts the organizational goals as the value premises of his decisions, is particularly sensitive and reactive to the influence upon him of the other members of his organization, forms stable expectations regarding his own role in relation to others and the roles of others in relation to him, and has high morale in regard to the organization's goals. What is perhaps most remarkable and unique about administrative man is that the organizational influences do not merely cause him to do certain specific things (e.g., putting out a forest fire, if that is his job) but induce in him a habit pattern of doing whatever things are appropriate to carry out in cooperation with others the organization's goals. He develops habits of cooperative behavior [Simon, Smithburg, and Thompson, 1950, p. 82].

This point, of course, returns us to the issue of rationality. Clearly, in

Simon's formulation, the price of achieving organizational rationality is individual autonomy. As the values of the organization replace those of the individual, it becomes apparent that one's contributions will be most helpful if they are consistent with the vision of the organization held by those in control. Consequently, obedience to the demands of those in authority is not merely efficient, it is rational. Simon (1957a, p. 198) puts it this way: "Since these institutions largely determine the mental sets of the participants, they set the conditions for the exercise of docility, and hence rationality, in human society."

Clarifying Terms

Although the rational model will be critiqued later in this book, its language needs to be clarified. Simon holds a scientific theory to be neutral and objective, without preference for any value. If a theory of administration is concerned with efficiency, then it is only rational to be efficient. Indeed, one can only be rational by being efficient. One can be most efficient by acting in accord with the design of the system, and that can best be accomplished by following the directives of those who designed the system. In this limited sense, rationality translates quickly into obedience to hierarchically superior authorities. Rationality is compliance. What began as a neutral and objective approach appears in fact to conceal strong preferences that favor organizational superiors, whoever they may be.

In many ways, the rational model of administration represents not a departure from earlier principles of public administration but rather a scientific legitimation of those principles. There remains the same concern for efficiency and, following from that, the same interest in authority and hierarchy as in previous works. And a full consideration of the role of public agencies in a democratic society is lacking, a consideration that might lead us to either a theory of individual responsibility in public organizations or a theory of the public role of administrative bodies. The extraordinary importance of the rational model is not to be denied, however. Within the context of technical rationality, Simon's exposition of the rational model is classic. If we accept efficiency as the ultimate criterion for evaluating public agencies, and if we accept the cognitive view of human beings as mechanistically responding to their environment by seeking greater utilities, then the conclusions of the rational model seem nearly inevitable. And, as has repeatedly been noted, a general acceptance of these assumptions has marked the recent history of public administration theory.

■ ─── ■

DECISION MAKING AND POLICY FORMULATION

To further illustrate the impact of the rational model, let us turn to two particularly important topics raised in Simon's work and see how these have been treated by later writers. Of all the issues posed by Simon, perhaps none has received as much attention in the literature on public administration as the process of decision making. Although Simon considered *Administrative Behavior* to be a study of decision making in organizations, he later came to state more directly what was certainly implicit in his earlier work, that decision making constituted the core of administration—indeed, that decision making was essentially the same as management itself. Of course, such a view was somewhat of a departure from previous work and suggested a new focus for students of public administration. In the past, under the influence of the politics-administration dichotomy, interest in decision making had been concentrated at the highest organizational levels, where broad policies are made. Simon argued, however, that decisions at this level simply lead to decisions at other levels, all the way down through the administrative system. From the decision of the chief executive to undertake a new program to the decision of the operative employee to carry out a given order, the same basic process of decision making occurs. To understand that process is to understand organizational behavior.

Simon (1967) saw that the decision-making process, at whatever level, consists of three parts: intelligence, design, and choice. By *intelligence,* Simon referred to those activities by which one scans the environment and arrives at occasions to make a decision; by *design,* he referred to finding or developing alternative courses of action; and, by *choice,* he referred to the selection of the alternative with the best chance of success. Of course, in real life, Simon acknowledged, these phases are not distinct; however, for analytical purposes, they seem to constitute the basic elements of decision making.

Given an interest in organizational efficiency, one would expect that decisions would be carried out in the most rational way possible, and, indeed, Simon's argument moved in just this direction. The ideal for rational decision making was the classical economic model, which assumes that the decision maker is completely informed of both the goals of the organization and the possible available alternatives and acts to maximize something (gains, profits, utilities, satisfactions, etc.). Unfortunately, the administrative decision maker can rarely approximate the kind of rationality required by the classical economic model. Rarely can the administrator count on full knowledge of the situation, including the consequences of various courses of action. For this reason, Simon's "administrative man," while seeking rationality (still defined in organizational terms), recognizes the limits of his capacity for rational behavior.

"Administrative Man" Versus "Economic Man"

In contrast to "economic man," "administrative man" seeks to "satisfice" (to find satisfactory solutions) rather than to maximize. Moreover, "administrative man" is content with a simplified and incomplete view of the world that can never, because of human limitations, approximate the complexity of the real world. As Simon (1957a, p. xxvi) points out, these two characteristics are quite significant: "First, because he satisfices rather than maximizes, administrative man can make his choices without first examining all possible behavior alternatives and without ascertaining that these are in fact all the alternatives. Second, because he treats the world as rather 'empty,' and ignores the 'interrelatedness of all things' (so stupefying to thought and action), administrative man is able to make his decisions with relatively simple rules of thumb that do not make impossible demands upon his capacity for thought." Simply put, although "administrative man" cannot achieve the ideal behavior of "economic man," he does the best he can with what he has.

Several remarks need to be made at this point. First, although "administrative man" is only capable of "bounded rationality," he also must seek rational (efficient) organizational actions. Second, the basic calculus remains the same for "administrative man" as for "economic man": to whatever extent possible, utilities are to be maximized. Third, in order to diminish the negative effects of human irrationality, the organization will impose its own standards of rationality on the individual. This may occur either through the substitution of organizational decision premises for those of the individual or through molding the individual's behavior around programmed decisions or standard operating procedures.

Lindblom's Incremental Method

For the student of public organizations, Simon's important discussion of decision making had at least two effects: it moved the focus of decision-making studies from the policy to the operational level; and it highlighted the tension between rational behavior and real behavior in human systems. This second point was soon examined in greater detail by Charles E. Lindblom (1959) in an article entitled, "The Science of Muddling Through." Here Lindblom outlined two approaches to policymaking (or decision making): the rational-comprehensive method and the "successive limited comparisons," or incremental, method (p. 81). He then suggested that, whereas the rational method had received the greatest attention in the literature, the incremental method was much more likely to be used in practice. Moreover, the use of the incremental method was not just a compromised version of the rational method but in fact held definite advantages for policy formulation in a democratic society.

Following the rational method, the policymaker would prioritize all relevant values and choose an objective, develop a list of alternative policies, examine these in light of their ability to achieve the desired goal, then select the alternative that would maximize the value chosen. Following another approach, the incremental approach, the policymaker would settle on a limited objective to be achieved by the policy, outline the few options that were immediately available, and make a choice that combined into one "the choice among values and the choice among instruments for reaching values" (Lindblom, 1959, pp. 79–80). The comparisons would be limited by the administrator's past experience and would likely achieve only partial solutions. For this reason, the policymaker would expect to repeat this incremental process repeatedly in response to changing circumstances.

Aspects of the Incremental Method

Several aspects of the incremental model stand out. First, Lindblom argues that, contrary to the ideal suggested by the rational method of decision making, it is never possible in real life to sort out and rank all the values of objectives related to a particular problem. Citizens, elected officials, and other administrators may differ as to their preferences and may have stated them in the first place. Moreover, in discussions of public policy issues, values quite often conflict with one another. For this reason, according to Lindblom, values or objectives must be stated in marginal terms with respect to particular policies. Since the administrator is concerned with the marginal difference between two or more policy alternatives in a given situation, "when he finally chooses between the two marginal values, he does so by making a choice between policies" (Lindblom, 1959, p. 83). Second, consistent with the pluralist model of democracy, Lindblom argues that the most effective public policies are those that are already in effect and that are agreed to by a wide range of competing parties. By seeking incremental or marginal changes in existing policies, Lindblom argues, the decision maker can simplify the process of choice to manageable proportions. No longer is it necessary, as in the rational-comprehensive model, to take everything into account. More important, such an approach to policy formulation is consistent with a political structure in which the major parties agree on fundamentals and offer only minor variations in their policy perspectives.

The incremental approach also helps the policymaker pursue the pluralist objective of reaching agreement among competing but balanced interests. Lindblom, for example, recognizes that policymakers often ignore important possible consequences of alternative policies, yet he contends that, if different groups ignore different consequences, a sense of balance will ultimately be achieved. Since "almost every interest has its watchdog," the interaction of various competing groups will eventually lead to policies that are responsible to a wide range of interests (Lindblom, 1959, p. 85). In this view, then, the only test of good policy is that it is agreed on: "For the method of successive limited comparisons, the test is agreement on policy itself, which remains possible even when agreement on values is not" (p. 83).

In Lindblom's view, policymaking that occurs through a series of incremental steps provides the administrator (and in turn the society) with a number of safeguards against error: "In the first place, past sequences of policy steps have given him knowledge about the probable consequences of further similar steps. Second, he need not attempt big jumps toward his goals that would require predictions beyond his or anyone else's knowledge, because he never expects his policy to be a final resolution of a problem. His decision is only one step . . . . Third, he is in effect able to test his previous predictions as he moves on to each further step. Lastly, he often can remedy a past error fairly quickly—more quickly than if policy proceeded through more distinct steps widely spaced in time" (Lindblom, 1959, p. 86). Ultimately, the method of successive limited comparisons does more than recognize the limitations of the hopefully rational decision maker, as did Simon; it argues on behalf of an approach to policymaking closely tied to the pluralist view of democracy.

Three Models of Decision Making

A more recent attempt to outline various approaches to the decision-making process is Graham T. Allison's account of the 1962 Cuban missile crisis, *Essence of Decision* (1971). In his book, Allison argues that most foreign policy analysts think about particular decisions, such as that faced by John Kennedy in the missile crisis, in terms of largely implicit conceptual models and that these models significantly affect their view of the decision-making process. Moreover, Allison contends that the classical, or "rational actor" model of decision making, though the most widely used, has serious deficiencies. Two other models, the "organizational process" model and the "governmental politics" model, may be employed to improve one's analysis and interpretation (pp. 4–7). Allison, after presenting the three models, examines the Cuban missile crisis from each perspective, noting the differences that result.

Allison describes the rational actor model in terms similar to those used by Simon and Lindblom—it involves a process of setting objectives, designing alternatives, examining consequences, and choosing the alternative that maximizes the objectives. "Rationality refers to consistent, value-maximizing choice within specified constraints" (p. 30). What is important about Allison's description of the rational actor model for our purposes is not the process itself, which we have encountered before, but rather the fact that Allison treats this process as the standard model of decision making. Clearly, Allison contends that most persons who analyze foreign policy decisions (and, by implication, other government decisions) utilize the perspective of the rational model. One actor (whether an individual, group, or agency) is taken as central to the analysis, then the behavior of the actor is analyzed as intentional and goal-seeking. The analyst's attention is drawn to such matters as whether the actor followed the best strategy or whether the actor deviated from what turned out to be the most rational approach. The rational actor model therefore directs the policy analyst, and presumably the policymaker, to a set of issues that focus on means rather than ends in the decision-making process and may have little to do with the real contexts in which decisions are made.

Despite what he sees as the prevalence of the rational actor model in the analysis of foreign policy decisions, Allison argues that other models are available, two of which he describes in some detail. The organizational process model is based on the premise that few major government decisions are exclusively the province of a single organization. Even decisions made at the highest levels of government require information and advice (in other words, policy direction) from several agencies. (Similarly, one could argue that decisions made by the head of an agency require direction from several divisions of the agency.) This being the case, an understanding of the way in which policies are eventually derived requires knowledge of how various organizational components generate outputs relevant to the policy in question.

Allison's understanding of organizational theory is based on the work of Simon as supplemented by the work of Cyert and March (1971) on "the behavioral theory of the firm." This view sees the organization as less interested in attaining specific goals or objectives than in operating within the framework of a set of constraints negotiated through the various components of the organization. Operating within these constraints, the organization attempts to reduce uncertainty in its environment and to seek out those alternatives that are immediate, available, and related to the problem at hand. Finally, although organizations are relatively stable, they do change to meet environmental demands, thus providing new and often unexpected outputs. In any case, according to Allison, the policy process cannot be understood without reference to the operations of public organizations.

A third model, the governmental politics model, recognizes that major government policies are not made by single rational actors or even by monolithic groups at the upper reaches of the bureaucracy. Rather, policy is the outcome of a process of bargaining among individuals and groups with diverse interests and varying degrees of power to support those interests. Where disagreements occur, parties contend with one another in a political game that leads either to a victory for one party or, more likely, to a mixed result different from what any party intended. "[What] moves the chess pieces are not simply the reasons that support a course of action or the routines of organizations that enact an alternative but the power and skill of proponents and opponents of the action in question" (Allison, 1971, p. 145). Like the other models, the governmental process model is important as a guide to analysis. A particular model directs our attention to certain topics and focuses our understanding of the decision-making process. We see the world in different ways, depending on which lens we choose.

■ ■

CLOSED SYSTEMS VERSUS OPEN SYSTEMS

The work of Lindblom and Allison represent two important shifts away from Simon's description of the decision-making process: far less emphasis is placed on rational choice, even choices made with "bounded rationality"; and far greater attention is paid to environmental factors. In part, these changes occur as the focus of attention is shifted back from individual decisions to major policy decisions (although all three writers seem to use decisions and policies interchangeably). At the higher level, the influence of nonrational factors is far more striking, and the impact of political bargaining is much easier to recognize. Here the organization is no longer seen as an isolated unit but is seen as subject to important influences from its environment.

Strategies for Studying Complex Organizations

These differences in perspective are treated more formally by James D. Thompson in his characterization of closed-system and open-system strategies for studying complex organizations. Thompson suggests that two fairly distinct approaches to the study of *Organizations in Action* (1967) have developed. The first of these, the closed-system strategy, is basically concerned with efficiency in the accomplishment of objectives. An attempt is made to employ the resources of the organization in a functional manner, with each component contributing to the "logic" of the system and with control mechanisms designed to reduce uncertainty. As examples of closed-system thinking, Thompson cites Taylor's scientific management, Gulick and Urwick's administrative management, and Weber's concept of bureaucracy. We might also include Simon's description of the rational model of administration, or at least those portions of the model most directly concerned with efficiency and control.

In contrast, the open-system strategy assumes that we cannot be fully knowledgeable of all the variables that may influence the organization, nor can we predict and control their influence. For this reason, the open-system approach suggests that we expect surprise or uncertainty. As a natural system, "the complex organization is a set of interdependent parts which together make up a whole because each contributes something and receives something from the whole, which in turn is interdependent with some larger environment" (Thompson, 1967, p. 6). The goal, the survival of the system, is attained through an evolutionary process of development. Although changes do occur, the overall tendency of the system is toward homeostasis or balance. As examples of this model, Thompson cites studies of informal organization and studies commenting on the relationship between the organization and the environment.

Within the field of public administration, at least two major case studies emphasizing relationships between the organization and its environment have been produced. In order to indicate the way in which they contrast with closed-system thinking, each will be examined briefly.

An Open-System Approach to Organizational Analysis

The first, a study of the emerging Tennesse Valley Authority, entitled *TVA and the Grass Roots* (1949), was undertaken by Philip Selznick in the mid-1940s. Selznick was particularly concerned with the grass-roots policy of the agency, a policy of decentralization and the involvement of already existing local and state agencies as an approach to democratic planning. However, in the course of his discussion, Selznick outlined an open-system, or institutional, approach to organizational analysis. This approach was also the basis for a later work on the organizational statesman entitled, *Leadership in Administration* (1957).

Although organizations are often conceived as instruments for the achievement of given purposes, according to Selznick (1957, pp. 1–22), they soon take on sociological characteristics that far exceed the closed-system interest in rationality or efficiency. In the first place, the members of the organization resist being treated as means; rather, they participate as whole personalities, each having a particular and unique set of experiences and desires. Second, the organization exists within an institutional framework that makes certain demands on it. Parties, interest groups, and other agencies all interact within the same matrix, meaning that no group is free from the influence of others. For this reason, organizations cannot escape the impact of these "nonrational" factors.

This condition requires that the organization be analyzed in structural-functional terms, that is, with an eye to discovering how the organization adapts to meet its basic needs for stability and self-preservation. Among such basic needs is "the stability of informal relations within the organization," a need that is fulfilled through the development of informal mechanisms that may accommodate the individual differences noted earlier (Selznick, 1949, p. 252). The informal system enhances the flow of organizational communication but also restricts the policy prerogatives of the leadership. Another need of the organization is "the security of the organization as a whole in relation to social forces in its environment" (p. 252). This need may be met at least in part by developing stable relationships with various actors in the environment, even relationships that may seem to compromise somewhat the organization's ability to determine its own directions.

The Process of Cooptation

One such mechanism, which lies at the core of Selznick's discussion of TVA, is called *cooptation*. Cooptation is defined as "the process of absorbing new elements into the leadership or policy-determining structure of an organization as a means of averting threats to its stability or existence" (p. 13). Cooptation is seen as a technique for securing the consent and commitment of potentially threatening groups in the environment. By bringing these groups into the structure of the organization (for example, by placing persons on advisory groups or by negotiating service agreements with other agencies), the organization seeks to gain support for its own policies and position. However, as Selznick points out, "the use of formal cooptation by a leadership does not envision the transfer of actual power" (p. 14). The organization does not, therefore, offer control, for to do so would be tantamount to handing over the organization to outsiders. Selznick sees the special role of the organization's top leadership as dealing with the institutional character of the group. "The art of the creative leader is the art of institution building, the reworking of human and technological materials to fashion an organism that embodies new and enduring values" (Selznick, 1957, pp. 152-153). As the transition is made from administrative management (which is concerned with productivity and efficiency) to institutional leadership, the executive is faced with new tasks that relate to attaching values and meaning to the actions of members of the organization. Decisions at this level are not routine but critical, much attention must be given to the definition of the group's purpose and the development of the organization's character, and the executive must develop effective relationships with those in the environment, relationships that both accommodate the demands of outside groups and maintain the essential integrity of the organization itself. "If there is a practical lesson for leadership here," writes Selznick (1957, p. xiii), "it is this: if you have to compromise, guard against organizational surrender."

The Impact of Environmental Factors

Another study indicating the importance of environmental factors in shaping the activities of a public organization was Herbert Kaufman's study of the United States Forest Service, *The Forest Ranger* (1960). Kaufman proposed to focus on one problem facing the Forest Service (as well as other large organizations), the problem of "administrative integration." Given the large distance between broad policy statements made by those at the top of the organization and the actions taken by those at the bottom, the potential always exists for substantial discrepancies between the policy announced and the actions taken. Kaufman therefore sought to examine: those factors beyond the organization's control that might lead field officers to deviate from the prescribed path of the organization; and those factors that could be employed by the organization to achieve greater consistency.

In the Forest Service, Kaufman found a number of things that might lead toward fragmentation, most being influences from outside the organization. For the rangers, "the customs and standards of the communities in which they reside and the preferences and prejudices they bring with them from their extraorganizational experiences and associations may lead them in a variety of directions" (p. 57). For example, rangers are occasionally faced with decisions that affect their local friends and neighbors. In such cases, the rangers' concern for these persons may play an important role in their decisions. Moreover, if firmly established local interests are involved, the ranger could be subject to serious pressures from the community. In either case, the unity of the Forest Service might be challenged.

In order to counter such centrifugal tendencies, the Forest Service, like other large organizations, utilizes various techniques of integration, which include using procedural devices (such as decision-making rules, financial and work-load planning, etc.); detecting and discouraging deviation (through reporting, inspections, and, where necessary, sanctions); and encouraging a certain degree of conformity (through selection and training). Again, following the same example, in order to prevent a ranger from being unduly influenced by members of the local community, field officers are encouraged to develop a high degree of identification with the service prior to assuming a position in a community. Moreover, personnel are frequently transferred from one location to another, thereby preventing local interests from becoming more important to the ranger than the interests of the service. Ultimately, in Kaufman's view, it is the capacity of the organization to increase the receptivity of field personnel to organization directives that determines the degree of administrative integration that is achieved.

Integrating Open- and Closed-System Approaches

At the beginning of this section, we noted that decision making might be viewed differently at different locations in the organization. Now that we have seen two illustrations of open-system thinking, we may return to this point and attempt to integrate our knowledge of open and closed systems with a concern for organizational levels. Again we may be aided by the work of James Thompson, who attempts a reconciliation of the closed- and open-system approaches based on three organizational levels of responsibility and control: technical, managerial, and institutional. In his view (1967, pp. 10–11), based on the work of the sociologist Talcott Parsons, each organization consists of various suborganizations: the technical suborganization is concerned with the effective performance of the actual task of the organization; the managerial suborganization is concerned with mediating between the technical group and the clients of the organization and with providing the resources necessary to accomplish the technical task; the institutional suborganization is concerned with the relationship between the organization as an institution and the wider social system of which it is a part.

Thompson argues that, since the closed-system logic of the rational model seeks to eliminate uncertainty, it would seem advantageous for organizations to attempt to apply such logic to the operations of the technical core. To the extent that variables affecting the task of the organization can be brought under control at this level, greater technical rationality (efficiency) is possible. At the other extreme, at the level of the institution, the organization must continually cope with a high degree of uncertainty. Here factors in the environment over which the organization has no control prove most difficult; thus, open-system logic, recognizing the influence of outside factors and the likelihood of uncertainty, is more appropriate. The role of the managerial level is to move back and forth between these positions. "If the organization must approach certainty at the technical level to satisfy its rationality criteria but must remain flexible and adaptive to satisfy environmental requirements, we might expect the managerial level to mediate between them, ironing out some irregularities stemming from external sources but also pressing the technical core for modifications as conditions alter" (Thompson, 1967, p. 12). In this way, Thompson sees the possibility of reconciling the interests of closed and open systems, certainty and uncertainty, determinateness and indeterminateness, and lays the groundwork for so-called contingency theories of management.

■ _____ ■

CONCLUSION

This chapter has examined the rational model of administration and some of the issues generated by the rational model. It is appropriate to conclude by noting once more the durability of the rational model. Although a number of challenges have been presented, the basic commitments of the rational model to a positivist interpretation of the "facts" of administrative behavior and the use of technical rationality (often translated as "efficiency") as the main criteria for evaluating organizational life remain at the core of thinking about public organizations. Indeed, as long as these assumptions are held, the rational model appears to be the only logical approach to understanding organizations. However, approaches now being developed are beginning to challenge these basic assumptions and, consequently, the rational model itself. Until recently, these approaches have been grouped together as the "human relations school." The following chapter deals with this perspective on organizational behavior.

■ _____ ■

REFERENCES

Allison, Graham T. _Essence of Decision: Explaining the Cuban Missile Crisis._ Boston: Little, Brown, 1971.

Barnard, Chester I. _Functions of the Executive._ Cambridge, Mass.: Harvard University Press, 1938.

Cyert, Richard, and March, James. _A Behavioral Theory of the Firm._ Englewood Cliffs, N. J.: Prentice-Hall, 1963.

Dahl, Robert A. "The Science of Public Administration." _Public Administration Review,_ Winter 1947, 7, pp. 1–11.

Horkheimer, Max. _Eclipse of Reason._ New York: Seabury Press, 1974.

Kaufman, Herbert. _The Forest Ranger._ Baltimore, Md.: Johns Hopkins University Press, 1960.

Lindblom, Charles E. "The Science of Muddling Through." _Public Administration Review,_ Spring 1959, 19, pp. 79–88.

Selznick, Philip. _TVA and the Grass Roots._ New York: Harper & Row, 1949.

Selznick, Philip. _Leadership in Administration._ Evanston, Ill.: New York: Harper & Row, 1957.

Simon, Herbert A. "The Proverbs of Administration." *Public Administration Review,* Winter 1946, *6,* pp. 53–67.

Simon, Herbert A. "A Comment on 'The Science of Public Administration.'" *Public Administration Review,* Summer 1947, *7,* pp. 200–203.

Simon, Herbert A. *Administrative Behavior: A Study of Decision-Making Process in Administrative Organization.* 2nd ed. New York: Free Press, 1957a.

Simon, Herbert A. *Models of Man.* New York: Wiley, 1957b.

Simon, Herbert A. *Organizations.* New York: Wiley, 1958.

Simon, Herbert A. "Administrative Decision Making." *Public Administration Review,* March 1965, *25,* pp. 31–37.

Simon, Herbert A. *The Shape of Automation for Men and Management.* New York: Harper & Row, 1967.

Simon, Herbert A., Smithburg, Donald W., and Thompson, Victor A. *Public Administration.* New York: Knopf, 1950.

Thompson, James. *Organizations in Action.* New York: McGraw-Hill, 1967.

5

ORGANIZATIONAL HUMANISM AND THE NEW PUBLIC ADMINISTRATION

As we have seen, the rational model of administration assumes that human beings actively make choices but that the range of their choices can be significantly affected by those at the top of the organization, the "controlling group." Although we may pursue those "utilities" or satisfactions that we personally desire, our behavior may also be modified by guidelines or "decision premises" imposed from above, which lead us to act in a way consistent with the organization's purpose as defined by those in charge. We may obey because we seek rewards, because we fear punishments, or simply because we have been conditioned to obey. But, in any case, our response is shaped by forces in the environment subject to managerial manipulation.

In contrast to this viewpoint, the individual may be seen as an active participant in the development of the social world, one whose needs, intentions, and self-worth play a major role in determining the course of human events. Here the individual is not seen as simply a consequence of social forces operating in the environment but is accorded a far more active and creative role. This view gives precedence to individual feelings and desires, recognizing that human values may sometimes be given priority over those of the organization. It is this approach to the development of the human personality that unites an otherwise diverse set of challenges to the rational model of administration, challenges that sprang from ideas that began to appear in the 1930s and have continued to the present.

This chapter will explore the development of these alternatives, characteristically more humanistic in their orientation yet still best seen as counterpoints to the prevailing theme of organizational rationality. Interestingly enough, although the more humanistic approaches to organizational life might have been expected to emerge first in writings on public rather than private management, exactly the opposite was the case: the main thrust of what came to be called the human relations approach occurred first in business administration and industrial psychology. Only recently have those in public administration taken up the themes of the human relations school (and related viewpoints) and added their own special perspective.

For this reason, the discussion will begin with an examination of the work of several writers typically associated with business rather than public administration, especially Chris Argyris, the theorist of this group who has had the greatest impact on public administration. This discussion will be followed by an explanation of the growing interest in organizational change—discussed in public administration largely under the heading of organization development and championed by Robert T. Golembiewski—and by a look at a recent humanistically based protest movement within public administration known as the new public administration. Throughout, both the possibilities and limits of organizational humanism will be noted.

■   ■

THEMES IN ORGANIZATIONAL HUMANISM

Organizational humanism has many loosely connected roots. On the one hand, scientific studies of worker behavior and informal organization led to the conclusion that more open, participatory styles of management would result in not only more satisfied workers but also more productive ones. Humanism was required by the demand for efficiency. On the other hand, examination of the process of organizational change led many to suggest that increased involvement on the part of lower-level participants (even the organization's clients) would facilitate moves to restructure or reinvigorate organizations. Humanism was required by the demand for change. Pointing in quite a different direction was a third stream of thought, primarily social commentary, which held that a humanistic approach to the individual in an organizational society was itself a priority, that the individual's efforts to maintain a sense of freedom and responsibility in an age of increasing organization should be encouraged for moral and ethical reasons alone. Humanism was required by the demand for humanism. Each of these perspectives deserves our attention.

Those students of business management who are generally credited with laying the groundwork for the human relations approach to management and organization developed their views in contrast to the prevailing administrative management perspective, which sought scientific principles of organizational design that would enhance the group's efficiency. Of these, Chester Barnard may be taken as representative of a group urging greater attention to informal actors in organizational life. In addition, the well-known Hawthorne studies illustrate an increased concern for the social or interpersonal climate of the organization.

Barnard on Informal Organizations

Although Barnard is often taken as a precursor of the rational model of administration (for his use of an inducements–contributions formula and the notion of a "zone of indifference"), his work also has interesting humanistic overtones. Especially in contrast to the structural emphasis of other writers in the later 1930s, Barnard's recognition of the complexities of human motivation is quite striking. Indeed, Barnard (1948, p. 21) begins his book *The Functions of the Executive* by arguing that organizational studies always imply a certain view of the individual—sometimes a view that sees the individual as a product of social forces, at other times a view that accepts the idea of "freedom of choice and of will." Barnard does not attempt to reconcile these two positions but instead makes their contradiction the cornerstone of his theory of organization. Defining a formal organization as "a system of consciously coordinated activities or forces of two or more persons" (p. 81), Barnard recognizes that such cooperative systems are dependent on the participation of the individual and that the wants and desires of the individual, whether rational or not, must be met in order for cooperation to result. "If the individual finds his motives being satisfied by what he does, he continues his cooperative effort; otherwise, he does not" (p. 57).

The maintenance of the organization, which is the chief function of the executive, depends less on the design of formal structures of authority than on an understanding of human motivation. For example, authority is defined not in terms of hierarchical position but as a form of communication or order capable of guiding the behavior of the individual. To achieve cooperation, one must take into account the social circumstances that affect the individual's willingness to cooperate. Among these is the informal organization that grows up alongside the formal structure of the organization. Barnard views this matter, like many others, somewhat dialectically: "Formal organizations arise out of and are necessary to informal organization; but, when formal organizations come into operation, they create and require informal organizations" (p. 120).

In addition to understanding that social factors underlie cooperative behavior, the executive must also recognize that these factors will be expressed in contradictory ways, as a contest between reason and intuition, independence and dependence, freedom and control. Rather than seeking the "one best way" of scientific management or the correct principle of administrative management, Barnard urges executives to understand the dialectical nature of human cooperation. "Cooperation and organization as they are observed and experienced are concrete syntheses of opposed facts and of opposed thought and emotions of human beings. It is precisely the function of the executive to facilitate the synthesis in concrete action of contradictory forces, to reconcile conflicting forces, instincts, interests, conditions, positions, and ideals" (p. 21). In this, the executive bears a moral responsibility to expand the field of cooperation and choice and to enhance the development of the individual. One cannot occur without the other.

The Hawthorne Experiments

Whereas Barnard based his conclusions on experience and philosophical reflection, another group of writers were developing similar positions based on rigorous scientific research. In 1927, a group of researchers from Harvard University began a series of studies of working conditions at the Hawthorne Works of the Western Electric Company in Chicago. The experiments, basically following in the scientific management tradition, were initially concerned with the relationship between working conditions such as lighting, temperature, and humidity, on the one hand, and aspects of worker productivity such as fatigue and monotony, on the other. In the conduct of the research, certain goups of workers were treated as an experimental group, isolated from others in the plant and asked to work under varying conditions. Both the conditions and the productivity of the workers were measured precisely. Yet, as the experiment proceeded, the expected relationships between working conditions and productivity failed to materialize. Indeed, despite all the variations in conditions, productivity generally continued to increase.

For this reason, the researchers turned to the informal or social factors that might be affecting the worker's motivation. The special attention accorded the test group, particularly the changes in supervisory practice required in the experiments, was apparently influencing productivity more than changes in physical conditions. A significant increase in the morale and solidarity of the test group was noted, as was a change in the relationship between the workers and their supervisors. Specifically, "social conditions had been established which allowed the operators to develop their own values and objectives" (Roethlisberger and Dickson, 1940, p. 561). These observations led the study team to important conclusions concerning both the nature of supervision and the influence of the informal organization.

The researchers moved to the theoretical position that any complex industrial organization serves two different purposes: the stated purpose of producing certain goods or services and the purpose of "creating and distributing satisfactions among the individual members of the organization" (p. 562). Among the satisfactions desired are not only monetary incentives and proper physical conditions but also social and psychological rewards. This

being the case, the form of supervision that utilizes effective human relations will be most effective. The role of the manager reflects the dual
purposes of the organization. On the one hand, the manager seeks to
accomplish the organization's purposes, but, on the other hand, the manager's job, just as Barnard said, is to maintain the equilibrium of the organization, to balance satisfaction and cooperation. One cannot underestimate the
role of the informal organization in achieving this end. Indeed, the
researchers concluded that "the limits of human collaboration are determined far more by the informal than the formal organization of the plant"
(p. 568).

The widely publicized Hawthorne experiments, like the work of Chester
Barnard, provide a sharp contrast to the prevailing 1930s interpretation of
organizations as dependent on carefully designed formal structures of
authority. These experiments held instead that the behavior of individual
workers is the key to organizational work and that securing the cooperation
of the employees is the central problem of organization. Moreover, they
held that both psychological satisfactions and the benefits of a positive social
environment influenced worker productivity. But, despite these shifts, it
was clear that the chief objective of the manager (and, not coincidentally,
the chief concern of the management scientist) was to find the most efficient way to secure worker compliance with the wishes of management.
This objective led to a search for the most effective techniques of human
relations, those that would increase worker satisfaction but, more important, increase the productivity of the organization.

McGregor's "Theory X and Theory Y"

Many students of human relations emerged in the following years, but
two of the most popular formulations were Douglas McGregor's "Theory X
and Theory Y" and Robert Blake and Jane Mouton's "Managerial Grid." In
his book, *The Human Side of Enterprise*, McGregor (1960, p. 561) pursues the
argument that successful management depends on "the ability to predict
and control human behavior" and that developments in the social sciences
are providing the basis for a new approach to more effective management.
This new approach to management is contrasted to more traditional forms
in terms of the basic assumptions it makes about human behavior. According to McGregor, managers in industry and writers on management traditionally have made the following assumptions about the worker:

1. The average human being has an inherent dislike of work and will avoid
   it if he can.
2. Because of this human characteristic of dislike of work, most people
   must be coerced, controlled, directed, threatened with punishment, to
   get them to put forth adequate effort toward the achievement of organizational objectives.
3. The average human being prefers to be directed, wishes to avoid

responsibility, has relatively little ambition, wants security above all. (pp. 33–34).

Based on these "Theory X" assumptions, an approach to management has developed that relies on rewards and punishments, incentives and threats, coercion and control. But McGregor holds that such an approach to management is ineffective, even in its "softest" versions, for it neglects the social and egoistic needs of individuals.

A recognition of these needs by modern social science results in an alternative set of assumptions about human behavior and leads to an alternative approach to management. These new assumptions are:

1. The expenditure of physical and mental effort in work is as natural as play or rest.
2. External control and the threat of punishment are not the only means for bringing about effort toward organizational objectives. Man will exercise self-direction and self-control in the service of objectives to which he is committed.
3. Commitment to objectives is a function of the rewards associated with their achievement.
4. The average human being learns, under proper conditions, not only to accept but to seek responsibility.
5. The capacity to exercise a relatively high degree of imagination, ingenuity, and creativity in the solution of organizational problems is widely, not narrowly, distributed in the population.
6. Under conditions of modern industrial life, the intellectual potentialities of the average human being are only partially utilized. [McGregor, 1960, pp. 47–48].

The organizational principle to which these assumptions point is integration, the creation of conditions under which the individual's own objectives will be obtained at the same time that he or she contributes to the attainment of the organization's goals. The worker is to be integrated into the organization—that is, managers must take care to determine the needs and desires of their employees, perhaps through more open and participatory modes of conduct, and then help orient those individual objectives so that they can be best obtained through work toward the organization's objectives.

Blake and Mouton's "Managerial Grid"

A similar tone prevails in Blake and Mouton's discussion of the "Managerial Grid." The Grid is created along two dimensions: the manager's concern for production and the manager's concern for people. This leads to several prototypical styles of management based on the various combinations of concern for productivity and people. For example, the combination of high concern for production and low concern for people is called the "authority-obedience" approach and assumes that minimizing the intrusion of human elements is the best approach to organizational efficiency. Blake and Mouton (1981, p. 128) argue, however, that another combination, high concern for production and high concern for people, is the most "positively associated with success, productivity, and profitability in comparison with any other theory." This approach, "team administration," emphasizes interdependence, trust, and respect between managers and workers in the pursuit of the organization's objectives. Like McGregor's Theory Y, team management seeks an integration of individual and organizational objectives through a more humane style of management.

Although Blake and Mouton argue that team management is indeed scientifically proved to be the "one best way" to manage, thus rejecting contingency theory, they leave open the possibility of "versatility" on the part of managers. Similarly, McGregor (1960, p. 56) seeks the implementation of Theory Y wherever possible but recognizes that this approach will not always work: "Authority is an appropriate means for control under certain circumstances—particularly where genuine commitment to objectives cannot be achieved." In the end, therefore, the human relations approach to management proves to be simply another technique for managerial control. Although the human relations approach provides a recognition of the human factors in organizational life, it ultimately treats these as just another set of inducements to be manipulated in the pursuit of managerial control. Where conflicts arise between the individual and the organization, managers are admonished to resort to hierarchical authority. Ultimately, this approach remains simplistic and unfulfilling and, in any case, hardly leads toward a true alternative to the rational model of administration. Though appearing humanistic, the human relations approach may simply be more subtle.

■ ─── ■

PERSONALITY AND ORGANIZATION: THE WORK OF CHRIS ARGYRIS

A far more sophisticated interpretation of the relationship between the individual and the organization, one more suggestive of alternative theoretical possibilities, is found in the work of Chris Argyris. Argyris gained early prominence with the publication of *Personality and Organization* (1957), a review and synthesis of previous literature on the interchange between the individual personality and the demands of the organization. Following this theoretical statement, Argyris (1962) then conducted a number of empirical studies related to various aspects of his theory, especially interpersonal competence and organizational effectiveness. More recently, Argyris has focused on management and organization development or, more broadly, what he terms organizational learning. In this section, the connections between Argyris's work and the work of other human relations theorists will be examined, as will some ways in which Argyris seems to be moving toward an alternative conception of organizational life.

Management Practice and Individual Growth

In *Personality and Organization,* Argyris argued that formal organizational structures and traditional management practices tend to be at odds with certain basic trends toward individual growth and development. Reviewing studies of personality development, Argyris (1962, p. 50) concluded that persons in our society tend, in their growth from infancy to adulthood, to move from passivity to activity, from dependence to independence, from a limited to a greater range of behaviors, from shallow to deeper interests, from a shorter to a longer time perspective, from a subordinate position to a position of equality or superordination, and from a lack of awareness to greater awareness. Movement along each of these dimensions constitutes growth in the direction of a more healthy adult personality.

In contrast, standard management practice, guided by the theory of formal organization, directly inhibits the growth of the individual. The specialization of tasks and the concentration of power and information that characterize formal organizations imply certain assumptions about the human personality, assumptions that better describe infants than adults. For example, in most organizations, employees have very little control over their work and are expected to be dependent, submissive, and limited in the range of their responses. Under such conditions, in which normal opportunities for growth and development are restricted, employees experience considerable frustration, which manifests itself in many ways, ranging from regression to hostility. Moreover, individuals employing these patterns of adaptation are given support by others similarly situated, and their behavior is thereby reinforced.

From the perspective of management, this behavior is highly dysfunctional, for it limits the contributions that the individual and the group make to the work of the organization. A typical response on the part of management is to crack down, to take strong actions to control what is seen as negative behavior. If managers assume (as in Theory X) that workers are basically lazy, then the apathy exhibited by a frustrated employee just confirms their view and calls for an authoritarian response. But, of course, such a response simply leads to further frustration on the part of workers, which is in turn met by further crackdowns by management, thereby continuing the cycle.

A healthier approach, both for management and for the worker, would begin with an understanding of the basic tendencies of individuals toward growth and development and would then seek to fuse these tendencies with the demands of the organization's task. Presumably, such an effort would provide an optimum self-actualization for both the individual and the organization. The difficult task of achieving this congruence or fusion of individual needs and organizational demands belongs to the executive.

The effective leader, according to Argyris (1962, p. 207), has a clear understanding of the organizational context: "There is no one predetermined correct way to behave as a leader. The choice of leadership pattern should be based upon an accurate diagnosis of the reality of the situation in which the leader is embedded." The key to such "reality-centered leadership" is the manager's capacity to observe a situation, to diagnose what is actually happening, and to learn from the experience. This requires that the manager develop "skill in self-awareness, in effective diagnosing, in helping individuals grow and become more creative, in coping with dependent-oriented . . . employees, and in surviving in a competitive world of management" (p. 213).

Argyris's emphasis on learning about self and others provides an important connection between his early work on personality and organization and his later work on organizational change and suggests an important distinction between Argyris's work and that of other human relations theorists. Certainly, much of Argyris's work, like the work of other human relations theorists, may be appropriated by management for the more sophisticated manipulation of organizational members. But such a use of human relations techniques does not involve any real sense of engagement between the leader and the group, no implication of fraternity or community. A commitment to learning, however, implies a relationship involving shared meanings and raises the possibility for creating not only conditions of trust, openness, and self-esteem but also conditions of community. This potentially radical implication of Argyris's work, an implication that Argyris himself has not fully developed, is pertinent to a discussion of his view of organizational change.

If most organizations today suffer from mistrust, closed communication, and excessive formalization, how may we introduce changes in the direction of greater interpersonal trust, more open communication, and a greater degree of personal and organizational flexibility? Argyris (1972) responds, following the social psychologist Kurt Lewin, that an unfreezing of older patterns of behavior must occur, followed by the adoption of new patterns that are then frozen in place. Obviously, such a process is difficult, especially where a projected change would deviate significantly from existing norms and thus involve a high degree of personal and system discomfort. In behavioral science efforts at planned change, often discussed as organization development (OD), Argyris finds an approach to move organizations and their members toward more positive and congruent relationships.

The Role of the Interventionist

Most organization development programs involve an interventionist, typically someone from outside the organization who works with those in the client system either to improve the effectiveness of existing interpersonal relationships or to facilitate the implementation of planned changes in the organization's operations. Although OD efforts may indeed move the organization's members toward greater openness and trust, there is always a possibility that they may simply enhance managerial control. Argyris's particular formulation of the tasks of the interventionist is suggestive of more democratic outcomes. Just as a manager's behavior should not create excessive resistance and dependency on the part of workers, neither should the interventionist's actions create those conditions in the focal organization. In order to avoid this, Argyris (1970, pp. 12–13) recommends that the primary tasks of the interventionist are three: "(1) to help generate valid and useful information; (2) to create conditions in which clients can make informed and free choices; and (3) to help clients develop an internal commitment to their choice." The role of the interventionist is to assist in personal and organizational learning, an issue that requires special attention.

Writing with Donald Schon, Argyris argues that individuals and organizations hold "espoused theories" (those theories of action we profess to follow in our behavior) and "theories-in-use" (those we actually do follow). For effective learning to occur—that is, for learning to affect action—our espoused theories and our theories-in-use must become more compatible and must be subject to change when we detect problems in their functioning. Where organization members discover problems that affect the ability of the organization to carry out its theories-in-use, they may make alterations that Argyris and Schon (1978) call "single-loop learning." But, where organizational inquiry attempts to set "new priorities and weightings of norms" or to restructure the norms themselves, "double-loop learning" is said to occur (p. 24). Beyond this, individuals and organizations engage in "deutero-learning," which is essentially learning about learning. Here people examine previous instances of learning or failing to learn. "They discover what they did that facilitated or inhibited learning, they invent new strategies for learning, they produce these strategies, and they evaluate and generalize what they have produced" (p. 27). In other words, they refine their theory of learning.

Argyris's point seems to be that organizations and individuals facing the complexities and turbulence associated with modern life must constantly inquire into their own capacities to learn effectively and that they may be assisted in this by an interventionist. The interventionist then becomes a researcher, an educator, and a change agent. But, of course, in an organization whose members are committed to learning, this role belongs to the manager. The interventionist and the manager then assume the same role, but this result poses a dilemma for Argyris. The manager is not a disinterested party but rather has a personal interest in the life of the organization. Moreover, the manager, being in a position of some power, has a stake in the status quo, a vested interest in maintaining the structure of power as it is. Where learning occurs that is critical of the existing normative structure of the organization, the manager must either choose to act authoritatively to preserve the organization as it is or to act democratically to assist in altering the group's norms. Obviously, a full commitment to double-loop learning would require the latter, yet Argyris is ambiguous on this point. He seems reluctant to follow the logic of his own work and to step beyond the limitations of traditional thinking.

Implications of Argyris's Work

The resulting ambiguity is particularly noticeable in an essay on the future of organizations written in the early 1970s in which Argyris (1973, p. 6) notes a general tendency toward organizational deterioration in terms not unlike the New Left critique of that period: "Public and private organizations seem to be full of internal conflict that cannot be surfaced or discussed, surrounded by an increasingly disappointed, if not hostile, environment designed with and managed through the use of concepts that tend to reinforce the forces toward ineffectiveness, a self-sealing cluster of trends slowly but surely leading to a social explosion." But, in spite of these critical circumstances, "the traditional pyramidal structure will not be discarded," any organizational changes will "begin at the top," and "the new organization will permit a whole range of participative and authoritarian leadership styles by defining the conditions under which each may be most effective" (p. 39).

In Argyris's work, we find one of the most sophisticated and comprehensive examinations of the relationship between personality and organization in the human relations literature. Yet, at its present stage of development, this work still seems bound to an instrumentalist perspective. Hopefully, Argyris's emphasis on learning will ultimately permit even more far-reaching conclusions than have yet been entertained, even by Argyris. It may even be possible to construct a new relationship between instrumentalism and critique (or learning). In any case, Argyris has clearly had a substantial impact on theories of public and private organization, especially with respect to the issue of organizational change.

ORGANIZATION DEVELOPMENT IN THE PUBLIC SECTOR: THE WORK OF ROBERT GOLEMBIEWSKI

An interesting public-sector parallel to the work of Chris Argyris is found in the extensive writings of Robert T. Golembiewski. From his early work on small groups and organizational behavior (*The Small Group* [1962]) as well as his work on ethics and management (*Men, Management, and Morality* [1967]), Golembiewski has moved to a more sustained focus on organization development as a perspective from which to view growth and change in public organization (*Renewing Organizations* [1972], *Organization Development in Public Administration*, Part 1 [1978], and *Approaches to Planned Change* [1979]). Most recently, and perhaps most relevant to our present study, is Golembiewski's argument in behalf of an approach to building a theory of public organizations from several alternative perspectives, or "miniparadigms" (*Public Administration as a Developing Discipline: OD as One of a Future Family of Miniparadigms* [1977]).

Moral Management

Golembiewski's early *Men, Management, and Morality* can be read in several different ways: as a beginning study in administrative ethics, as another attempt to integrate the individual and the organization, or as a prelude to behavioral science applications to planned change. Golembiewski begins with the standard human relations argument that traditional theories of organization, with their emphasis on top-down authority, detailed supervision, and organizational routine, do not allow for the simultaneous development of the individual. But, whereas Argyris based his argument on increasing the psychological maturity of the individual, Golembiewski raises a different issue: that the failure of formal theories of organization to address the question of individual freedom reveals an insensitivity to the moral posture of the individual worker. In contrast, Golembiewski (1967, p. 53) argues that more recent research indicates that "moral sensitivity can be associated with satisfactory output and employee satisfaction."

Specifically, Golembiewski (1967, p. 65) points to five values associated with economic life that, he says, follow from the "Judeo-Christian ethic: (1) Work must be psychologically acceptable to the individual . . . . (2) Work must allow man to develop his own faculties . . . . (3) The work task must allow the individual considerable room for self-determination . . . . (4) The worker must have the possibility of controlling, in a meaningful way, the environment within which the task is to be performed . . . . (5) The organization should not be the sole and final arbiter of behavior; both the organization and the individual must be subject to an external moral order."

These values are then examined in light of new ways of organizing that are said to lead to the enhancement of the Judeo-Christian ethic, while, not incidentally, also being associated in the behavioral science literature with high employee satisfaction and high output. For example, the first value is discussed in terms of job rotation and job enlargement, and so forth.

Individual Freedom Versus Managerial Control

Although Golembiewski's stated objective in this review is "to enlarge the area of discretion open to us in organizing and to increase individual freedom," in the end, it seems that much more of the former than the latter has been accomplished (1967, p. 305). The managerial techniques discussed hardly extend beyond a litany of human relations efforts in complex organizations. Very little is omitted. Theory X and Theory Y, the Managerial Grid, Argyris's work on personality and organization, all are present and contribute to a general view of more open and more participatory management leading to greater worker satisfaction and organizational productivity. One is left to wonder, however, given Golembiewski's concern for the individual and the Judeo-Christian ethic, whether worthwhile efforts might be made to increase individual freedom, even if they were only possible at some cost to organizational productivity. But this possibility is not considered. In the absence of such a discussion, one is again left with the feeling that the human relations school is simply providing, even if unintentionally, a greater range of techniques for managerial control, techniques that can be sold to workers on an ethical basis.

For Golembiewski, the dilemma is most clear (though still unresolved) in his discussion of the fifth value—that the organization must not be the final arbiter of behavior, that an external moral order should be used to evaluate both the individual and the organization. Golembiewski correctly points out that, as long as complex organizations are permitted to do so, they will develop their own moral standards, which may be at considerable odds to those of the individual or the larger society. But, rather than confronting the task of building a sociopolitical ethic based on democracy, socialism, or whatever, Golembiewski (1967) chooses instead to discuss the issue of centralization and decentralization in organizations, positing decentralization as the answer to "the central moral question." "Decentralization is the creature and creator of this entire analysis" (p. 286). Presumably, individuals in decentralized organizational structures would have greater moral latitude. Although this might be true, the ethic of the organization would still assert itself, especially since "freedom to act in a decentralized structure is paid for by adherence to corporate policies" (p. 273). The freedom of the individual would still be defined by the organization; there would be no external moral order to which both the individual and the organization could be held accountable.

Although Golembiewski's *Men, Management, and Morality* falls far short on this point, one might certainly make a more positive evaluation of this work, especially in the interest of building a theory of public organizations. In contrast to the increasingly strong positivist orientation in public administration, a tradition to which he largely subscribes, Golembiewski directly opens the question of morality in organizations. Unlike those who seek a strict separation of fact and value, he seeks an integration of the two, one might even say a connection between objectivity in theory and ethics in practice. Moreover, it is noteworthy that Golembiewski's analysis ultimately leads to the issue of decentralization. Although his treatment of decentralization is far too narrow to constitute the basis for an external moral order—one could hardly base such an order, as he does, on the fact that DuPont seems to have profited from decentralization—the issue of decentralization does point in two interesting directions. First, it implies that the relationship between the individual and the organization (or the society) must be resolved in moral and political terms rather than in terms of managerial technique. Second, it raises the question of how organizations might be reformed to extend the moral benefits of decentralization while maintaining the material benefits of increased productivity. It would have been interesting if Golembiewski had chosen to emphasize the former in his later work; instead, he chose to emphasize the latter.

"Metavalues" and Organizational Change

Golembiewski's approach to organizational change is stated most clearly in his book *Renewing Organizations*, published in 1972 and revised and extended in 1979 under the title *Approaches to Planned Change*. In these works, Golembiewski relies on his earlier examination of the dynamics of small group behavior to detail a laboratory approach to organizational change—that is, an approach dependent on changes in learners induced through the experience of the learners themselves in direct social encounters such as T groups. Golembiewski sees the laboratory approach as the larger genre from which organization development (OD) activities flow, and, in his discussion of organization development techniques, Golembiewski (1972, p. 112) deviates little, if at all, from mainstream OD practice. He does, however, pay considerably more attention than many other writers to the value implications of his work. Since these issues have direct consequences for building a theory of public organizations, as we see in Golembiewski's own work, there will be less focus in this discussion on specific techniques of organization development, survey feedback, team building, and career development, than on the value implications of such work.

Golembiewski (1972, pp. 60–66) sees five "metavalues" guiding the laboratory approach to personal and organizational change: (1) acceptance of inquiry based on mutual accessibility and open communication; (2) expanded consciousness and recognition of choice, especially the willingness to experiment with new behaviors and choose those that seem most effective; (3) a collaborative concept of authority, emphasizing cooperation and willingness to examine conflicts openly and with an eye toward their resolution; (4) mutual helping relationships with a sense of community and responsibility for others; and (5) authenticity in interpersonal relationships. These values not only define the structure of the laboratory situation (e.g. the T group) but also provide a model for the organization as a whole. These values are both the guiding principles of the interventionist and the ultimate values that he or she seeks to establish in the organization.

Since these values stand in considerable contrast to the traditional values of bureaucratic management, they would seem to urge an alternative to such approaches, at least at the level of theory. Golembiewski argues that the traditional pyramidal values are indeed often dysfunctional and in need of replacement. In contrast, he outlines a collaborative-consensual system of management emphasizing openness, confrontation, feedback, and shared responsibility. Yet this new model never appears to be a direct substitute for bureaucracy. Rather, following the logic of contingency management, it appears to be a convenient alternative in certain circumstances.

In certain kinds of organizations, such as the Strategic Air Command, mechanical or functional systems may be required. "Inducing aspirations about consensus in such organizations, consequently, may be foolhardy. Or inducing such aspirations may even be cruel, if compelling considerations require a structure within which only centralized conventions for decision making are realistic; (1972, p. 571). But who is to determine whether considerations are compelling? More likely the manager than the interventionist, and more likely either of these than the worker. Organization development efforts do not envision greater worker freedom or satisfaction at the cost of productivity. Indeed, "the implied exchange is that, as individuals can approach those multiple humanistic values in organizations, so also will they be fuller and freer contributors to the organizational task . . . . OD does not contemplate some kind of free ride, in short" (1978, p. 11).

Organization development seeks certain metavalues, including those that are at odds with traditional bureaucratic concerns; yet it also seeks "narrower organization goals that are managerially desired" (1972, p. 10). The potential conflict between the two and the potential conflict between the interventionist and the manager raise moral questions that date to *Men, Management, and Morality,* but they also raise political questions. Whereas some organization development practitioners, such as Argyris, seem careful not to impose their own values, Golembiewski seems to urge his followers to do so. That their values might initially appear more attractive to those interested in democratic systems makes their imposition no more a matter of choice than the imposition of other values.

"Miniparadigms" in Public Administration

This point becomes especially important if we entertain Golembiewski's recent argument that organization development be viewed as one of a series of miniparadigms competing for prominence in the field of public administration. Golembiewski's use (or calculated misuse) of the notion of paradigms comes from a work in the history of science that has had a surprisingly important impact on the field of public administration, Thomas Kuhn's *The Structure of Scientific Revolutions* (1970).

Kuhn argues that certain coherent traditions or patterns of scientific inquiry are produced within various scientific disciplines and constitute models for more detailed experimentation within those disciplines. According to Kuhn, such paradigms of scientific endeavor do not develop incrementally with the addition of new concepts to the basic theory. Rather, paradigms compete for acceptance by scientists working within the particular field. The discovery of anomalies leads to the postulation of alternatives. Only through a social process involving substantial conflict does a new paradigm come to replace an earlier one. The result of this process is what Kuhn terms a "scientific revolution."

In the field of public administration, Golembiewski argues, a disciplinary longing for the emergence of consensus around any one paradigm is premature, if not impossible. It is premature because there is no one viewpoint currently proposed that can effectively unify the study of public organization; it may be impossible in the long run because public administration may be a professional field of study rather than a discipline capable of developing its own coherent and integrated approach. Golembiewski argues that scholars, rather than wasting time seeking the impossible dream of paradigmatic agreement, should focus on the aggressive development of several peripheral approaches, or miniparadigms, hoping that eventually these somewhat independent studies will define a center. Not surprisingly, Golembiewski finds the laboratory approach to organization development just such a leading focus for the study of public administration.

This approach poses a number of difficulties, not the least of which is Golembiewski's failure to clarify how social scientific knowledge develops. Indeed, through his contorted treatment of Kuhn, Golembiewski seems to end up confirming what he attacks. In the review of theories of public organization presented in this book, a pattern of theoretical development has been revealed in which various positions compete for prominence rather than building on one another directly, thus suggesting a dialectical process rather than an evolutionary one. That a single approach has not "won" does not contradict Kuhn but in fact confirms his view that "it remains an open question what parts of social science have yet acquired such paradigms at all" (1970, p. 15). Questions even remain among Kuhn's interpreters as to whether any of the existing social sciences are capable of developing agreement around a particular model of scientific activity.

This raises an important point that Golembiewski seems to miss—a paradigm is not a theory but rather an approach, a model, or a pattern of activity that serves as an example to others. Agreement on a paradigm may or may not include agreement on a comprehensive theory; rather, it implies agreement within the scientific community on the appropriate questions to ask and the appropriate ways to go about answering them.

Now, if public administration is a discipline, as Golembiewski would seem to conclude, that somehow seeks agreement on theories and approaches, what is gained by referring to various orientations as miniparadigms? Why not call them either alternative theories or competing candidates for paradigm status? The logic in favor of *miniparadigms* seems shallow indeed. Moreover, to suggest that organization development is just such a miniparadigm—perhaps thereby implying that it might eventually grow into something larger—seems especially problematic. Although organization development is an approach to organizational change based on certain humanistic values, it remains today more technical than theoretical. Certainly, until organization development can resolve the dilemma of individual freedom and organizational control, neither its explanatory nor its ethical import will be fully realized.

Implications of Golembiewski's Work

Despite its many shortcomings, Golembiewski's discussion may, in one important way, carry more significance for the field than even he recognizes. Let us assume for a moment that students of public administration have indeed reached some agreement about the appropriate questions to ask and the ways in which to ask them—in other words, that a paradigm is currently in operation. This would suggest that the theoretical differences have occurred within the framework of some greater agreement about the field. How might we describe this agreement? As we have seen, most theories of public administration are concerned with the efficiency of public organizations in elaborating public policies through generally hierarchical structures within which various mechanisms are employed to achieve compliance. Moreover, students of public administration share a general concern for developing their field through an application of objectivist or positivist social science based on the observation of manifest behavior and on the propositional frameworks constructed from the resulting data. These two thrusts in turn imply a particular view of the relationship between theory and practice in public administration. Whether or not this area of general agreement is called paradigmatic in Kuhn's terms, it becomes clear that existing approaches to theory have much more in common than is apparent on the surface.

If this is the case, we would expect the greatest turbulence in the discipline to be caused not by those developments, such as the rational model of administration or mainstream organization development, that are consistent with this basic pattern but instead by those perspectives that appear to challenge fundamental and unquestioned beliefs. One body of work that has had just such an effect on the field of public administration is the "new public administration." For that reason, before the possibilities for agreement in public administration are explored further, it will be helpful to consider the anomalies cited by the new public administration.

THE NEW PUBLIC ADMINISTRATION

Some care and discretion must be exercised in any discussion of the new public administration, for that movement has been subject to wide-ranging interpretations and has become, for many, a topic highly charged with emotion. Some feel that the new public administration sought a comprehensive alternative to the existing patterns of research and teaching in public administration, that the new public administration represented a paradigmatic challenge to the field. Others feel that its work was more limited, that its proponents pointed out certain problems in existing approaches but lacked a specific alternative focus. I tend toward the latter view. Although I feel that the new public administration held and continues to hold great significance for the field of public administration, its significance lies more in its discovery of anomalies within the framework of traditional theories than in the presentation of some new alternative. Moreover, the diversity and internal conflict within the new public administration ultimately prevented an effective resolution of the issues raised—a task that still remains.

The Minnowbrook Perspective

To begin with, the so-called new public administration was a far more modest effort than either friends or foes like to believe. If it can be said to have constituted a movement, it did so only symbolically, as a result of the attributions of others rather than any coherence among its members. The new public administration began with a conference, held in late 1968 at Syracuse University's Minnowbrook Conference Center, designed to bring together a number of the most promising young scholars in the field of public administration to discuss their interests and approaches and, by implication, to consider how those might differ from the approaches of more established writers in the field. Papers and comments presented at the conference were collected and published under the title *Toward a New Public Administration* (1971), a volume that its editor, Frank Marini, heralded as presenting the Minnowbrook perspective. Since the movement now had a name, the name had to have a movement. Thus, despite the remarkable diversity of the papers in the Minnowbrook volume (and in a related work, *Public Administration in a Time of Turbulence* [1971]) a movement was born, a movement from the beginning more fictional than real.

Although some who identified with the new public administration had leftist tendencies, this movement was hardly as radical as those that arose in nearly all other social science disciplines during that period. For example, unlike their counterparts in other disciplines, the younger students of public administration sought neither a radical caucus within the field nor alternative journals to express their views. Intellectually, there was also little coherence. Although certain themes dominated the Minnowbrook discussions and many that followed, those themes were largely adaptations of more general demands for relevance, equity, and participation. No single approach to understanding public organizatons emerged to challenge the existing pattern of agreement within the field. Yet the demands were clearly troublesome in that existing approaches to the field apparently could not respond—a fact discomforting to many (not only intellectually but also personally).

Politics and Administration

If any vestiges of the old politics-administration dichotomy remained by the mid-sixties, they were effectively eliminated by the new public administration. It did so not by arguing, as earlier scholars had, that the dichotomy was a fiction, that administrators *do* make policy, but by arguing instead that administrators *should* make policy. In part, this argument was a response to the failure of other political agencies, such as the executive or the legislature, to address in any satisfactory fashion such issues as poverty, racism, and war; if they could not (or would not) do so, then perhaps the time was right for administrators to take matters into their own hands. But the new public administration also directed its challenge closer to home, for it was apparent that scholars in public administration and in political science were unable to provide knowledge relevant to these problems. The preoccupation of public administration with administrative management and the fascination of political science with behavioralism had prevented scholars from approaching public problems in a way that would help society resolve those problems that were most pressing. "Contemporary public administration exists in a state of antique maladapted analytical models and normative aridity. There is almost no basis for rejecting or accepting either substantive problems or analytical models save political-administrative crises or academic fashion. Teaching and research tend to be based on past problems or instant response to present 'establishment' problem definitions. Both bases have limited utility in developing administrative vision, political leadership, or intellectual vigor and a kind of wandering relevance to students, practitioners, and the future" (LaPorte, 1971, p. 21).

For the field of public administration, the question was not simply the "recovery of relevance," to borrow Todd LaPorte's phrase. After all, as many of those who objected to the new public administration pointed out, the study of public administration had always been closely tied to the practical operations of government, especially to efforts at government reform. Indeed, the standard charge made by most other academics was that public administration as a field of study was too practical, too relevant. The agenda that the new public administration actually urged, therefore, was not to recover relevance but to become relevant in broader terms, to become relevant to the political system as well as to its administrative elements.

One of the Minnowbrook participants (Crenson, 1971, p. 88) put it this way: "Public administration is not merely the instrument for executing public policy but one determinant of the way in which the public sees the world—particularly the political world—and their own place in it." Though perhaps intended as an instrument for carrying out the will of the executive and the legislature, the public bureaucracy in modern society—simply by virtue of its immense presence and complexity—impacts the political system in many ways. Not only are important issues decided within the bureaucracy; public organizations direct the attention of the public, play a significant role in setting the public agenda, and help to establish the values of the society. Public organizations are therefore not only on the periphery of politics but also in its mainstream.

This being the case, the study of public administration must be drawn away from narrow studies of administrative procedures to a broader concern for the way in which policies are shaped, confirmed, and managed in a democratic society. The closed-system view must give way to an open-system perspective that would help in understanding the policy process more completely. In part, such a study would be empirically based, and several of the Minnowbrook papers discussed how this might come about; but it would also be normative. It would involve both students and practitioners of public administration in an effort to prescribe the appropriate directions for the society and the ways in which those directions might be pursued. In facing this issue, the new public administration confronted the old fact-value distinction.

Fact-Value

According to the new public administrationists, social scientists had in part failed to produce relevant knowledge because their commitment to positivism had limited their activities to data collection and statistical manipulation leading toward empirically based theory. While not overtly challenging this approach (except in one case noted below), the new public administration sought a recognition of the values at play in the research process and a stronger advocacy role for social scientists. For example, it was pointed out that the values of both the scientists and their subjects often impinge on the value-free ideal of positive social science and that a recognition of this potential might both clarify the research process and make it more relevant to the solution of social problems. A scientist, it was noted, chooses a topic of study that is of personal interest, not one dictated by the discipline. Presumably, scientists with a heightened sense of social awareness would address problems of importance to the society. Moreover, recognition of the possibility of bias enables the scientist to be more careful in protecting the objectivity of the research and therefore the validity of the result.

The next step for the scientist is to use the knowledge gained through the research activity for improvements in social conditions. The scientist's responsibility does not end with the production of knowledge but rather includes its dissemination, especially to those in a position to influence public policy in the chosen direction. Students of public administration were urged, therefore, to make themselves available to policy makers and, based on their greater understanding, to become advocates for change. The new public administration, then, was explicitly normative in its thrust. Although research might be empirically based, normative conclusions were seen as not only inevitable but also necessary.

Was the new public administration, through its greater attention to normative concerns, raising a basic challenge to positivism or merely urging its reform? The latter seems to be the position of George Fredrickson, who commented in the Minnowbrook volume that the new public administrationists were neither antipositivist nor antiscientific but merely interested in using their scientific and analytical skills to understand the impact of various policies and to explore new ways of satisfying client demands. Fredrickson described the new public administrationists at Minnowbrook with some accuracy as "second-generation" behavioralists, a term much like Gary Wamsley's later postulation of a "new social science" (1976, p. 391). Though writing a critique of the new public administration, Wamsley seemed to summarize well the position of many at Minnowbrook by arguing for a positive social science that recognizes that "values and norms occupy a premier role that guides the direction and sets the agenda for the scientific study" (pp. 393–394).

For the most part, the new public administrationists seemed concerned with reforming positivist social science. But there was an exception, and, in a manner consistent with the confusion of appearance and reality that seemed to characterize the new public administration, the exception came to be viewed as the rule. That exception was Larry Kirkhart's contribution to the Minnowbrook papers, an attempt to outline a theory of public administration from the standpoint of existentialism and phenomenology. In his article, Kirkhart (1971) noted that new developments in the social sciences, especially in sociology, epistemology, and growth psychology, might provide the groundwork for transcending the traditional Weberian view of rational bureaucracy. These developments, which Kirkhart felt directly challenge the positivist approach to social science, make possible several "non-bureaucratic variants," one of which Kirkhart called the "consociated" model. The epistemological viewpoint underlying Kirkhart's work was explicitly antipositivist in conception and in many ways foreshadowed certain important efforts in public administration a decade later. (These efforts will be examined in a later chapter.) However, it is unfair to label the new public administrationists "phenomenological," as a group. At best, their hope was for an enlightened science of public administration that would examine norms and values and act on them. The question remains as to which values were found most attractive.

Efficiency Versus Equity

Being highly attuned to normative issues, the new public administrationists were quick to point out some of the values that supported earlier theories of public organization, chief among these the criterion of efficiency. They correctly noted (as has chapter 4 of this book) that efficiency is a value chosen from among a larger set of values and that the adoption of the value of efficiency precludes attention to others, such as equity or participation. Moreover, they noted the tendency toward technicism that seems to be implied in a heavy dependency on efficiency as a basic value—in pursuit of rational efficiency, there is a tendency toward depersonalization and objectification. In contrast, they sought a different or at least complementary basis for the study of public administration. At the center of their alternative was the concept of social equity.

Equity, of course, involves a sense of fairness or justice—specifically, the correction of existing imbalances in the distribution of social and political values. In contrast to equal treatment for all, equity proposes that benefits be greater for those most disadvantaged; in contrast to efficiency, equity emphasizes responsiveness and involvement. Moreover, in the new public administration, the concept of equity is applied not only to the activities of the executive, legislative, and judicial bodies but to administrative agencies as well, leading to a considerable redefinition of what public administration is all about. For example, compare the earlier definitions of public adminis-tration of Willoughby or White with the Minnowbrook definition of Todd LaPorte (1971, p. 32): "the purpose of public organization is the reduction of economic, social, and psychic suffering and the enhancement of life oppor-tunities for those inside and outside the organization." Or note Fredrick-son's charge that "a public administration which fails to work for changes which try to redress the deprivation of minorities will likely be eventually used to repress those minorities" (1971, p. 211). Thus, to the traditional concerns for efficiency and economy, the new public administration adds a concern for equity.

The most careful elaboration of the concept of equity as an ethical guide-line for public administrators is probably David K. Hart's (1974) discussion and application of John Rawls's *Theory of Justice* (1971). Hart notes that the existing ethical standard for public administration is that of impartial administration, which holds that policies be applied equally to all without regard for circumstances not specifically related to the policy at hand. Social equity would recognize the different needs and interests of different people and therefore would result in differential treatment. As a philosophical basis for this approach, Hart examines Rawls's concept of "justice as fair-ness," an attempt to secure rights "not subject to political bargaining or to the calculus of social interests" (pp. 3–4). As a way of illustrating his theory, Rawls suggests an intellectual device, the "original position," in which binding decisions are made concerning the structure of society. If such choices are made under a "veil of ignorance" in which none of the parties knows its place in society, its class or social status, each party will take care to create circumstances that it will find acceptable regardless of its eventual position in the society. As a consequence, "the collective efforts of the society [will] be concentrated in behalf of its least advantaged members" so that at least a minimum of rights and respect, income and wealth, will be guaranteed to all" (Hart, 1976, p. 7).

As a rough example, imagine a city council that has just been given a grant of $10 million for street improvements. One approach the council members might take, out of self interest, would be to concentrate the money in their own neighborhoods so that they would receive the greatest advantage. Another approach, the impartial approach, would be to distribute the funds equally to all neighborhoods, to spread the benefits to all parts of the city. A third approach, based on social equity, would be to concentrate the money in those neighborhoods most in need of street improvements. If the council members acted under Rawls's "veil of ignorance," that is, if they acted on the basis of fairness rather than self-interest, they would be significantly more likely to choose the third alternative, which would promote social equity in the community.

Hierarchy Versus Participation

In addition to their interest in social equity, the new public administrationists placed considerable emphasis on the value of participation, either the participation of clients in the operation of agency affairs or the involvement of lower-level organizational participants in organizational decision making. The first of these themes was, of course, consistent with mid-sixties efforts toward citizen participation—for example, the "maximum feasible participation" of the poor in antipoverty programs—and even more in keeping with the radical cry for "power to the people." Certainly, the involvement of clients in agency affairs had often been attempted before: one need only recall Selznick's discussion of *TVA and the Grass Roots* (1949), cited in chapter 4. But the new public administrationists recognized that such efforts were often attempts to coopt client groups rather than to involve them substantially in the decision-making process. As an alternative, they sought more open organizational structures having permeable boundaries and marked by confrontation and exchange.

Among those who focused most directly on this issue was Orion White, whose earlier work, "The Dialectical Organization" (1969), had suggested the importance of an active and continuing interchange between agency personnel and client groups in pursuit of policies and procedures taking all interests into account. In the Minnowbrook volume, White (1971) pursued this notion by describing administrative adaptation in terms of confrontation and consensus around ethical values rather than in terms of negotiation and bargaining leading either to the imposition of a solution by the most powerful or to a compromise between the interests of both (see also Thayer, 1973). In pursuing his alternative (a "politics of love"), White argued for adaptation through open communication, equality through a functional distribution of power, and a conscious recognition of the ideological principles that guide action. How this alternative might work in practice was unclear.

The second theme, involving lower-level participants in organizational decision making, was frequently voiced by new public administrationists, although, in the end (again with the possible exception of Kirkhart), it could hardly be seen as more than an extension of earlier work in human relations. The new public administrationists certainly struggled with the issue of how organizations might be restructured to achieve greater involvement and participation without such efforts becoming simply devices for managerial manipulation; however, their results were mixed. As in many other areas, the new public administrationists were here accused of providing a radical critique—in this case, an antihierarchical, antibureaucratic critique—but offering few solutions or alternatives.

■ _____ ■

CONCLUSION

The work of the organizational humanists marks a curious chapter in the development of public administration theory. Although they correctly identified many limitations of the rational perspective, their interest in more open participatory styles of management was all too easily subsumed under the rational approach. That is, the techniques of worker involvement (even organization development) were soon appropriated as simply more subtle and sophisticated techniques to secure worker compliance. At the same time, the organizational humanists—such writers as McGregor, Blake and Mouton, Golembiewski, and Argyris—were raising questions of great importance, especially to those interested in public organizations. Their plea for a new role for workers and clients in the direction of the organization came very close to being an argument for democratic administration. Yet, in the end, these theorists seemed constrained by their managerial perspective and by their epistemological viewpoint from fully embracing that notion. Although they suggested issues that were not being fully addressed in the context of mainstream social science, their work eventually entered into the mainstream.

The more pressing questions, at least for those interested in public organizations, remained for the new public administrationists to ask. Yet they too provided few answers. Contrary to the views of many, the new public administrationists did not urge a new alternative paradigm for the study of public administration. Rather, their work was a loosely knit collection of commentaries on the condition of public administration theory and practice that pointed out the problems existing in the field and called for action to correct those problems. Although the language of public administration today is less shrill and the proposals less stark, the anomalies revealed by the new public administrationists continue to occupy the attention of both theorists and practitioners. There remains a substantial concern for understanding the integration of policy and administration through a more relevant policy science, and there continue to be attempts to derive a new epistemological base for the study of public administration that would reconcile the often contending empirical and normative interests of the discipline. Theorists and practitioners alike seem to share a feeling that our understanding of life in public organizations is incomplete, that there is something more or something different that we need to know in order to make sense of our lives and our work. In establishing this shared consciousness and concern, the new public administrationists played a major role.

■   ■

REFERENCES

Argyris, Chris. *Personality and Organization.* New York: Harper & Row, 1957.

Argyris, Chris. *Interpersonal Competence and Organizational Effectiveness.* Homewood, Ill.: Dorsey Press, 1962.

Argyris, Chris. *Intervention Theory and Method: A Behavioral Science View.* Reading, Mass.: Addison-Wesley, 1970.

Argyris, Chris. *The Applicability of Organizational Sociology.* Cambridge, Mass.: Harvard University Press, 1972.

Argyris, Chris. *Organizations of the Future.* Administrative and Policy Study Series, Vol. 1. Beverly Hills, Calif.: Sage, 1973.

Argyris, Chris, and Schon, Donald. *Organizational Learning: A Theory of Action Perspective.* Reading, Mass.: Addison-Wesley, 1978.

Barnard, Chester I. *The Functions of the Executive.* Cambridge, Mass.: Harvard University Press, 1948.

Blake, Robert, and Mouton, Jane. *The Academic Administrator Grid.* San Francisco: Jossey-Bass, 1981.

Crenson, Matthew A. "Comment: Contract, Love and Character Building." In *Toward a New Public Administration: The Minnowbrook Perspective,* edited by Frank Marini, pp. 83–88. San Francisco: Chandler, 1971.

Fredrickson, H. George. "Toward a New Public Administration". In *Toward a New Public Administration,* edited by Frank Marini, pp. 309–331. San Francisco: Chandler, 1971.

Golembiewski, Robert T. *The Small Group.* Chicago: University of Chicago Press, 1962.

Golembiewski, Robert T. *Managerial Behavior and Organization Demands.* Chicago: Rand McNally, 1967a.

Golembiewski, Robert T. *Men, Management, and Morality.* New York: McGraw-Hill, 1967b.

Golembiewski, Robert T. *Renewing Organizations.* Ithaca, Ill.: Peacock, 1972.

Golembiewski, Robert T. *Public Administration as a Developing Discipline.* New York: Dekker, 1977.

Golembiewski, Robert T. *Approaches to Planned Change.* New York: Dekker, 1979.

Golembiewski, Robert T., and Eddy, William, eds. *Organization Development in Public Administration.* Part 1. New York: Dekker, 1978.

Hart, David K. "Social Equity, Justice, and the Equitable Administrator." *Public Administration Review,* January-February 1974, 34, pp. 3–10.

Kirkhart, Larry. "Toward a Theory of Public Administration." In *Toward a New Public Administration: The Minnowbrook Perspective,* edited by Frank Marini, pp. 127–163. San Francisco: Chandler, 1971.

Kuhn, Thomas S. *The Structure of Scientific Revolutions.* Chicago: University of Chicago Press, 1970.

LaPorte, Todd. "The Recovery of Relevance in the Study of Public Organization." In *Toward a New Public Administration: The Minnowbrook Perspective,* edited by Frank Marini, pp. 17–47. San Francisco: Chandler, 1971.

McGregor, Douglas. *The Human Side of Enterprise.* New York: McGraw-Hill, 1960.

Marini, Frank, ed. *Toward a New Public Administration: The Minnowbrook Perspective.* San Francisco: Chandler, 1971.

Rawls, John. *A Theory of Justice.* Cambridge, Mass.: Belnap Press of Harvard University Press, 1971.

Roethlisberger, Fritz, and Dickson, William. *Management and the Worker.* Cambridge. Mass.: Harvard University Press, 1940.

Selznick, Philip. *TVA and the Grass Roots.* Berkeley: University of California Press, 1949.

Thayer, Frederick E. *An End to Hierarchy! An End to Competition!* New York: New Viewpoints, 1973.

Waldo, Dwight, ed. *Public Administration in a Time of Turbulence.* San Francisco: Chandler, 1971.

Wamsley, Gary. "On the Problems of Discovering What's Really New in Public Administration." *Administration and Society,* November 1976, *8,* pp. 385–400.

White, Orion F. "The Dialectical Organization: An Alternative to Bureaucracy." *Public Administration Review.* Winter 1969, *29,* pp. 32–42.

White, Orion F., Jr. "Administrative Adaptation in a Changing Society." In *Toward a New Public Administration: The Minnowbrook Perspective,* edited by Frank Marini, pp. 59–62. San Francisco: Chandler, 1971.

6

THE POLICY EMPHASIS IN PUBLIC ADMINISTRATION

In recent years, students of public administration have been attracted to the more general field of public policy, or policy analysis, as a way of understanding the role of public organizations in expressing social values. Experts in policy studies who have followed this path see the policy process as central to the operations of government. Policies are seen as the outcomes of government activity, and, for this reason, policy formulation and policy implementation are seen as central to the political process. If the work of government is to produce policy, then the proper study of government is the study of public policy. But, to some, this study of public policy has come to be viewed as embracing (and perhaps even replacing) the field of public administration as a focus for education and practice. Not only does it provide a new set of categories for viewing government action (typically, those categories associated with systems analysis), it also suggests a new set of skills to be required of those entering the public service—the most advanced positivist techniques of analysis and evaluation. The classical "administrative man," bound by his rationality and the range of his interests, is to be replaced by the more modern, more rational, and more influential policy analyst.

Viewing public organizations as a part of the policy process opens new avenues for theories of public organization. First, there is the possibility that public organizations might be considered integral to the political process. That is, rather than viewing administration as separate from politics, the policy perspective confirms that members of public organizations play an important role in formulating public policy, that their influence is widely felt in the designing of policies and programs, and that they continue to shape public policies through their efforts at implementation even after formal policies have been stated by the legislature, the executive, or the judiciary. In such a view, the politics-administration dichotomy is hard to justify. Second, in a related vein, the policy orientation suggests at least the potential for casting the study of public organization in a value-critical rather than an instrumental mode. As we have seen, other views of public organizations, especially those consistent with the rational model of administration, are based on a separation of fact and value and on an interest in the factual analysis of goal-oriented behavior within organizations. If public organizations are taken as central to the policy process, however, then such a view is obviously too restrictive. The role of public organizations in expressing societal values becomes paramount, and, correspondingly, an approach to public organizations that focuses on and critiques the valuational basis of such organizations is far more appropriate.

Unfortunately, the full promise of the public policy approach has not been realized. Despite its comprehensiveness, the policy orientation has not fundamentally altered our approach to theory. Both a reemergence of the politics-administration dichotomy and a continuation or even an extension of the instrumentalist conception of organization have been maintained, at least in some works. Students of public policy have differentiated between policy formulation and policy implementation in much the same way that earlier students of public administration separated their work from the study of politics. Similarly, those embracing the public policy orientation have largely maintained their commitment to mainstream social science, including a positive view of science and an instrumental conception of organization. In order to understand these arguments, however, we must first examine the development of the public policy orientation and two issues that have been central to policy studies, responsiveness and effectiveness.

DEVELOPMENT OF THE PUBLIC POLICY ORIENTATION

Many early theorists of public organizations were critical of the politics-administration dichotomy, which they saw as failing to recognize the influence of the bureaucracy on the formation of public policy. Paul Appleby, in *Policy and Administration* (1949), complained that the tendency to separate policy and administration left no policy making role for administrators other than the chief executive. To the contrary, he argued, "administrators are continually laying down rules for the future and are continually determining what the law is, what it means in terms of action" (p. 7). In addition to this exercise of discretion, administrators have access to important information about policy questions and are often called upon to relate recommendations for legislative action. In these ways, Appleby said, "public administration is policy making" (p. 170).

Similarly, Norton Long (1962, p. 67) wrote, "The bureaucracy is in policy and major policy to stay: in fact, . . . bureaucracy is likely, day in and day out, to be our main source of policy initiative." By this time there was no question among students of public administration that public organizations played an important role in defining public policy. The "initiatives" of public agencies, furthermore, required a solid base of analysis on which recommendations could be built. This meant that the study or analysis of public policy, especially the consequences of proposed policies, became highly important. Students and practitioners of public administration, then, had very practical reasons to engage in the study of public policy.

But theoretical concerns existed as well, concerns that were voiced more clearly by political scientists less centrally involved with public administration. These persons, following trends in social science generally and in political science specifically, urged on their colleagues a view of policy studies more relevant to the issues of the day. In the more liberal interpretation, it was argued that political scientists had previously neglected social problems, such as poverty or urban decay, and consequently bore some responsibility for those problems. In its more conservative interpretation, it was argued that careful and rational techniques of analysis (such as those in the McNamara Defense Department) should provide a model for the rest of the government and the raw material for a reconstructed science of politics. In either case, traditional political science was assailed for being too concerned with the institutions of government and the behaviors of government actors. What was being overlooked, it was argued, was a careful analysis of the content and impact of public policies.

Political Scientists View Public Policy

Among political scientists, there were at least two distinct orientations toward the emergence of public policy. Quite early, Harold Lasswell and others of the "policy science" approach (Lerner and Lasswell, 1960) felt that systematic inquiry into the policy making process could establish relationships between instrumental policies and end values. Normative choices about the ultimate direction of society would be followed by prescriptive recommendations as to the way in which such goals might be attained. In a somewhat similar vein, Yehezkel Dror (1968, p. 8) argued that policy science is principally directed toward improving the "design and operations of policymaking systems." In his view, knowledge about specific policies should be integrated with knowledge about the policy making system itself, with how it operates and how it might be improved.

A second approach popular among political scientists was one that would utilize studies of public policy to generate empirically based knowledge about the political process. Thomas Dye (1970), for example, held that a sharp distinction between normative and empirical models should be maintained and that the study of public policy, though guided by normative interests, could only provide empirical explanations of public policy. "By choosing to employ an empirical model, we are committing ourselves to the task of explanation rather than recommendation" (p. 25).

In Dye's view, public policy is simply "whatever governments choose to do or not to do" (1976, p. 1). Policy analysis in turn is "finding out what governments do, why they do it, and what difference it makes" (p. 1). The study of public policy can focus either on the causes of particular policies— that is, the political, social, or economic circumstances that have created particular kinds of policies—or on the consequences of policies—for example, the effect a particular policy will have on a particular kind of problem. In either case, the goal of the policy analyst is the same: to provide a description and explanation of the causes or consequences of various policies. This information may be useful to the policy maker; however, that use is incidental to its purpose of building a broader theoretical understanding of governmental action. The political scientist has the role of scientist, not advocate.

Especially important in the development of a political science perspective on public policy was David Easton's model of the political system. Easton (1965, p. 110) argued that the political system consists of the patterns of interaction of political actors, those persons concerned with the "authoritative allocation of values" for the society. From the environment flow various demands on and various supports for the system, which are converted into outputs in the form of public policies. These outputs are then fed back to the environment and affect future inputs into the system.

Responsiveness and Effectiveness

For the student of public organizations, Francis E. Rourke (1969) provided a careful analysis of the way in which the bureaucracy asserts its influence on the policy process. Rourke contended that three factors are central to the ability of an agency to influence the system. First, agencies depend on external support, the development of constituencies that assist in promoting their viewpoint. Such support may come from outside the government—for example, from educators who support the Department of Education or conservationists who support the Forest Service—or from other agencies within the government, as in the case of interdepartmental projects. Second, agencies vary in their impact on the policy system based on the amount of information or expertise they possess. Such expertise may be brought to bear either by trained and experienced agency personnel who are able to influence political decision makers (including appointed officials within the bureaucracy as well as legislators and other elected officials) or by administrators who exercise discretion in applying their expertise to the execution of existing policies. Third, bureaucracies differ in their impact based on internal characteristics of the agencies, especially the vitality of the organization and the effectiveness of its leadership. This point is especially well illustrated by the traditional battles between the Department of State and the Department of Defense, battles that have often been decided by the skill of one secretary in urging his agency's position.

Rourke's work is important not only in outlining ways in which agencies effectively influence policy outcomes but also in drawing attention to the ethical and political implications of this process. Rourke noted two issues that are of concern to students of the policy process: *responsiveness,* the extent to which the system "promotes a correspondence between the decisions of bureaucrats and the preferences of the community or the officeholders who presume to speak for the public"; and *effectiveness,* the degree to which policies lead to decisions that "are more likely than alternative choices to bring about the outcomes . . . desired" (p. 3).

Later in this chapter, we will examine the ways in which each of these issues have been discussed by students of public policy. However, it is important to note, with Rourke, that these two concerns are often at odds with one another, and neither can be dealt with in isolation. For example, Rourke noted that secrecy in national security matters potentially affects both responsiveness and effectiveness. In the case of John and Carol presented in chapter 1, the issues of responsiveness and effectiveness were not only central but in apparent opposition. Ultimately, as we will see, the two issues merge into a concern for how effectively those in public organizations are able to manage change processes to express societal values. As such, these two issues are at the core of any theory of public organization.

However, the positivist influence on the study of public policy (deriving primarily from mainstream political science) has increasingly come to dominate policy studies, focusing attention on issues of effectiveness rather than issues of responsiveness. This view has limited its concern to the most effective means to the ends being sought, to issues of fact rather than value. Although many scholars have been attentive to the issue of responsiveness, the continued reliance on the methods and techniques of positivist social science has limited the scope of the growing field of policy analysis. Each of these areas will now be examined in greater detail.

■ _____ ■

RESPONSIVENESS IN PUBLIC POLICY

The issue of responsiveness has drawn the attention of a wide variety of scholars and has ranged across many concerns. Certainly, if the public bureaucracy substantially influences public policy, it would seem only proper to consider ways of assuring that actions of the bureaucracy reflect the values of the society. But what exactly does this mean? Does it mean that those in public organizations should limit their own influence to matters of little consequence, seeking neutrality and deferring always to others? Does it mean that they should seek to match the mood of the legislators, the supposed representatives of the people? Should this occur even where the bureaucrat has information that would show the legislators to be misguided on a particular issue? Or should those in public organizations arrive at their own view of what constitutes the public interest, perhaps majority opinion, measured through polling or other procedures? Or do they have a responsibility to lead rather than to follow, to use their knowledge and expertise to act in the public interest, even when the public is not ostensibly interested? And, as if these questions were not difficult enough, is it sufficient that the resulting policies correspond to the values of the society, or must the process through which they are developed itself necessarily be democratic?

Redford's "Democratic Morality"

Emmett S. Redford states the issue well in his book *Democracy in the Administrative State* (1969). Redford argues that democratic morality rests on three key issues, each of which must be examined in light of the impact of large administrative organizations with substantial influence over the development of public policy. First, democratic morality assumes that the person, the individual, is the basic measure of human value. It is in the realization of the fullest potential of the individual that we come to judge our political and social system. Second, it is recognized that all persons have full claim to the attention of the system. Differences in wealth or position are not valid reasons for giving undue advantage to one group or another. All persons are created equal. Third, it is assumed that individual claims can best be promoted through the involvement of all persons in the decision-making process and that participation is not only an instrumental value, helpful in attaining other ends, but is essential to the development of democratic citizenship. The ideal of universal participation may take various forms; however, Redford indicates some basics: "Among these are (1) access to information, based on education, open government, free communication, and open discussion; (2) access, direct or indirect, to forums of decision; (3) ability to open any issue to public discussion; (4) ability to assert one's claims without fear of coercive retaliation; and (5) consideration of all claims asserted" (p. 8).

In contrast, those large and complex organizations that so dominate modern society appear to be marked by far different assumptions: that the goal of the organization exceeds the purpose of personal development; that an arrangement of unequal offices in a hierarchical fashion best serves the interests of the organization; and that participation is of limited value, important only in an instrumental sense when it provides additional information to improve the quality of decision making or when it improves the possibilities of successful implementation (Denhardt, 1981). Recognizing that such organizations not only provide the settings in which most of us play out our lives but also influence quite directly the development of public policies, one might well ask: What are the potential dangers to the preservation of democracy? Have our basic commitments to democratic morality been affected or supplanted? Have we now chosen an alternative, organizational morality? If not, what steps do we need to take to preserve the basic tenets of democracy?

Although these questions could (and should) be directed to all organizations, whether traditionally considered private or public, Redford (1969) focuses his response on those administrative agencies directly a part of government. These organizations, he asserts, have been built around a structural-functional approach that has led to a governmental system of specialized program areas, each with certain responsibilities for policymaking and policy execution, each with specialists directing their attention to a fairly narrow set of issues, and each supported by specialized interest groups. Moreover, within these organizations, not all persons have equal influence on policy decisions. Those in higher offices and those with particular professional skills constitute a small minority within which the power of the organization is concentrated. Policies, however, are rarely the province of a single individual but rather the result of the interaction of many persons and indeed many organizations. Redford concludes that "the attainment of the democratic ideal in the world of administration depends . . . on the inclusiveness of the representation of interests in the interaction process among decision makers" (p. 44). With Redford, we may conclude that the growth of the administrative state has indeed restructured the problem of democratic morality, yet it has not made it less important. As long as we are committed to the ideal of democracy, the administrative state will never attain legitimacy until it can demonstrate its capacity to enhance individual worth, equality among all citizens, and universal participation. It is along these lines that we must examine the responsiveness of public organizations and specific theoretical and practical efforts to ensure responsiveness.

Influencing the Bureaucratic Character

Very broadly speaking, theorists of public organization have developed two different approaches to the question of responsibility in public agencies. One seeks to assure responsibility by influencing the character of the bureaucrat, either through socialization, training, or professional standards. The other, perhaps a little less trusting of the good will of bureaucrats, suggests more formal mechanisms ranging from requirements for class representation among bureaucrats to removal from office for cause. Obviously, these two approaches are not exclusive of one another in either theory or practice. However, differences in the two are suggestive of the complexities involved in securing responsibility in public agencies.

Many early attempts to specify the character required of the public servant took their cue from Appleby, who often repeated (and apparently demonstrated by his example) the set of personal qualities most appropriate to government service. Appleby (1945, p. 4) hoped for a "special attitude of public responsibility" that would be transmitted to those entering the field of public administration, through either their background or their training. That special attitude went beyond the qualities generally considered desirable in other fields of management, such as interpersonal effectiveness, the ability to delegate, a focus on decision and action, and personal dynamism. Rather, it had to do with "democratic spirit". "The . . . enlistment of all the energies and abilities of the persons in an organization; getting their full and zealous participation" (p. 46).

This same spirit was sought by Stephen K. Bailey (1966, p. 24), who interpreted Appleby's work to indicate that administrators need an understanding of the moral ambiguity of public policies, a recognition of the moral priorities and paradoxes of the public service, and the moral qualities of "(1) optimism; (2) courage; and (3) fairness tempered by charity." Similarly, Marshall Dimock (1936, p. 132) "hoped for . . . loyalty, as well as honesty, enthusiasm, humility, and all the other attributes of character and conduct which contribute to effectual and satisfying service."

Obviously, these attempts to spell out the desired characteristics of the public servant remained somewhat distant from practice. Questions and dilemmas immediately arose: How can we ensure these qualities in our administrators? What happens when equally public-spirited officials disagree? How can terms such as "fairness tempered by charity" (Bailey, 1966) be made specific enough to be meaningful? To what extent can we trust the administrator's own conception of the public interest?

Standards of Responsibility

The typical answers given by the early writers on responsibility were consistent with the administrative management approach: the bureaucrat was to be strictly responsible to the legislature and to the chief executive. Specific centers of authority and responsibility were to be defined and obeyed. Responsibility was important, indeed central to public service, and responsibility was to be found in "a definite, hierarchical chain of command, reaching unbroken to the political heads of agencies and to the president, the Congress, and the general public" (Appleby, 1952, p. 250). Although such a process was made more difficult by the increase in layers of authority and responsibility in a big democracy, the answer remained essentially the same: the resolution of critical issues must occur in a central authority politically responsible to the people.

Others, however, recognized the difficulty of such an approach. For a particular administrator, competing and sometimes conflicting centers of power and responsibility are often demanding to be heard, and these may vary in scope and intensity from one decision to the next. The matter of responsiveness becomes exceedingly complex, and the administrator may indeed be left to his or her own preferences in making policy decisions. Therefore, it is not enough simply to argue for an abstract set of virtues to be adopted by all "good" administrators. At a minimum, we would expect that some general guidance would be provided by the administrator's training, by standards of the profession, or by reference to certain general principles of justice.

Objective Versus Subjective Responsibility

A classical debate between Carl Friedrich and Herman Finer centered on a similar issue: the difference between *objective responsibility*, or accountability to another person or group, and *subjective responsibility*, felt responsibility that causes one to behave in a particular way. In the debate, Friedrich (reprinted 1972) took the position that the complexity of modern government and the need for creative and unusual solutions to problems made specific objective mechanisms of control much more difficult. Increasingly, administrators are called upon to make decisions not based on precedent or direction from a superior body but on the basis of their technical expertise and their understanding of "popular sentiment" (p. 320). Where this is the case, the administrator's own sense of responsibility, what John Gaus called the "inner check," is often determining (p. 321). Fortunately, wrote Friedrich, the growing influence of professionals in government permits us to be more secure, for well-trained professionals imbued with the spirit of democratic responsibility will be attentive to public needs. Especially in the case of scientific professionals, the fellowship of science can be counted on to maintain a proper balance of competence and concern.

This same feeling was echoed later by Frederick C. Mosher (1968), who also saw government being placed increasingly in the hands of professionals; their background and training and the standards they adopted would be critical to the future of democratic government. But how can we be sure, asked Mosher, that the standards of the professions are consistent with those of democracy? After all, in many professions, there is a tendency to become isolated from the public, to become preoccupied with technical rather than human concerns, and to become self-interested rather than public-spirited. Mosher's answer lay in education. Through the universities, especially the professional schools, the values of future professionals would be shaped. And, through broader, more humanized programs of professional education for administrators, "the universities offer the best hope of making the professions safe for democracy" (p. 219).

Even if we assume that public-spirited professionals are the best hope for the maintenance of democratic government, we may wonder whether the professions or the schools that produce professionals will in fact undertake to communicate and enforce a sense of democratic responsibility. Certainly, many professions have established codes of ethics or similar standards of professional conduct; however, it remains unclear whether these include the kinds of commitments to democratic responsibility hoped for by Friedrich and Mosher and whether they are sufficiently precise to be enforced in any meaningful way. Similarly, universities, especially schools of public administration, have been more attentive in recent years to issues of ethics and responsibility in their curricula. But it remains to be seen whether such efforts are merely short-term reactions to recent political events like Watergate or whether they will have a more sustained influence on the development of public service professionals.

Ethical Studies

In the last several years, ethical studies in the field of public administration have taken two approaches. One has introduced students to philosophical studies in ethics, then sought applications to public-sector problems. As mentioned in chapter 5, for example, the work of John Rawls has been adapted to support a concern for justice and equity in the public service. Although such philosophical work has the advantage of considerable sophistication, it is often resisted by students, who cite its obscurity and alleged lack of relevance to public problems. Nevertheless, a thorough understanding of the question of democratic responsibility will clearly require that theorists and practitioners alike be prepared to seriously engage the ethical issues raised by philosophers.

A second approach—more direct and accessible, though somewhat less rigorous, than the first—is presented by John Rohr in his book *Ethics for Bureaucrats* (1978). Rohr argues that bureaucrats have an ethical obligation to support what he calls "regime values." Since "bureaucrats have taken an oath to uphold the Constitution that brought this regime into being and continues to state symbolically its spirit and meaning," they should look for guidance to the Constitution, or, more specifically, to Supreme Court interpretations of the Constitution, in exercising discretionary authority (p. 67). Clearly, an examination of Supreme Court opinions would give more specific meaning to such abstract concepts as justice and equality, yet one might question whether the Supreme Court itself always reflects the general views of the citizens, or even whether it should. Moreover, the Court shifts its own views from time to time, and, although examining the reasoning for such shifts would be helpful in understanding the various arguments involved in a particular issue, the Court does not always give firm guidance to the administrator. Finally, the Court necessarily depends on precedents in its review of cases, whereas administrators, as noted earlier, must often chart new territory, not reviewing or relying on precedent but developing innovative approaches to public problems. The guidance of the Court would not be especially helpful in these cases.

Limitations of Subjective Responsibility

In any case, the search continues for ways to ensure that professionals in government, including professional administrators, maintain a sense of democratic responsibility. Yet, as a means of securing the public interest, this approach to the question of responsiveness has certain limitations. Finer's argument of forty years ago comes to mind: leaving matters in the hands and minds of individual bureaucrats, professionals or not, does little to ensure responsiveness to the will of the people. Certainly, some members of public organizations, perhaps even a majority, will act with an appropriate concern for the norms of democracy, but others may not. Whether for reasons of personal gain or simply through a misguided sense of their professional duties and responsibilities, a minority may act without regard for the public interest and consequently do damage to that interest. For Finer (1972, p. 328) the issue was simple: "Are the servants of the public to decide their own course, or is their course of action to be decided by a body outside themselves?" His answer was the latter: legislators should be permitted and indeed expected to provide a precise definition of their intent based on careful consideration of the available technical evidence and to exercise frequent review of the implementation of policy. Only through the supervision and control of the bureaucracy by elected officials can responsiveness to the electorate be achieved. A sense of subjective responsibility may seem sufficient, but more objective means of accountability are in fact necessary to preserve the interests of the society from the occasional whims of government professionals. Moral responsibility is fine in theory, but political responsibility is required in practice.

Although Finer's argument is overdrawn, especially with respect to the capacity of the legislature to deal in specifics (or even the desirability that it do so), his analysis suggests that more formal institutional methods of promoting responsibility should be examined. Two such approaches, representative bureaucracy and public participation, have received special attention in recent years and serve to illustrate the theoretical importance of this issue. (Focusing on these two approaches, however, does not diminish the practical importance of other reforms, ranging from ombudsman programs and ethics commissions to open-meeting laws.)

Representative Bureaucracy

The proponents of representative bureaucracy, a term apparently coined by J. Donald Kingsley (1944), argue that decisions emerging from bureaucratic agencies will more nearly approximate the wishes of the public if the staffs of those agencies reflect the demographic characteristics of the general population. Kingsley hoped that a less elite, less class-biased British civil service would limit the possibility of bureaucratic dominance by the middle and upper classes in that country. Especially difficult would be a situation in which a party representing lower-class interests would come to power yet be stymied in its reform efforts by a recalcitrant public bureaucracy. As the notion of representative bureaucracy has been applied to the American experience, it has more often come to focus on race, sex, and ethnic background, though still suggesting that persons from particular groups would represent the interests of those groups as members of public agencies.

For several reasons, the logic of representative bureaucracy seems somewhat flawed. For example, studies of the policy preferences of the higher civil service have indicated that the correlation between background and attitude is weak. One cannot assume that persons coming from a particular group will in fact represent the interests of that group. They may represent the bureaucracy itself or the professional groups of which they are a part rather than the interests of their demographic group. For all these reasons, the issue of representative bureaucracy is considerably more complicated than its advocates (e.g., Krislov, 1974) sometimes seem to recognize.

Although representative bureaucracy has limitations as a means of securing responsiveness, we should not be led to question the need to involve a wide range of groups in the governmental process. To argue, as some have, that affirmative action programs for the recruitment, retention, and advancement of minorities and women do not ensure the representativeness of bureaucracy is not sufficient reason to limit such programs. In the first place, although such persons may not represent the interests of their demographic group on all issues, they may indeed represent such interests on key issues, thus providing a check on the potential excesses of the majority. Moreover, the involvement of such persons provides both a symbolic and a practical signal to others that centers of decision making are accessible and that, while agencies cannot necessarily be expected to respond automatically to the interests of previously disadvantaged groups, those agencies can be influenced. Someone should at least be willing to listen.

Citizen Involvement and Implications of Responsiveness

Significant efforts to achieve real participation were, of course, undertaken in the early 1960s. The history of the movement toward "maximum feasible participation" or "widespread citizen participation" has been well documented and need not be considered at length here. Although the idea of public participation had certain historical precedents and a firm intellectual basis, its incorporation into the final drafting of the Economic Opportunity Act of 1964 gave special impetus to the idea in this country. But the practice of involving the poor in antipoverty efforts quickly became an extremely volatile issue, especially in cases where the active participation of the poor led to confrontation with existing structures of power. However, by the time these conflicts were recognized, the principle of public participation seemed well established.

Other agencies had already begun to follow the lead of the Office of Economic Opportunity and to work toward citizen involvement. In 1966, the notion of public involvement in program planning and execution was incorporated in the Demonstration Cities Act, a move at least partially consistent with the previous and related urban renewal practice of public involvement in advisory capacities. Also, local school boards began to recognize the need for decentralization and for the involvement of students, teachers, and parents in the operations of school systems. At the university level, student demands for involvement in university decision making were at the heart of student activism in the late 1960s and early 1970s.

In all such cases, however, questions continued to arise as to whether real power was being shifted to client representatives or whether the real power remained with those who had previously controlled the organization's activities. For example, would the latter form alliances to maintain their control over client representatives, or would the skills and technical knowledge they possessed permit them to continue their domination of client groups? In many cases, client representatives, if not politically skilled on entering decision-making bodies, gained skills quite rapidly, to the point that their voice was often effective against surprisingly great odds. Still, the power of such representatives was probably exaggerated. Yet in many instances where cooptation was tried, participants reacted so strongly that real and meaningful power resulted.

Whether responsiveness is sought through the selection of particular types of persons to staff public organizations or through the imposition of external controls on their behavior, the issue of responsiveness must be recognized as central to any modern theory of public organization. If public organizations by definition seek to express societal values, then their members bear a responsibility to examine, understand, and interpret public values to the best of their ability. Beyond this, however, one might argue that those in public organizations have a responsibility to assist the public in articulating its needs, to identify important, though often hidden, needs, and to express a desire for their solution. In this view, the notion of responsiveness goes beyond simply reacting to those values that are publicly stated; it involves a certain amount of leadership in bringing issues forward for examination, debate, and possible solution. But our discussion of responsiveness has still another implication: that responsiveness in a democratic society involves not only seeking socially desirable ends but doing so in a way consistent with democratic values. This position would mean, for example, that we would not pursue justice in an unjust way. It might also mean that we would not seek democratic ends through nondemocratic (elitist, hierarchical, authoritarian) organizations. To meet all these criteria, we would require a theory of democratic administration far different from those currently found in the literature on public administration. However, there are some indications of continuing work on such a theory, examples of which will be presented later in this chapter and in the one that follows. First, however, we must examine the issue of effectiveness.

■ ── ■

EFFECTIVENESS IN PUBLIC POLICY

In addition to their concern for responsiveness, students of public policy have also been attentive to the effectiveness of policy decisions and of the actions taken to implement those decisions. This section will focus on the emerging field of policy analysis as an approach to improved policy decisions; the following section will examine a special body of literature that brings together a concern for responsiveness and a concern for effectiveness in its study of implementation processes. Work in the general field of public policy will not be summarized here. Rather, several prominent themes in that field will be identified, themes that would seem most directly to influence developing theories of public organization. Specifically, focus will be on public policy in the context of the larger political system and on contemporary approaches to the analysis and evaluation of public policy.

Lowi's "Interest Group Liberalism"

In contrast to those who encourage more representative processes of administration, Theodore Lowi, in *The End of Liberalism* (1969), argues, in effect, that responsiveness now depends on the restoration of effectiveness in government. Lowi contends that the vast expansion of government in recent years occurred because the political system succumbed to the interests of organized groups in society that were able to force their views on the government. The government in turn assumed responsibility for the programs sought by those groups and created vast agencies to carry out those programs. These agencies, Lowi asserts, have taken on far too much discretionary power, although they have been able to justify their power by claiming that they represent the popular will. To Lowi, such a situation undermines the formality and direction required for effective policy planning; it calls for the development of a far more legalistic or "juridical" democracy.

Lowi traces the roots of our current approach to government to the early twentieth century, a time when the values of capitalism prevailed to the near exclusion of popular rule. Although the industrialization of society led to material benefits for some, it also created problems that it could not solve. The failure of capitalism to secure the broad range of social benefits that it promised eventually led to its demise as a public philosophy. Its replacement, which Lowi terms "interest group liberalism," grew from two related sources, each feeding on the other. The first was an increasing concern for rationality in social and political processes, a rationality modeled by developments in technology and industrial organization. The rationalization of society, which Weber had discussed, was well illustrated in industrial America, with its emphasis on hierarchy and the division of labor. But rationalization also meant control, the ability to regulate and order human as well as mechanical activities. Following this logic, the concern for individual prerogative was soon displaced by a concern for social control. In government, this trend supported a more "positive" role for government, one in which government would act to balance the potential excesses of management and labor, technology and industrialization. This new attitude, called *statism*, began, especially in the Roosevelt years, to dominate the thinking of most political leaders in this country.

A second trend affecting the development of a new public philosophy was the rise of many competing organized groups, each promoting its own special interest. There were labor and management, to be sure, but also racial and ethnic groups, trade associations, consumer groups, and even religious organizations. Government was itself one such interest group, perhaps the most important, but still just one among many. And, in all cases, the rise of administration provided special support. All groups shared an interest in administration and organization; all sought to impose administrative structures and processes on their internal operations and on as much of their environment as they could. The group, converted by administration into organization, now became the center of attention and, correspondingly, the interplay of groups and organizations became much more important. Indeed, market competition was increasingly displaced by group competition, or *pluralism*.

The combination of these two trends, statism and pluralism, led to the rise of interest group liberalism, which Lowi (1969, p. 51) defines in this way: "It is liberalism because it is optimistic about government, expects to use government in a positive and expansive role, is motivated by the highest sentiments, and possesses a strong faith that what is good for government is good for society. It is interest group liberalism because it sees as both necessary and good a policy agenda that is accessible to all organized interests and makes no independent judgment of their claims."

Government Coercion

By adopting the functions of regulation and redistribution, the government gained more direct and coercive power over citizens.

Elsewhere Lowi (1974) defines four functions of government: regulatory, redistributive, distributive, and constituent. These four types are derived from differences in the coerciveness of government power: coercion may be either remote or immediate; it may be directly applied, or it may work through the environment. Those policies that involve immediate and direct coercion are termed *regulatory*. Regulatory policies prevent individuals from exceeding acceptable limits of behavior and range from criminal laws restricting individual behavior to federal prohibitions of unfair labor practices and workplace safety. *Redistributive* policies apply immediate coercion but do so through the environment. They typically involve taxing one group in order to provide benefits for another—for example, through welfare, health care, or subsidized housing policies. *Distributive* policies, the most common in the federal government, involve remote coercion of individual conduct. Such policies use general tax revenues to provide for individual needs, such as farm subsidies (which offer benefits if certain actions are taken), environmental research, and government insurance (such as flood insurance). *Constituent* policies employ remote coercion applied through the environment. These are especially difficult to define, ranging from such policies as reapportionment, which touch the citizen only indirectly, to such policies as national defense, which see the government as a constituent to which agencies deliver services. Although government agencies influence all types of policies, their impact in the increasingly important areas of regulatory and redistributive policy are felt most clearly where they establish special information, expertise, or client support—that is, where they amass the chief resources of interest group liberalism.

But coercion requires legitimation, which interest group liberalism seeks "by avoiding law, . . . by parsoning out to private parties the power to make public policy," and by promoting a new ideology of representation (Lowi, 1969, p. 44). This ideology seeks to apply notions of popular role to a more active and more coercive government and especially to the administrative agencies through which it exercises its power (p. 63). No longer is the legislature the primary organ for policy making; instead, the development of policy has been shifted to implementing agencies. Formal and authoritative rule making is replaced by a system of bargaining and negotiation. "Liberalism has opposed privilege in policy formulation only to foster it quite systematically in the implementation of policy" (p. 297). Such a government can be neither responsive nor effective.

Lowi's answer is a new emphasis on legislative enactment and administrative rule making that would codify as many relationships as possible, thus eliminating the need for discretion and the bargaining and negotiation that it allows. Obviously, such a solution merely fights fire with fire; it urges more systematic and detailed regulation (or rationalization) as a cure for the ills of regulation (or rationalization). Moreover, it asserts the role of the legislative body but does so in a way that would create still another interest group, the legislature itself; in order to act in the comprehensive and detailed way suggested by Lowi, the legislature would obviously require considerably more staff or administrative support.

But these concerns are of less significance than Lowi's implicit endorsement of elite rule, the rule of a privileged few holding the reigns of power and having only limited institutional constraints on the exercise of that power. In this view, representation is at best an election-year phenomenon, less important than the effort to centralize and formalize government power in pursuit of greater government effectiveness. As the ends of government and popular involvement in determining those ends come to be taken for granted, and as Lowi concentrates on the means to attain those ends, he ends up offering the same vision of an administered society as the administrative management theorists—one in which centralized powers seek not only to achieve rationality but indeed to define it.

■   ■

THE DISCOVERY OF POLICY IMPLEMENTATION

Just as Lowi is critical of the role of government agencies in policy implementation, others have taken that role as given and sought to understand
how efforts at implementation might redirect the intended course of
government policy. As students of the policy process more carefully examined the issue of effectiveness, that is, the ability of politics to bring about
desired outcomes, it became clear (as Lowi noted) that simply declaring a
policy by legislative decree or executive order was not enough. Just as
policies are not made in a vacuum, they are not carried out in a vacuum.
Rather, a complex set of environmental factors affect the execution of
public policies. Moreover, even in the relative absence of environmental
influences, the bureaucratic agencies charged with executing particular
policies sometimes simply fail to do so. For whatever reason—limited
resources, inadequate organizational structures, ineffective communications, or poor coordination—the policies of the policymakers are not put
into action in the way that had been intended. These limits on policy
execution have been discussed in a growing body of literature focusing on
policy implementation.

This new interest in problems of implementation has several important
implications for the development of a theory of public organizations: it
suggests greater attention to important environmental or interorganiza-
tional influences on organizational work; and it places the study of public
administration in the larger context of public decision making, thus
acknowledging the role of the public bureaucracy in expressing public
values. However, in other ways, the study of policy implementation represents a regression in the study of public organizatons: the distinction
between policymaking and policy implementation exactly parallels the old
politics-administration dichotomy; and the uncritical acceptance of such a
distinction by many students of the policy process neither recognizes the
role of the bureaucracy in framing public values nor addresses the issues of
democratic accountability raised by activity. Moreover, the apparent naiveté of certain students of policy implementation with respect to developments in public administration over the past thirty to forty years leaves
their work sounding far more like that of the early students of administrative management than the work of more recent and more sophisticated
writers.

Policy Formation and Policy Execution

One of the earliest studies to use the implementation focus was a book by
Jeffrey Pressman and Aaron Wildavsky, *Implementation: How Great Expectations
in Washington Are Dashed in Oakland; or Why It's Amazing that Federal Programs
Work at All* (1973). *Implementation* is a lengthy description and analysis of a
particular economic development program in the Oakland area that, as the

subtitle of the book indicates, was something less than a complete success. Pressman and Wildavsky's basic point seems to be that a simple relationship between policy formation and policy execution is deceiving. For example, they conclude that, in this case, "what seemed to be a simple program turned out to be a very complex one, involving many participants, a host of differing perspectives, and a long and tortuous path of decision points that had to be cleared" (p. 94). Even what appeared to be fairly straightforward programs consisted of many distinct and competing interests representing widely divergent views on many different though interrelated issues. At many points, these interests undermined the process of implementation.

Pressman and Wildavsky's response to this finding is bound up in a somewhat confusing discussion of the relationship between policy formation and policy implementation. Using language remarkably similar to that of Frank Goodnow more than fifty years earlier, Pressman and Wildavsky (1973) argue that policy and implementation may be separated for analytical purposes: "*Implementation* . . . means to carry out, accomplish, fulfill, produce, complete. But what is it that is being implemented? A policy, naturally." But Pressman and Wildavsky (1973, p. 143) also hold that implementation should not be separated from policy and indeed that many of the problems encountered in the Oakland project might have been avoided if a greater concern for implementation had been evidenced in formulating the original programs: "The great problem, as we understand it, is to make the difficulties of implementation a part of the initial formulation of policy." One way to do this would be to establish systems at the outset that minimize the number of intrusions into the implementation process, for example, by reducing the number of clearance points required. A second way of incorporating implementation considerations in the original formation of policy "would be to pay as much attention to the creation of organizational machinery for executing a program as for launching one " (pp. 144–145). In either case, the requirement seems to be that policymakers acknowledge the difficulties of implementation and take steps to reduce the possibility of interference from others who might wish to influence the direction of the program.

Stating this point in more extreme fashion, one might say that, against the vagaries of an open (democratic?) system, the best protection is closure. But, obviously, to resolve the formation–implementation dichotomy by giving greater control to the policymakers is a solution that reduces the influence of local and regional groups. And, of course, what is a failure of implementation for one person may be a triumph of democracy for another. Just as the concern for effective implementation underlying the Pressman and Wildavsky position is undeniable, the administrative management solution they offer is difficult to ignore. Placing more value decisions in the hands of policymakers does not transcend the formulation-implementation dichotomy but simply changes its terms. Choices are made by those in charge and carried out by those who are subordinate—just another version of the politics-administration split.

Games Policymakers Play

An interesting contrast to the Pressman and Wildavsky interest in control is provided in Eugene Bardach's more recent book, *The Implementation Game* (1977). Bardach too is concerned with the multiple interests represented in the combination of federal, state, and local relations and with those connecting the public sector at all levels to private and semiprivate groups and organizations. Viewing the interactions of all these groups, Bardach recognizes some of the limitations of seeking more effective policy processes through greater centralized control and turns instead to the metaphor of games to describe the process by which implementation occurs. Specifically, the idea of games "directs us to look at the players, what they regard as the stakes, their strategies and tactics, their resources for playing, the rules of play (which stipulate the conditions for winning), the rules of fair play, . . . the nature of communications (or lack of them) among the players, and the degree of uncertainty surrounding the possible outcomes. The game metaphor also directs our attention to who is not willing to play and for what reasons and to who insists on changes in some of the game's parameters as a condition for playing" (p. 56).

Following the "games people play" metaphor, Bardach analyzes the various kinds of bargaining and negotiation that occur in the implementation process. The result is a more clear and conceptual view of the implementation process and especially those games that interfere with the effective execution of public policies. For example, Bardach notes that the politics of implementation, which is distinguished by the existence of a policy, is therefore highly defensive. A concluding paragraph, however, is perhaps most telling. Here Bardach puts the study of implementation in perspective by commenting, "The most important problems that affect public policy are almost surely not those of implementation but those of basic political, economic, and social theory" (p. 283).

Political and Economic Factors

Whereas many studies of policy implementation have concentrated on the interrelationships between the various agencies and interests represented in the policy process, others have focused on the characteristics of specific agencies that influence their ability to effect desired outcomes. In *The Political Economy of Public Organizations* (1973), Gary Wamsley and Mayer Zald seek to place public organizations in an appropriate political and economic context, then to examine their internal operations and the "consequences of organizational structure and process for policy implementation" (p. 11). Although their work fails in its rather grandiose claim to assert "a systematic empirical theory of public administration" (p. 93), amounting instead to little more than a convenient way of describing and categorizing various aspects of organizational life, its directness and simplicity have proven quite appealing to some students of the policy process.

Wamsley and Zald's limited use of the term *political economy* simply suggests that organizations, especially public organizations, are influenced by both political and economic factors. The political factors are generally those recognized in the pluralist tradition, established values arrived at through the interplay of power and interest; economic factors are those that focus on the market and its exchange of goods and services. Political and economic factors are then seen to affect both internal and external aspects of the organization's functioning. The juxtaposition of the politics-economics dichotomy and the internal-external dichotomy results in a four-cell classi- fication of organizational structure and process through which Wamsley and Zald propose to analyze the workings of public organizations.

The external political environment is much like that discussed in other studies of policy implementation; it refers to the interplay of largely self-in- terested groups and agencies both inside and outside government as they affect the efforts of any particular organization to achieve its objectives. The economic environment, in contrast, focuses on input and output char- acteristics of the organization: what it takes from the environment in terms of personnel, resources, etc., and what it returns to the environment and to the larger "industry structure" of which it is a part (Wamsley and Zald, 1973, p. 21). The internal policy refers to the institutionalized structure of power and authority within the organization as well as claims against that structure of power. (Downs also details this organizational power structure in his book *Inside Bureaucracy* [1967].) The internal economy also involves patterns of authority, but chiefly those associated with task accomplish- ment: "It focuses upon organizational means rather than upon definition of goals" (Wamsley and Zald, 1973, p. 22).

Toward a Political Economy

Using this classification system, Wamsley and Zald proceed to illustrate various aspects of the political economy of public organizations with case studies and vignettes familiar to most students of public administration. Although the scheme itself appears useful, it tends to conceal the interac- tion between politics and economics, an interaction that Wamsley and Zald themselves acknowledge. Perhaps there is indeed a political economy separ- ate from either politics or economics as they are defined in the liberal tradition, and perhaps an investigation of that phenomenon would prove beneficial in developing a theory of public organizations. Or it may be that the mechanisms of exchange implied in Wamsley and Zald's definitions of both politics and economics suggest that the political economy approach would best be viewed in the tradition of the public choice theorists and their counterparts in public administration, such as Vincent Ostrom. (For the present, Wamsley and Zald would appear much closer to the latter.) In any case, if the political economy approach has merit, it is likely to be found in its connection with one or the other of these richer, more complete streams of thought.

One brief methodological note might be appropriate at this point. Following in the positivist tradition of most students of the policy process, Wamsley and Zald seek to develop an empirical theory, but one with normative overtones. In this view, which Wamsley (1976, p. 391) elsewhere labels the "new social science" (though citing "new social scientists" back to Weber), the scientist would make a choice of research topics based on normative preferences, then become totally objective in the remainder of the investigation. The many difficulties of such a position relate to both value neutrality and theory-practice issues, but, more important, they are suggestive of the difficulties facing the positivist approach to policy research. A truly relevant study of public policy able to connect issues of theory and practice seems a highly desirable goal; yet studies based on traditional positivism or even on a "reformed" social science seem ultimately limited in their ability to achieve these goals. Implicit in the positivist approach, as we noted in our discussion of Marx, Weber, and Freud, is an emphasis on control. Thus, it is hardly surprising to find policy studies based on the positivist tradition asserting the traditional interests of hierarchical domination in complex organizations.

Preconditions For Successful Implementation

Such an effort, one that clearly seems to return the study of public administration to its roots, is George Edwards's recent analysis, *Implementing Public Policy* (1980). Edwards begins with the now standard argument that "public policies are rarely self-executing" (p. 1). (Woodrow Wilson [1887, p. 200] had said, "It is getting harder to run a constitution than to frame one.") If policy implementation is the stage between the establishment of policy and its impact on the citizenry, then one might well ask, what are the preconditions for or obstacles to successful policy implementation? Edwards responds that four factors should be considered: communications, resources, dispositions or attitudes (of the implementers), and bureaucratic structures. The discussion of these factors that follows might best be described as an enlightened administrative management approach, differing little, if at all, from the writings of Willoughby, White, and Gulick in the 1930s. For example, we are told that orders must be clear and accurate, that resources must be sufficient, that authority must be equal to responsibility. The chapter on bureaucratic structure is especially familiar: here we are told that organizational fragmentation restricts the effectiveness of policy implementation. "The more actors and agencies involved with a particular policy and the more interdependent their decisions, the less the probability of successful implementation" (p. 134). The answer would obviously be the same as that provided by the administrative reorganization movement: the concentration of power and responsibility in a single center of executive authority exercised through a chain of command with a short span of control. The material sounds quite familiar, yet it is presented as a new discovery; one has the impression that the work of at least four decades of public administration theorists has been forgotten or neglected and that we find ourselves once more in the days of politics-administration and POSDCORB (see chapter 3).

However, such a result may be inevitable, to some extent; the particular perspective adopted by most students of public policy may restrict their vision to certain types of outcomes—most notably, those associated with authority, hierarchy, and control. The repeated associations between positive social science and hierarchical patterns of authority may be suggestive of something far deeper. Perhaps something about this perspective prevents both scholars and practitioners from recognizing a broader range of possibilities for the expression of societal values through public organizations. Although the recent emphasis on policy studies in political science and public administration correctly points to the importance of environmental concerns and the valuational implications of both policy and administration, this perspective may be limited by its own epistemological commitments and thus cannot adequately comprehend the full implications of its own message.

■ ─── ■

METHODS OF POLICY ANALYSIS

Although Lowi and the implementation theorists differ on several matters, they agree on two key points: policy making is crucial to the governmental process and should therefore be centralized and rationalized. Modern policy analysis directs its efforts toward responding to these needs in its examination of social action. But, over the last several years, policy analysis has proven to be a social force of some importance itself. The policy analysis movement—which, with its own networks and organizations, journals and monographs, is certainly more of a movement than the new public administration ever aspired to be—represents the epitome of policy thinking in this country. The message of the movement is clear: the key to effective government is the specification of the most rational means for obtaining the agency's objectives; the methods of positive social science are best able to specify such means; and individuals trained in the use of those methods (policy analysts, not managers) will best be able to guide the future.

The Ideal of Rationality

We have already examined the concept of rationality in our discussion of the rational model of administration. To review briefly: technical or objective rationality describes the most efficient means toward a given end. Dahl and Lindblom (1953, p. 38), for example, write, "An action is rational to the extent that it is 'correctly' designed to maximize goal attainment. Given more than one goal (the usual human situation), an action is rational to the extent that it is designed to maximize net goal attainment." Given such an orientation, the problem facing the decision-maker is fairly straightforward: alternative choices must be examined in the light of their contribution to the desired goals, and the alternative that maximizes gains should be chosen.

1. The decision maker is confronted with a given problem that can be separated from other problems or at least considered meaningful in comparison with them.

2. The goals, values, or objectives that guide the decision maker are clarified and ranked according to their importance.

3. The various alternatives for dealing with the problem are examined.

4. The consequences (costs and benefits) that would follow from the selection of each alternative are investigated.

5. Each alternative, and its attendant consequences, can be compared with the other alternatives.

6. The decision maker will choose that alternative and its consequences that maximize the attainment of his goals, values, or objectives [Anderson, 1979, pp. 9-10.]

As we have seen, however, the classical model of rational choice is rarely attainable in practice, and, for this reason, several theorists have suggested variations on the theme of rationality. Among these, Simon postulated the notion of "bounded rationality" leading to "satisficing" behavior, and Lindblom argued that most policy choices are merely "incremental" changes in the status quo, arrived at through a "disjointed" process (see chapter 3).

At first glance, these alternative descriptions of decision making or policy making may seem to be at odds with the classical model of rational choice. However, that is not entirely true. The main alternatives to classical rationality do not challenge the basic concern of that model. Their critiques are aimed at the comprehensiveness of the decision-making process, not at the concept of rationality per se. Simon's "administrative man" is limited in his rationality, but he does the best he can to approximate rationality through his participation in complex organizations. Lindblom's incrementalist may "muddle through," but, where analysis is available to support a particular course of action, that information is of great value. In either case, the ideal of rationality, that human actions might serve as means to organizational goals, is preserved. (The confusion is especially manifest in the challenging work of Aaron Wildavsky [1979, p. 18], who argues on the one hand for a view of policy analysis involving artistry and craftsmanship yet finally comes down on the side of rationality: "Policy analysis is about the realm of rationality and responsibility, where resources are related to objectives. Rationality resides in connecting what you want with what you can do, and responsibility in being accountable for making that connection." The search for a true alternative, which Yehezkel Dror has termed "extrarational," falls by the wayside.

An "Extrarational" Alternative

Interestingly enough, Dror treats the failure of theorists to concern themselves with extrarational processes such as intuition and judgment as a theory-practice question. Accusing modern behavioral scientists of reducing leadership in policy making to a set of environmentally determined functions, Dror (1968, p. 149) notes that "experienced policymakers, who usually explain their own decisions largely in terms of subconscious processes such as 'intuition' and 'judgment,' unanimously agree and even emphasize that extrarational processes play a positive and essential role in policymaking." Again mainstream social science appears to have constructed a view of the world quite at odds with the way that actors in that world experience it. As we will see in the next chapter, other approaches to the question of knowledge acquisition may correct this problem, leading to an integration of theory and practice.

Such alternatives, however, are not a part of the contemporary study of policy analysis. The same concern for achieving rational solutions to means-ends problems found in the classical model and its variations is central to modern policy analysis. Although policy studies began with Harold Lasswell (Lerner and Lasswell, 1960, p. 8) arguing for the development of policy sciences that would focus upon "the fundamental problems of man in society rather than upon the topical issues of the moment," the recent policy analysis movement has taken a decidedly more rational, technical direction. What one writer (Ostrom, 1974, p. 132) has called the "new political science . . . needed for a new world" is clearly based on inferential and empirical processes designed to "use human reason to derive conclusions, to think through problems, and to communicate meaningfully with one another."

Positive Social Science and Policy Analysis

From its commitments to instrumental rationality flow the methodological perspectives of policy analysis, exactly those of mainstream, positive social science. Stuart Nagel (1980, p. 3), one of the prime movers in the movement, defines policy analysis as "the how-to-do-methods associated with determining the nature, causes, and effects of government decisions or policies designed to cope with specific social problems." Elsewhere he writes: "Sometimes, policy analysis is more specifically defined to refer to the methods used in analyzing public policies. The main methods, however, are no different from those associated with social science and the scientific method in general, except that they are applied to variables and subject matters involving relations among policies, policy causes, and policy effects. In that sense, policy analysis is not something new methodologically" (Nagel and Neef, 1980, pp. 15–16).

The method is the study; the study is the method. And, as a method, a technique, policy analysis is devoid of content, a procedure to be applied with equal force to any circumstance. The language of policy analysis is the language of positive social science, with its concern for the measurement of quantitative data and its desire to establish cause-effect relationships. The specific questions asked by the policy analyst may vary: What causes a given policy? What social forces are responsible for what policies? What effects do given policies have? What policies will best achieve a given objective? However, the basic interest in a rational determination of cause and effect remains. Yet there is also the implication that analysis provides more than explanation, it provides solutions. For example, in cases of policy evaluation or optimization (the third and fourth questions above), it is assumed that the analysis will produce the "best" solution, that which maximizes benefits in relation to costs (Nagel and Neef, p. 27). By viewing the study of public policy as a set of methods or techniques and by reducing human needs and desires to a calculus of economic costs and benefits, modern policy analysis represents the ultimate extension of positivist social science into the realm of human choice.

Limitations of Policy Analysis

Although many obviously welcome such a development, there are clearly certain dangers in the application of policy analysis to all phases of social and political life. For our purposes, an even greater danger is that the method might be elevated to the status of a model or a theory of public organization. At least three problems come readily to mind. First, policy analysis promotes an uncritical acceptance of existing goals. By concentrating on the means to achieve given ends, policy analysis, like other instrumental sciences, diverts attention away from an exploration of the ends themselves. Societal values are taken as given, frozen in time, rather than as products of human interaction. Such a viewpoint obviously reinforces the existing values of society, making change appear neither warranted nor even possible. But, even if change were possible, there would be no normative standard to guide our actions. The world of instrumentalism makes no provision for moral consciousness.

Second, a preoccupation with objectification leads one to consider only those topics that can be analyzed in the terms of the method itself. For example, one prominent policy analyst (Scioli, 1979, p. 42) recently argued in behalf of a "new consciousness" among analysts, one that would allow them to operate in terms of "objectives and measurable outcomes." Presumably, those policies that cannot be objectively measured should not be undertaken. The result is that the method begins to structure social and political relationships rather than reflect them. And the structure toward which it tends is its own, one that places means-ends relationships in a hierarchical order to achieve systematic explanation, prediction, and control.

Third, policy analysis seeks to resolve the theory-practice dichotomy by forcing practice to correspond to theory rather than vice versa. Many have addressed the theory-practice question by seeking alternative ways of conceptualizing the relationship between theory and practice, an effort examined in more detail in the next chapter. However, if theory and practice diverge, another response is to develop a practice that corresponds to the theory—in this case, to produce a set of analysts throughout government whose professional allegiance is to the scientific method. That seems to be exactly the intention of the policy analysis movement.

The movement calls for a new profession of rational and practical policy analysts extending from the universities and policy centers (think tanks) to all areas of the government bureaucracy and even into the halls of Congress (see Meltsner, 1980, p. 249). The new analysts are to be rational in the sense of being thoroughly trained in the techniques of positive social science and in their application to human affairs. They are to be practical in the sense of being responsive to the concerns of the bureaucracy (and, presumably, accepting of its definition of goals and problems). If, as Waldo said, instrumental thinking has a tendency to extend its power to all realms of human activity, then, surely, modern policy analysts are some of its primary and not-so-secret agents.

■   ■

VINCENT OSTROM'S "INTELLECTUAL CRISIS"

The implications of this critique will be explored later; at this point, we should return to the argument made at the beginning of this chapter: that the study of public policy, though holding forth significant promise for advances in our understanding of public organization, has largely failed to live up to its promise. One possible exception to that evaluation, however, is the work of Vincent Ostrom. Yet even here the results are mixed. Ostrom in some ways represents the best in policy studies—he is concerned with fundamental social and political values, he understands something of the relationship between these values and the organization of public agencies, and he seeks an extension of democratic norms in the operations of public organizations. At the same time, his methodological commitments seem to prevent him from extending his analysis as far as he otherwise might. On balance, however, Ostrom provides important material for the student of public organization, and his work should be examined with some care.

Key Elements of Public Choice Theory

Ostrom (Ostrom and Ostrom, 1971) seeks to move away from what he sees as a preoccupation with bureaucracy in American public administration toward a broader conception of collective action. He suggests that the mainstream of public administration theory from Wilson through at least Simon has been too concerned with the efficiency of the administrative process, efficiency generally sought through mechanisms of centralization and control. The result has been an "intellectual crisis" in American public administration, in which theorists and practitioners lack both a clear sense of identity and the confidence to deal with the increasingly difficult problems they now face (p. 205). Ostrom seeks a solution to this contemporary crisis in the work of theorists of public choice.

This work is based on three key elements, the first of which is the concept of "methodological individualism," the presumption that the individual—that is, a representative individual decision maker—is the basic unit of analysis. The individual decision maker, comparable in most respects to the classical "economic man," is assumed to be self-interested, rational, and seeking to maximize his or her own utilities. By "self-interested," Ostrom means that each individual has distinct preferences that may differ from the preferences of others; by "rational," Ostrom means that individuals can rank alternative choices in a transitive manner; by "maximization," Ostrom assumes a strategy in which the individual seeks the highest net benefit in any decision situation (p. 205). Like Simon's "administrative man" or the classical "economic man," Ostrom's individual decision maker does not represent the behavior of any particular individual but suggests what we might expect a rational (or mostly rational) individual to do, given certain conditions. (It should be noted that Ostrom is not critical of Simon's work in this respect but only considers it unfortunate that Simon did not extend his concept beyond the bounds of the organization to embrace all collective action.)

A second feature of public choice theory lies in "the conceptualization of public goods as the type of event associated with the output of public agencies" (p. 205). Public goods are distinguished from private goods (those that can be measured, marketed, and contained) by virtue of the fact that they are highly indivisible. A public good provided for one person or group will be available for use by all. For example, once national defense is provided for some in a country, it is provided for all. Somewhere between private and public goods lies a range of intermediate situations in which the production and consumption of goods and services involves spillover effects, or "externalities," which are not contained in the normal mechanisms of the market. In their pursuit of these various forms of goods or benefits, individuals devise differing strategies. Among these, individuals might, under certain circumstances, form enterprises to engage in collective action seen as resulting in individual benefits. "Public agencies are not viewed simply as bureaucratic units which perform those services which someone at the top instructs them to perform. Rather, public agencies are viewed as a means for allocating decision-making capabilities in order to provide public goods and services responsive to the preferences of individuals in different social contexts" (p. 207).

The third feature of work in public choice is the idea that different kinds of decision structures (decision-making rules or arrangements) will have different effects on the behavior of individuals seeking strategies of maximization. For the student of public organization, the key question is whether an individual would expect to gain more from a single integrated bureaucratic structure or from a multiorganizational arrangement. Ostrom follows the logic of public choice to the latter conclusion: "If a domain that is relevant to the provision of a public good or service can be specified so that those who are potentially affected can be contained within the boundaries of an appropriate jurisdiction and externalities do not spill over onto others, then a public enterprise can be operated with substantial autonomy," assuming the prohibition of coercive power being used to deprive certain persons of their rights (p. 211).

Obviously, such a solution is at odds with what Ostrom perceives to be the mainstream view in American public administration, which emphasizes centralization and control. To the contrary, Ostrom's analysis suggests a constitutional arrangement that would feature multiorganizational arrangements with overlapping jurisdiction and fragmentation of authority operating at many different levels of government. (Interestingly, Ostrom finds ample historical support for such a view of the federal system in the works of the Founding Fathers, although he recognizes that other interpretations have attributed a more centrist viewpoint.)

Theory of "Democratic Administration"

What Ostrom draws from the work of public choice theorists is an argument for the development of multiorganizational arrangements in the public sector that resemble public enterprises operating with considerable independence and based in significant measure on the mobilization of client support. The basic unit, the enterprise, would operate at the lowest level consistent with the nature of its work. Where externalities spill over into other domains, there could be recourse to a second level of organization, and so forth; such arrangements as transfers or grants-in-aid could be used to facilitate the relationship between the various levels and between interrelated units at the same level.

In this view, notions of hierarchy and centralization, long central to mainstream public administration, no longer appear workable in all situations. Indeed, they no longer even appear to be the most efficient mechanisms for the distribution of public goods. In their place, Ostrom (1974, pp. 111-112) proposes the theory of "democratic administration," a theory founded on premises such as the following:

1. Individuals who exercise the prerogatives of government are no more ... [or] less corruptible than their fellow men.
2. The exercise of political authority—a necessary power to do good— will be usurped by those who perceived an opportunity to exploit such powers to their own advantage and to the detriment of others unless

authority is divided and different authorities are so organized as to limit and control one another.

3. The structure of a constitution allocates decision-making capabilities among a community of persons; and a democratic constitution defines the authority inherent in both the prerogatives of persons and the prerogative of different governmental offices, so that the capabilities of each are limited by the capabilities of others. The task of establishing and altering organizational arrangements in a democratic society is to be conceived as a problem in constitutional decision making.

4. The provision of public goods and services depends upon decisions taken by diverse sets of decision makers, and the political feasibility of each collective enterprise depends upon a favorable course of decisions in all essential decision structures over time. Public administration lies within the domain of politics.

5. A variety of different organizational arrangements can be used to provide different public goods and services. Such organizations can be coordinated through various multiorganizational arrangements, including trading and contracting to mutual advantage, competitive rivalry, adjudication, as well as the power of command in limited hierarchies.

6. Perfection in the hierarchical ordering of a professionally trained public service accountable to a single center of power will reduce the capability of a large administrative system to respond to diverse preferences among citizens for many different public goods and services and [to] cope with diverse environmental conditions.

7. Perfection in hierarchical organization accountable to a single center of power will not maximize efficiency as measured by least cost expended in time, effort, and resources.

8. Fragmentation of authority among diverse decision centers with multiple veto capabilities within any one jurisdiction and the development of multiple, overlapping jurisdictions of widely different scales are necessary conditions for maintaining a stable political order which can advance human welfare under rapidly changing conditions.

As a replacement for the Wilsonian paradigm, which Ostrom decries as inconsistent with the ideals of American democracy, a theory of democratic administration will shift attention from "a preoccupation with the organization to concerns with the opportunities that individuals can pursue in a multiorganizational environment" (p. 132). Supported by a new policy analysis that would focus on the limitations of existing organizational arrangements, the theory of democratic administration would finally assure the flexibility and responsiveness that were originally a part of the American dream.

Ostrom's work provides a fascinating juxtaposition of several important themes in public administration theory, in a sense turning the rational model of administration on its head. Ostrom accepts the same assumptions of classical rationality that had been used, in the works of previous theorists, to support centralized hierarchical power; however, by taking the logic of rational choice to the extreme, Ostrom comes to far more democratic conclusions. In this sense, his critique of earlier work in public administration theory is much more radical than the critiques of many human relations theorists who argue for cosmetic changes in management style while doing little to alter the real distribution of organizational power. Similarly, while seemingly accepting the analytical thrust of modern policy studies, Ostrom puts policy analysis to work in the critique, rather than the justification, of existing organizational structures. In doing so, he returns the study of public policy to its older and more fundamental role in the expression of basic societal values. Most important, while clearly writing within the tradition of public administration theory, Ostrom moves both outside and inside the standard unit of analysis, the organization, to consider the reformation of those social structures through which we distribute public goods and to discover ways in which those new enterprises might be made more responsive to the preferences of individuals.

The Ostrom-Golembiewski Exchange

Despite its scientific and ethical appeal, Ostrom's work leaves several important questions unanswered. These questions, essential to a comprehensive theory of public organization, have been discussed at length in an exchange between Ostrom (1977) and Golembiewski (1977). Although that discussion need not be repeated here, several summary points should be made. The first is empirical: the assumption of classical rationality sacrifices the individual actor for a methodological construct that even public choice theorists admit does not accurately reflect reality. In effect, they argue that such and such would be expected if people were rational. But, of course, real people only approximate rationality from time to time. To rest theoretical propositions on assumptions that only remotely correspond to reality raises serious questions about the validity of those propositions. What is developed is a logical progression based on untested and indeed unlikely hypotheses about how human beings actually behave. Norton Long (1974, p. 804) makes this point sharply by concluding that public choice theorists "argue with elegant and impeccable logic about unicorns."

In any case, such an approach concentrates on rationality to the exclusion of other important dimensions of human experience. Why not presume a normative model and attempt to derive the moral basis for democratic administration? Why not focus on feeling or intuition, aspects of humanity every bit as important as rationality? The answer probably lies in the assumption of an economic model of choice and its focus on utility maximization. The public choice theorists advise us to concentrate on the market distribution of economic goods and services and in turn on the way individuals and groups maximize the pursuit of their own objectives. But such a focus has important implications. Not only does a dependence on an economic model eliminate other bases for choice, such as emotional or political considerations, but it also presumes that the ends we pursue are well established and not subject to change.

This latter point is illustrated in the Golembiewski-Ostrom discussion of "self-interest." Golembiewski (1977, p. 1496), following an earlier discussion by DeGregori, points out that the public choice notion of self-interest contains neither a concept of self nor a concept of interest; it says little about what individuals can, do, or should seek to maximize. To say that a particular choice was a reflection of self-interest does not tell us what that interest was, and, without such knowledge, we can hardly derive expectations about future behavior. Moreover, a matter of moral choice is involved, the choice of which "utilities" one might wish to maximize—money? pleasure? concern? charity? Ostrom (1977, p. 1515) replies that, whereas his work assumes a certain cost calculus from which certain propositions flow, "a different type of intellectual venture is involved when the question is posed as to what criteria should be used to evaluate or guide a decision, e.g., to weigh and select from alternative possibilities." Ostrom even footnotes John Rawls's theory of justice at this point, suggesting that it is one such effort to provide a proper set of criteria for choice. Such an admission certainly seems to open the possibility of an integration of various theories, yet Ostrom does not pursue the matter, and his theory seems to remain dependent on the maximization of economic benefit alone.

Implications of Ostrom's Approach

However, certain beliefs and values creep into the analysis—not surprisingly, the beliefs and values of the theorist—most notably at two points. First, law and order is assumed. The operations of the public choice model occur only within the context of a legal system that prevents individuals from using force or violence to impose their will on others. But such a legal system would obviously imply certain values: at a minimum, a respect for private property. And, of course, any legal system contains preferences: one person's order is another person's prison. Second, the notion of democratic administration carries obvious value connotations, some of which extend far beyond the public choice preference for decentralized or federal structures. To describe a federal system, even one that incorporates noncentral "mechanisms of partisan mutual adjustment, cooperation, and conflict resolution" (Ostrom, 1977, p. 1521), is not to ensure a system that produces democratic outcomes with respect to such values as equality or justice. Indeed, considerable evidence indicates that decentralized structures can become highly authoritarian within their limited realms. Yet Ostrom describes his theory as democratic.

In either of these cases, Ostrom might well respond that a different kind of theory is required to complement and perhaps complete this work. That kind of theory would fill out the valuational character of a system of democratic administration, seeking an understanding of the meaning of personal experience and relying on a critical evaluation of both substantive and procedural issues. Ostrom's work is far less rigid and narrow than that of others who have pursued the policy emphasis in public administration. Indeed, he seems to invite us to seriously entertain a phenomenological or critical approach equally as radical as his inversion of the rational model. Just such an approach has interested a group of theorists who have recently attempted to move beyond the rational model of administration in its many variants and to construct a critical understanding of life in public organizations.

■ ■

REFERENCES

Anderson, James E. *Public Policy Making.* New York: Holt, Rinehart and Wilson, 1979.

Appleby, Paul. *Big Democracy.* New York: Knopf, 1945.

Appleby, Paul. *Policy and Administration.* University: University of Alabama Press, 1949.

Appleby, Paul. *Morality and Administration in Democratic Government.* Baton Rouge, La.: Louisiana State University Press, 1952.

Bailey, Stephen, "Ethics and the Public Service." In *Public Administration: Readings in Institutions, Processes, Behavior,* edited by Robert T. Golembiewski, Frank Gibson, and Geoffrey Cornog, pp. 22–31. Chicago: Rand McNally, 1966.

Bardach, Eugene. *The Implementation Game.* Cambridge, Mass.: M.I.T. Press, 1977.

Dahl, Robert, and Lindblom, Charles. *Politics, Economics, and Welfare.* Chicago: University of Chicago Press, 1953.

Denhardt, Robert B. *In the Shadow of Organization.* Lawrence: Regents Press of Kansas, 1981.

Dimock, Marshall E. In *The Frontiers of Public Administration,* edited by John M. Gaus, Leonard D. White, and Marshall E. Dimock, pp. 116–132. Chicago: University of Chicago Press, 1936.

Downs, Anthony. *Inside Bureaucracy.* Boston: Little, Brown, 1967.

Dror, Yehezkel. *Public Policymaking Reexamined.* San Francisco: Chandler, 1968.

Dye, Thomas. "A Model for the Analysis of Policy Outcomes." In *Policy Analysis in Political Science,* edited by Ira Sharkansky, pp. 21–38. Chicago: Markham, 1970.

Dye, Thomas. *Policy Analysis.* University: University of Alabama Press, 1976.

Easton, David, *A Framework for Political Analysis.* Englewood Cliffs, N.J.: Prentice-Hall, 1965.

Edwards, George C. *Implementing Public Policy.* Washington, D.C.: Congressional Quarterly Press, 1980.

Finer, Herman. "Administrative Responsibility in Democratic Government," In *Bureaucratic Power in National Politics,* edited by Francis Rourke, pp. 176–186. Boston: Little, Brown, 1972.

Friedrich, Carl J. "Public Policy and the Nature of Administrative Responsibility." In *Bureaucratic Power in National Politics,* edited by Frances Rourke, pp. 165–175. Boston: Little, Brown, 1972.

Golembiewski, Robet T. "A Critique of 'Democratic Administration' and Its Supporting Ideation." *American Political Science Review,* December 1977, 71, pp. 1488–1507.

Kingsley, Donald. *Representative Bureaucracy: An Interpretation of the British Civil Service.* Yellow Springs, Ohio: Antioch University Press, 1944.

Krislov, Samuel. *Representative Bureaucracy.* Englewood Cliffs, N.J.: Prentice-Hall, 1974.

Long, Norton. *The Polity.* Chicago: Rand McNally, 1962.

Lerner, Daniel, and Lasswell, Harold, eds. *The Policy Sciences.* Stanford, Calif.: Stanford University Press, 1960.

Lowi, Theodore. *The End of Liberalism.* New York, N.Y.: Norton, 1969.

Lowi, Theodore. "Four Systems of Policy, Politics, and Choice." *Public Administration Review,* July-August 1974, *33,* pp. 298–310.

Meltsner, Arnold J. "Creating a Policy Analysis Profession." In *Improving Policy Analysis,* edited by Stuart S. Nagel, pp. 235–249. Beverly Hills, Calif.: Sage, 1980.

Mosher, Frederick. *Democracy and the Public Service.* New York: Oxford University Press, 1968.

Nagel, Stuart S. *The Policy Studies Handbook.* Lexington, Mass.: Lexington Books, 1980.

Nagel, Stuart S., and Neef, Marian. "What's New About Policy Analysis Research?" In *Improving Policy Analysis,* edited by Stuart S. Nagel, pp. 15–33. Beverly Hills, Calif.: Sage, 1980.

Ostrom, Vincent. *The Intellectual Crisis in American Public Administration.* University: University of Alabama Press, 1974.

Ostrom, Vincent. "Language, Theory and Empirical Research in Policy Analysis." In *Problems of Theory in Political Analysis,* edited by Phillip M. Gregg, pp. 9–18. Lexington, Mass.: Lexington Books, 1976.

Pressman, Jeffrey, and Wildavsky, Aaron. *Implementation: How Great Expectations in Washington Are Dashed in Oakland: Or, Why It's Amazing That Federal Programs Work at All.* Berkeley: University of California Press, 1973.

Redford, Emmett S. *Democracy in the Administrative State.* New York: Oxford University Press, 1969.

Rohr, John. *Ethics for Bureaucrats.* New York: Dekker, 1978.

Rourke, Francis E. *Bureaucracy, Politics, and Public Policy.* Boston: Little, Brown, 1969.

Scioli, Frank P., Jr. "Problems and Prospects for Policy Evaluation." *Public Administration Review.* January-February 1979, *39,* pp. 41–45.

Wamsley, Gary. "On the Problems of Defining What's New in Public Administration." *Administration and Society,* November 1976, *8,* pp. 385–400.

Wamsley, Gary, and Zald, Mayer. *The Political Economy of Public Organizations.* Lexington, Mass.: Lexington Books, 1973.

Wildavsky, Aaron. *Speaking Truth to Power: The Art and Craft of Policy Analysis.* Boston: Little, Brown, 1979.

Wilson, Woodrow. "The Study of Administration." *Political Science Quarterly,* June 1887, *2,* pp. 197–222.

7

■ BEYOND RATIONAL ACTION ■

In previous chapters, we have reviewed a wide variety of approaches to understanding public organizations and have seen some of the arguments used in defense of various positions. Public administration theorists seem to dispute endlessly about their work, hence, there seems little possibility of developing anything approximating a paradigm in the field. This confusion has been described in a number of interesting ways. Years ago, for example, Dwight Waldo (1961, p. 210) referred to organization theory as an "elephantine problem." More recently, Waldo (1968), Golembiewski (1977), Ostrom (1974), and others have commented on the "crisis of identity" in public administration, a situation in which disagreement about the direction of the field prevents us from addressing certain problems.

There is indeed an identity problem in public administration theory, although I would describe it instead as a crisis of legitimacy, in which the agreed-on bases of theory fail to reflect or respond to the needs of actors in the field—theorists, practitioners, and citizens. In fact, I would argue, there is considerable, though often implicit, agreement as to the proper direction of public administration theory, but questions of the legitimacy of theory arise when attempts are made to relate mainstream theory to practice. The thread that ties otherwise disparate theories together grows directly from the Weberian intellectual heritage, with its emphasis on rational bureaucracy, and the Wilsonian political heritage, with its emphasis on politics-administration. The result is an attempt to construct a rational theory of administration based on a positivist understanding of human behavior set within a framework of democratic accountability.

This curious combination of Weberian social science and Yankee industrialism has several different components. First is the view that the proper study of public administration is the study of how to operate public organizations most efficiently, that is, how to achieve given objectives with the least cost. In this view, goals and objectives are determined by responsible public officials (typically legislators) to whom members of the bureaucracy are accountable. The means to achieve those ends may vary, but, by and large, the integration of the various subparts of the organization requires a hierarchical structure leading upward to a single central authority. All kinds of devices are then employed to secure the compliance of organizational members, with this rational pattern of activity derived from the organization's mission. In this effort, science is the key. Science, it is said, can provide causal explanations that will permit greater control over the organization and its members by those with access to knowledge and resources, those in positions of power.

Although most mainstream public administration theorists differ on details, they seem to agree on these basic concerns. For example, Simon's classical description of the rational model of administration moved beyond earlier theories of administrative management yet did so in a way that preserved much of the politics-administration (now translated into fact-value) dichotomy as well as the hierarchical pattern of the administrative management viewpoint. Similarly, the human relations theorists, while purporting to move beyond the rational model, may have simply provided a more sophisticated array of techniques for managers to use in securing compliance. Finally, the policy analysts, though recognizing the increased role of bureaucracy in policymaking, concentrate on the scientific assessment of the impact of established or proposed policies while suggesting implementation strategies that return us directly to the days of administrative management.

In contrast to this mainstream set of commitments in public administration theory, there has always been a less well-understood counterpoint of interests in democratic administration. In the last decade, this interest has emerged as a specific and direct critique of the rational model in all its guises and as an attempt to move public administration theory beyond merely rational action. This chapter will examine this new critique of the rational model, then turn to two alternative perspectives now beginning to be discussed, one based on phenomenology, the other on critical social theory. What may be emerging is a viewpoint drawing more readily from the intellectual traditions of Marxist humanism and Freudian psychoanalysis and the political tradition of Jeffersonian democracy. Most important, theorists moving in this direction place very strong emphasis on the integration of theory and practice, seeking to develop theories that will serve as meaningful guides to life in public organizations.

■ ■

A CRITIQUE OF THE RATIONAL MODEL

Mainstream public administration theory appears to be centered on the rational model of administration. However, the rational model and related theories have several important limitations, which have been noted throughout this book. At this point, it is appropriate to summarize our critique of the rational model in terms of three important problems: (1) the rational model is based on a limited and confining view of human reason; (2) the rational model is based on an incomplete understanding of knowledge acquisition; and (3) theorists working within the framework of the rational model fail to adequately connect theory and practice. Each point will be examined in some detail.

Restricted View of Human Reason

The first issue—that the rational model is based on a limited and confining view of human reason—can be approached from either an historical or a more immediate perspective. In his recent book *The New Science of Organizations,* Alberto Guerreiro Ramos (1981) connects the modern concept of instrumental rationality to the growth of a market economy and then summarizes some of the consequences of such a development. Modern organization theory, according to Ramos, is a by-product of organizational processes arising with the development of a market-centered society. In order to meet the demands of the market (including demands that are artificially created), those in control of large organizations seek greater efficiency through a rationalized production process. But this approach has serious consequences for the individual and the society. Only in the market society is the production process so ordered that the individual is reduced in significance to the mere status of a jobholder, one who fills a position in the hierarchy for a given period of time. In the prevailing form of organization, which Ramos terms the "economizing" organization, the mechanical design of production, based on instrumental or technical rationality, transforms the individual into the laborer, who is in turn subject to a new market mentality.

But, Ramos argues, the expansion of the market may now have reached the point of diminishing returns in terms of both personal development and social stability. Rationalized organization leaves little place for self-actualization; where self-actualization occurs, it is merely incidental to the production process (contrary to certain human relations theorists). Moreover, that process leads us further and further toward "psychological insecurity, degradation of the quality of life, pollution, and waste of the planet's limited resources" (p. 23). (Ramos finally argues for a "delimitation" of the market system based on new allocative criteria that would be sensitive to ecological and psychological effects.)

Let us examine some of these points in greater detail. If the rational model draws our attention to the means to attain given ends, then it also draws our attention away from the ends themselves. In concentrating on efficiency alone, we might fail to fully examine and participate in decisions that are of importance to us, thus failing also to meet our democratic obligations. Acting in this way, we would hardly be facilitating the expression of societal values. Rather, we might simply be trying to achieve at minimum costs the objectives presented to us. Although operating quite efficiently, we might find ourselves pursuing objectives that, if properly understood, would be seen to be at odds with the values of our society—our values.

These considerations are of special importance in discussing public organizations. The rational model's distinction between means and ends clearly connects to the politics-administration dichotomy, in which the role of public organizations is simply to discover the most efficient means toward politically given ends. But, as we have seen, the politics-administration dichotomy neither reflects practice nor correctly states the role of administration in a democracy. Whereas one might argue (though wrongly, I think) that the determination of objectives in private organizations should be made only by those in positions of power, public organizations, since they are involved in the expression of societal values, must give their members a share in decision making. And, in doing so, they must certainly emphasize the necessity of widespread communication and participation in decision making. Members of public organizations bear a special responsibility to promote the democratization of the policy process beyond simply acting efficiently.

Those in public organizations also bear an obligation to act with fairness, understanding, and humanity, but even this obligation is made more difficult by a solely rational perspective that ignores such other aspects of human life as emotion and intuition. Emotion is said to interfere with rational planning and decision making; intuition is said to detract from reason and order. But emotion and intuition are important aspects of human existence, and they should be, particularly because these areas of our experience connect most clearly to our feelings and our values. Robert Dahl and Charles Lindblom (1976, p. 252) made this point many years ago: "A bias in favor of a deliberate adaption of organizational means to ends requires that human relationships be viewed as instrumental means to the prescribed goals of the organization, not as sources of direct prime goal achievement. Joy, love, friendship, pity, and affection must all be curbed— unless they happen to foster the prescribed goals of the organization."

Such an attitude obviously results in the depersonalization of the individual in complex organizations, a theme prominent in a number of works, ranging from William Whyte's *The Organization Man*, (1956) to such more recent books as William Scott and David K. Hart's *Organizational America* (1979) and my own *In the Shadow of Organization* (1981). These writers seem to agree that the control mechanisms of complex organizations trivialize personal interaction so that individuals are merely objects to be used in the production process. Each becomes an instrument to be manipulated by the other in the efficient pursuit of organizational goals. More important, each loses that sense of self-reflection and self-understanding that is essential to creativity and personal growth. Again, these concerns are even more pronounced in public organizations than in others. The commitment of those in public organizations to seek life, liberty, and the pursuit of happiness, to aid all citizens in their own development, and to provide an education for citizenship itself can only occur through the interaction of persons, not objects.

A final problem with the concept of reason employed by the rational model of administration is that it omits any concern for the moral context within which action can occur. As noted earlier, several theorists have viewed the rationalization of society as a process in which broader questions of human values, represented by such terms as *freedom, justice,* and *equality,* are losing their importance as criteria for judgement, replaced by a specific calculus of costs and benefits, means and ends. The deliberative, communicative, and participative functions seem of little importance when the only issues to be discussed are measures of efficiency. Yet, if public organizations are to fulfill their promise of supporting and promoting democratic governance, their members must be willing to think in terms of larger questions, such as those that enable us to establish a sense of personal responsibility or mutual action. We simply cannot secure a moral context for our actions, including our organizational actions, within the limited framework of instrumental rationality.

Incomplete Understanding of Knowledge Acquisition

The rational model seems to assume that there is only one way in which true knowledge can be obtained—through the rigorous application of the methods of positive science to social and technical relationships within organizations. Whether or not this assumption is valid, we should be clear about both the strengths and weaknesses of this approach to knowledge acquisition.

Let us first review and summarize more formally the basic premises of the positive science model: (1) A single approach to knowledge acquisition is considered appropriate to both natural and social events; hence the social scientist should use the model of scientific inquiry of the more "advanced" natural sciences. (2) All knowledge that is not purely conceptual must be based on sensory experience, and, in turn, all statements about such experience must be based on direct observation, subject to agreement among observers, of the behavior of social actors. (3) There is a strict separation of fact and value, a distinction between what is and what ought to be; the role of the scientist is to gather facts, not to speculate on values. (4) The goals of scientific inquiry are explanation, prediction, and control. *To explain* means that one must discover the causes that propel events; explanation enables prediction, and prediction enables control. (5) The relationship between theory and practice is remote, at best. The role of the scientist is to conduct investigations that provide the data on which theoretical frameworks can be constructed. The scientist has neither interest in nor responsibility for the application of knowledge. Rather, he or she simply tries to create knowledge, while others determine its use.

Several readily apparent limitations of the positive science model have been debated back and forth over the years and should at least be reviewed here. (A more complete philosophical analysis of this debate is contained in Richard J. Bernstein's *The Restructuring of Social and Political Theory* [1976].) One of the most pointed criticisms of the positive science model is that human behavior is culturally or historically determined, that it varies from place to place and time to time. If this were the case, the behavior of one group would not necessarily be the same as that of another, and the development of broad generalizations applicable to all cultures at all times would be extraordinarily difficult. One variant of this criticism, of course, is that human beings do in fact change their behavior based on new information, including scientifically derived information. This shift in habitual patterns of behavior could occur in several ways. On the one hand, people might be inclined to behave in ways consistent with theories of human behavior. For example, the human relations emphasis on self-actualization as a goal of human behavior might lead persons to consciously model their behavior after characteristics identified as self-actualizing (Maslow, 1962, 1971). Or, on the other hand, people might stop acting in ways that appear contrary to theory. For example, persons encountering the rational model of administration, with its implicit critique of emotion, might seek to suppress their own feelings in organizational situations. In any case, the variability of human behavior from place to place and time to time limits the positive science pursuit of lawlike statements applicable to a wide range of human behaviors.

A second major criticism of the positive science approach to knowledge acquisition concerns the role of subjective experience in human life. One aspect of this critique focuses on those who are the objects of study, arguing that people have purely subjective reasons for their actions, reasons that are not accessible to those observing their behavior from the outside. In this view, the values and intentions of individuals move their actions every bit as much as the external influences to which they are subjected. Whereas the latter can be observed, the former cannot; thus, the capacity of positive science to gain a complete view of human action is limited. A similar objection focuses on the values of the scientist: the scientist is also a human being, subject to the same interplay of emotions and values as other human beings and therefore incapable of complete objectivity in his or her consideration of the behavior of others. The scientist's own values creep into the research process at several points, especially in the selection of topics for observation and in the assessment and evaluation of evidence. In either case, the scientist's own values intrude on the objectivity sought by the positive science model. (One variant of this criticism is that human beings may react subjectively to the very act of being observed, that the intrusion of the scientist into an everyday situation for the purpose of observation changes that situation.)

These concerns have been elaborated by Jay White in his examination of the limitations of the positive science model as a guide to the study of public organizations and especially public policy. White (1982, p. 128) argues first that an instrumental approach to knowledge acquisition fails to comprehend the normative structures of society, "the reasons, motives, intentions, shared meanings and shared expectations of social actors." The scientific attitude selects those aspects of human experience that can be objectively understood, leaving behind the world of subjective experience, the world of values, which is very important in policy studies. Second, and in a related vein, White suggests that positive science can contribute little to our moral understanding. Although policy analysis can tell us the causes of a problem and the probable consequences of various alternative actions, it can give little guidance as to what we ought to want or what we ought to do to change the situation. "Developing . . . that logic is the task for a normative ethics of public policy analysis" (p. 130).

Third, White charges that the positive science approach tells us little about the aesthetic dimensions of public policy; indeed, the logic of cost-benefit analysis and similar techniques is totally incongruent with discussions of aesthetics. The logic of objectivity disregards the quality of our experience, as if we were forced to judge the value of a painting simply on the cost of the canvas, brushes, and paint. White argues, in contrast, that "aesthetic experience and judgment [is] a valid basis from which to theorize about society" (p. 132). Fourth, White holds that instrumental science is ahistorical, that policy analysis based on a positive science lifts issues out of their broadest cultural and historical context and therefore has no sense of history.

Fifth, and most important, White argues that mainstream policy analysis, based on positive social science, is "unable to comprehend and to overcome the crisis tendencies of societal development" (p. 135). White draws the notion of social crisis from critical social theory, which will be outlined more fully later in this chapter, and suggests that a crisis occurs in a society when ideological constraints prevent the society from reaching a normal, healthy state. Moving beyond such limitations, according to White, requires more than a simple instrumental explanation of the society's condition. It requires an approach to knowledge that gets to "the source of feeling of the crisis" and is therefore simultaneously both revealing and compelling (p. 137). To clarify this point, a parallel may be drawn to individual behavior, where often an objective explanation is insufficient as a form of knowledge to compel a change in one's behavior. For example, many people who rationally understand the dangers of smoking cigarettes continue to smoke; however, someone who experiences the cancer-related death of a close friend may be so deeply touched that a new pattern of behavior will be initiated. This point returns us to the notion of a crisis of legitimacy in the study of public organizations and to a final limitation of the rational model.

Inadequate Link Between Theory and Practice

The seeming gap between theory and practice, between academics and practitioners, has practically become a joke, but it conceals a deep unrest, a dissatisfaction with the way in which we have sought to understand our work and make it meaningful to us. Unfortunately, the mainstream positive science approach to acquiring knowledge about public organizations provides very little help; indeed, it may be the root of the problem.

What do practitioners want from theory? Two things, I think: explanations and understandings from which new approaches to administrative work can be fashioned, and a framework in which the individual's experience can be seen as a meaningful part of something larger and more important. The rational model of administration, in its many variants, has some capacity to meet the first need. It is concerned with instrumental explanations that permit more effective prediction and control, and it has over the years provided a number of very useful explanations that have been seized on by practitioners. Budget techniques, incentive patterns, management styles, and many other topics have been commented on by theorists working out of the rational model, and their explanations have been of considerable interest and value to practitioners. Communication has broken down at times, most pointedly in the excessive jargon and quantification that seem to be associated with the pursuit of positive social science. But, for the most part, social scientists, practitioners, and theorists have pursued the same explanatory goals.

On the second point, the rational model and positive social science are more vulnerable. An approach to knowledge acquisition that seeks to objectify human experience can hardly be expected to comment on the meaning of that experience; indeed, it detracts from that meaning. The meaning of experience, the value it has to us individually and as a society, is based on our subjective and intersubjective world. To objectify that experience is to rob it of the very character or texture that makes it significant to us. When the practitioner asks, therefore, that theory be meaningful, that it comment on matters of real importance to human beings, the request simply cannot be met by those who follow a model in which individuals respond to social forces as one billiard ball responds to another. Even the act of evaluation by which we impute importance to the inquiry is denied by the rational model. Any individual with humanitarian concerns wishes more than this from theory.

These practical issues serve well to introduce the theoretical problem. Theorists following the rational model are interested in explanation, prediction, and control, but they are not necessarily interested in whether their theories directly correspond to reality. If satisfactory explanations can be produced by assuming that all people are fully rational in pursuing their self-interests, then it makes little difference to theorists whether individuals act in this way or not. Moreover, following the positive science model, the scientist bases theoretical propositions on the observation of manifest behavior, behavior as viewed from the outside. But behavior viewed from the outside may not correspond at all to the actions intended by the individual. Similarly, the practitioner who must act on the information presented by the scientist must assume responsibility for that action and so would like guidance that is both instrumentally effective and morally sound. But the scientist working out of the positivist tradition assumes no responsibility for the way in which the accumulated knowledge is used and thus fails to provide a basis for moral action. In all these ways, the theorist following the rational model and its commitment to positive social science makes conscious choices that have the direct effect of severing the experience of the individual from the process of inquiry. The result is that theory and practice are separated. The theory-practice dichotomy, therefore, is not an accident but is a consequence of specific choices, specific commitments to one particular approach to knowledge acquisition.

Fortunately, the positive science approach is not the only available approach to knowledge acquisition (although it has been made to appear that way). In fact, other approaches now being explored offer, among other things, the possibility of a better correspondence between theory and practice. Two such approaches will be examined in the remainder of this chapter; first, however, the importance of seeking such alternatives should again be noted. Any science that accurately portrays the experience of individual actors and directs itself to the issues they find important will obviously be considered more reliable. Moreover, commitment to a mode of knowledge acquisition that neither objectifies nor depersonalizes is a far better model for the relationship between theorists and practitioners and between public servants and their clients than a mode that does. The rational model can only carry us so far. Until certain important questions are addressed, the study of public organizations will be suspect, and the crisis of legitimacy will continue.

■ ─── ■

INTERPRETIVE/ACTION THEORY

Near the end of the discussion of Marx, Weber, and Freud in chapter 2, it was indicated that, depending on the purposes to be served by knowledge, one might choose among different approaches to the question of knowledge acquisition. Among these, the prevailing positivist viewpoint is oriented toward instrumental explanations that enable the prediction and ultimately the control of human affairs. Now we have found that, in its application to the study of public organizations, the positive science approach is incomplete. Not only has the explanatory power of the rational model proven limited, we have now found that mere explanation is not all we want from theory. We also seek theories that will help us understand the meaning of human action and enable us to act with greater skill and clarity in pursuing our personal and societal goals. Fortunately, there are modes of inquiry more suited to these purposes; the remainder of this chapter will examine two such efforts in the field of public administration.

Phenomenological Roots

Interpretive social theory—or action theory, as some public administration theorists have come to call it—has its roots in the philosophical work of Edmund Husserl around the turn of the century. Husserl, a mathematician by training, sought a philosophical basis for scientific inquiry that would strip away the presuppositions or assumptions on which positive science was based and move directly to an understanding of human meaning. This approach, called phenomenology, seeks to suspend the definitions or characterizations of human behavior imposed on the actions of human beings from the outside by scientific observers and to apprehend instead the exact meaning of those actions from the standpoint of the actors themselves. In this effort, attention is focused on the way individuals interpret their everyday existence, sometimes called "life-world." Interpretive social science seeks "the greatest possible clarification of what is thought about the social world by those living in it" (Schutz, 1967, p. 222). Human beings are now seen as conscious beings who act intentionally and thus give meaning to their actions.

The world of meaning became central to the phenomenologist and represented a critical break with the techniques of the natural sciences. All consciousness is consciousness of something: we seek something, we hope for something, we remember something. Every act of consciousness, as we reflect on it, bestows upon our world meanings to which we in turn give order. The human capacity to endow action with meaning sets the reality to be examined by the social scientists quite apart from the reality of the natural scientist, and, therefore, the methodology of the natural scientist cannot be copied by the social scientist. Rather, the social scientist must seek ways to understand the structure of consciousness, the world of meanings of the social actor.

The connection between meaning and intentionality leads to a view of human beings as active agents in a social world rather than as passive respondents to that world. Intentionality is the active directing of consciousness toward a specific object and itself stands at the very heart of consciousness. Through our intentions, we give meaning to the world around us and in effect construct that world. Husserl uses the somewhat awkward term *essences* to refer to the pattern of unities of intended meanings that we build up either as individuals or as groups. For example, the notion of a university brings to mind for each of us and for us as a society a certain constellation of meanings. From both a personal standpoint and a scientific standpoint, the understanding of such patterns of meaning is far more important than explanations built around the mere descriptions of observed behavior. (As noted before, the term *action* is often reserved by interpretive theorists to indicate the intentional nature of action as opposed to the reactive nature of behavior. Hence, the term *action theory*.)

By connecting consciousness and intentionality, Husserl and other phenomenologists move both behind and beyond the mainstream positivist interest in manifest behavior. Phenomenologists recognize that the conceptual knowledge with which we often deal is founded on a preconceptual (or prepredicative) basis. It is on the basis of these clusters of intentions that we build our more formal and reflected view of the world. The political theorist Hwa Yol Jung (1971, p. 544) comments on the practical implications of this position as follows: "The felt dimension of our experience plays an important function in what we think, observe and perceive and in how we behave. Meaning involves experiencing which is preconceptual, presymbolic and preverbal (that is, something felt)." To recognize the preconceptual basis of experience considerably broadens the realm of our understanding, but phenomenologists also recognize the possibilities that various classes of meaning may hold. A set of meanings is not viewed by Husserl as important merely as something already actualized but as an indication of the realm of possibilities or alternative directions. This realm, which is not reality but irreality, is seen as the true ground of knowledge, a point neglected by many action theorists examining public organizations.

An Intersubjectively Comprehensible World

For the social scientist and for the student of public organization, perhaps the most important contribution of phenomenology has been its restoration of the relationship between subject and object and its elaboration of the role of this relationship in constituting an intersubjectively comprehensible world, a world in which we all can share. As we have noted, the relationship between subject and object was severed by positive science through the argument that objectivity can only be obtained through a separation of fact and value. Interpretive social scientists—in particular, Alfred Schutz—have argued, to the contrary, that the subject and the object are one: "I can, on the one hand, attend to and interpret in themselves the phenomena of the external world which present themselves to me as indications of the consciousness of other people. When I do this, I say of them that they have objective meaning. But I can, on the other hand, look over and through these external indications into the constituting process within the living consciousness of another rational being. What I am then concerned with is subjective meaning" (Schutz, 1967, p. 37). Since what is observable is always related to the awareness of the actor, the two aspects, objective and subjective, can never be fully separated. And, since the act of understanding implies evaluation, the same is true of fact and value.

In such a situation, we can relate to one another in various ways. Although there are some persons with whom we do not interact face-to-face and whom we treat somewhat anonymously, there are also those whom we consciously recognize and view as a subject (a Thou relationship) and those who reciprocate in such a recognition (thus constituting a We relationship). What is most important about the We relationship is that it necessarily involves a mutual recognition and even a mutual disclosure of motives. No matter how much I might try to objectify or impersonalize our relationship, awareness of you as a conscious being interacting with me discloses our common humanity—exactly the point that the rational model fails to comprehend. Thus, from the phenomenological standpoint, not only is the instrumental reduction of human beings to the status of objects improper, it is impossible. Any study based on such an assumption would fail to acknowledge that individuals are open possibilities, intentional and reflective, engaged in the continuing and mutual task of establishing social reality (Berger and Luckmann, 1966).

The Consociated Model

To minds trained in a world that values objectivity and explanation, the language of phenomenology may initially seem foreign and inaccessible. However, important lessons can be drawn from this work that are both theoretically and practically relevant to the study of public organizations. One of the earliest applications of phenomenology to the study of public organizations was Larry Kirkhart's contribution to the new public administration papers mentioned in chapter 5. In his article, Kirkhart (1971) examines various alternatives to mainstream social science, with particular attention to Schutz's phenomenological interpretation of Weber's concept of social action. Specifically, Kirkhart attempts a reconstruction of Weber's ideal-type bureaucracy based on Schutz's notion of the We relationship. Proposing a model in which trust and mutual disclosure are central (as in the We relationship), Kirkhart outlines his "consociated" model of organization based on the adaptability of the organization and on noncompetitive, trusting interpersonal relationships. Among the features of this model are (1) the project team as the basic work unit, (2) an authority structure without permanent hierarchy and dependent on diverse authority patterns, (3) social relationships characterized by open communications, (4) the representation of clientele in the organization, and (5) professional orientations requiring not only technical competence but also skills in maintaining the kind of ambiguity useful to problem solving.

Kirkhart argues that his consociated model is only one of many possible alternatives to traditional bureaucratic structures, and his work is most important in suggesting the possibility that employing different approaches to the question of knowledge acquisition might lead to reconstructing traditional views of organization. Although Kirkhart's work has not been adequately elaborated, his analysis stands as one of the most creative recent efforts in the field of public administration.

Silverman's Action Analysis

A similarly distinctive work, David Silverman's *The Theory of Organisations* (1971), appeared at about the same time as Kirkhart's. Silverman follows Berger and Luckmann in developing the view that reality is socially constructed and maintained. Individuals within and around organizations help create those organizations by assigning meaning to their own actions and to the actions of others. The resulting pattern of established meanings and of actions based on those meanings constitute the organization. Consequently, the relationship between the organization and its environment is governed by the way in which the situation is perceived by participants. Change in turn arises through the interaction of persons inside and outside the organization and is governed by the flow of meanings assigned to various patterns of action.

This view leads Silverman to indicate six areas that should be investigated by an action analysis of organization:

1. The nature of the role system and pattern of interaction that has been built up in the organization, in particular, the way in which it has historically developed and the extent to which it represents the shared values of all or some or none of the actors.

2. The nature of involvement of ideal-typical actors (e.g., moral, alienative, instrumental) and the characteristic hierarchy of ends which they pursue (work satisfaction, material rewards, security). The way in which these derive from their biographies outside the organizations (job history, family commitments, social background) and from their experience of the organization itself.

3. The actors' present definitions of their situation within the organization and their expectations of the likely behavior of others, with particular reference to the strategic resources they perceive to be at their own disposal and at the disposal of others (degree of coercive power or moral authority; belief in individual opportunity).

4. The typical actions of different actors and the meaning which they attach to their action.

5. The nature and source of the intended and unintended consequences of action, with special reference to its effects on the involvement of the various actors and on the institutionalization of expectations in the role system within which they interact.

6. Changes in the involvement and ends of the actors and in the role system and their source both in the outcome of the interaction of the actors and in the changing stock of knowledge outside the organization (e.g., political or legal changes; the varied experiences and expectations of different generations) [Silverman, 1971, p. 154].

Although Silverman writes from a perspective informed by phenomenology, his work in the *Theory of Organisations* remains closer to the instrumentalist perspective than one might at first recognize. Certainly, Silverman seems to acknowledge a high degree of order and regularity apparently built through some sort of exchange between individuals and their society. Not only is reality socially constructed, it also seems to do some of the constructing. We are thus led to two different ways of analyzing more familiar phenomena. For example, efforts to change organizations are described as "the outcome of the relative capacity of different actors to impose their definition of the situation upon others"—perhaps a more sophisticated way of viewing the issue of power, yet one that does not alter the basic distribution of power or the way in which power is used in organization. In contrast to Kirkhart's more challenging work, Silverman's action frame of reference fails to draw out the implications of phenomenology as an alternative way of viewing the world, a way that not only recognizes that the world is socially constructed but also suggests a new construction of that world. (In fairness, it should be noted that Silverman's more recent work extends beyond *The Theory of Organisations* to provide a more radical critique of organizational life.)

HARMON'S ACTIVE-SOCIAL PARADIGM

By far the most comprehensive application of phenomenology to the field of public administration is Michael Harmon's *Action Theory for Public Administration* (1981). Harmon resurrects Kuhn's notion of scientific paradigms, arguing that public administration today requires a new paradigm capable of both a value theory and a theory of knowledge different from those implied by the rational model of administration. Harmon describes what he calls an alternative paradigm (although his alternative is really more theory than paradigm) based on the assumption that human beings are naturally active rather than passive, and social rather than atomistic. The active view of human nature supposes that individuals impute meaning to their own activities and consequently determine the circumstances that are of importance to them. Rather than simply responding to factors in the environment, as in the passive interpretation of human nature, the active conception holds that individuals interact with their environment in a reciprocal relationship.

People both influence and are influenced by the circumstances around them. The ability of people to conceive of the world in symbolic terms, to reflect on events, distinguishes their active nature from the passive nature of physical objects. Consequently, the capacity of human beings for self-reflection must be taken into account in any interpretation of human activity. The social conception of the individual sees the person as a product of social interaction. In this view, meaning is constituted not merely by the individual but also by the individual interacting with others in face-to-face situations. Mutual awareness leads to mutual participation in the construction of social reality. Language, which is the basis of the individual's capacity to symbolize, is itself intersubjective. (In this view, the face-to-face situation rather than the individual or the collective becomes the basic unit of analysis; thus, Harmon opposes both the methodological individualism of Ostrom and the systems orientation of both rational and humanistic organization theory.)

Toward an Alternative Epistemology

Harmon's active-social view of the self leads in two directions: toward an alternative epistemology that might form the basis for a new understanding of organizational life and toward a normative theory that would permit a more complete understanding of democratic accountability and personal responsibility. Harmon adopts the epistemological position of Schutz, especially as modified by Berger and Luckmann. Following these theorists, Harmon argues that the active-social individual is one who attributes meaning to action and who acts intentionally in the world. Although Harmon appears to be ambiguous on the issue of whether the social world is merely a reflection of human meaning or exists objectively—holding, on the one hand, that "the social world is real only by virtue of the actions that make it real" and, on the other, that it is useful "to conceive of environments initially as existing independent of administrators' perceptions of them"—he adopts the distinction between action and behavior mentioned earlier and argues that social science must be attentive to intended action rather than manifest behavior (1981, pp. 45, 67). As a consequence, organizational studies require "attention to how organizational actors make sense of their world, decide what is worth doing, and reflect on the meaning of their own and other's actions" (p. 53). Harmon then suggests a paradigm based on work in phenomenology, symbolic interactionism, and critical theory (p. 70).

Revising The Basis For Accountability

In addition to a new epistomology, Harmon argues that the active-social conception of self requires a new normative basis for accountability in public organizations. Holding that public administration is distinguished by "making and legitimating decisions in public organizations," Harmon asserts that public administration theory must address the relationship between substance and process and between individual and collective values (p. 5). Following other process theorists, Harmon argues that the value of human action is found in the action itself rather than in the ends produced by that action. For example, evaluation of issues such as justice and freedom can ultimately be determined not by specific substantive outcomes but by the degree to which democratic procedures—that is, procedures that are open to and involving of citizens—are followed. More pointedly, Harmon contends that what we usually regard as substantive outcomes are themselves simply objectifications resulting from agreement among people concerning the facticity of those outcomes. The quality of the process is based in turn on "the extent to which definitions of the problem are shared and understood, mutual trust is developed, and solutions are arrived at free of coercion or domination" (p. 102). (Note that this view is far different from that of the rational model, which would hold processes as merely instrumental to the accomplishment of given ends.)

Moreover, the relationship between individual encounters and larger collective values must be addressed. Harmon argues that the notion of mutuality or community is the basic normative premise guiding the face-to-face relationship. In the same way in which Kirkhart employed the inherent mutuality of the We relationship in constructing his consociated model of administration, Harmon suggests that, in relationships characterized by mutuality, individuals take into account the wishes of others and are open to influence by others. Moving from the face-to-face encounter to the realm of larger social systems, Harmon argues that a parallel normative theory must be developed. "The idea of social justice is the logical extension of mutuality applied to social collectivities and should therefore be regarded as the normative premise underlying 'aggregate' policy decisions made by and implemented through public organizations" (p. 84). While generally pursuing Rawls's notion of justice, Harmon holds that justice is a natural outgrowth of our active-social nature. The fundamental question that arises, therefore, is "how to strengthen the natural bonds among people so as to promote a kind of social order that enables, more than it constrains through domination, acts of individual freedom and social cooperation" (p. 83).

Reformulating Administrative Responsibility

This question leads to a critique and reformulation of the classical notion of administrative responsibility, which holds that accountability is maintained in public agencies through a correspondence between the actions of those agencies and the intentions of the legislature. Such a view holds to an instrumental relationship between means and ends, with administrative agencies seen as constrained to execute the desires of the governing body. Moral obligations lie somewhere outside the individual and are enforced through various constraints, either those imposed externally by law or regulation or those internalized by administrative professionals. In contrast to this view, Harmon argues that the active-social nature of the self implies an alternative mode of responsible administrative action, specifically, personal responsibility. "Personal responsibility implies that actors are agents who must bear the moral brunt of their actions rather than shift the blame or responsibility to other people or external standards of 'correctness'" (p. 125).

This view, however, is not meant to imply that individual administrators should act with total discretion. Rather, Harmon maintains, since administrative action is necessarily interaction, personal responsibility implies social responsibility as well—individuals should be guided by community interests as well as their own discretion. Such a view, however, once again raises the confusion between self and society, with the possibility that social expectations might come to guide personal responsibility rather than personal responsibility lying at the basis of social responsibility. More important, issues of practicality come into play. In some (perhaps many) cases, there is great difficulty in arriving at consensual definitions and consequently in executing personal responsibility. For this reason, Harmon argues, mechanisms of accountability are still required for the more extreme cases. One is left with the impression of a contingency model of value: that is, wherever possible, personal responsibility framed in a context of mutual understanding should be the basis for administrative action. However, since such an approach is only rarely possible, traditional mechanisms of accountability must be followed in most cases. (A similar confusion arises where Harmon argues that "organization structures must be free of superior-subordinate relationships," but does not reject systems of hierarchical accountability, which he defends in terms of the practical difficulties of working without hierarchy [pp. 103, 107].) In any case, Harmon sees a tension between accountability and discretion that requires a continual "negotiation of meaning."

Role of the Action Theorist

The role of the action theorist who, in working with specific practical problems, becomes an action "therapist" is to assist in this process in order to facilitate cooperative action (Harmon, 1981, p. 180). The theorist becomes one who seeks to clarify the meanings, intentions, and values of administrative actors in order to help administrators better understand one another. Presumably, when clarity is achieved, and especially where disaggregated decisions are possible, consensual decision-making rules will permit mutually satisfactory solutions.

In any case, the building of theory must be based on the world as conceived by the administrator. To the extent that the administrative theorist imposes a particular view on the administrator's world, the theorist does injustice to the active social concept of the individual. But, certainly, one might ask whether accepting the administrator's own view of the world enables one to critically evaluate that view. Harmon would seem to agree that individuals may be led to the acceptance of false ideologies, particularly as they are subject to domination by others who impose a sense of reality on them; yet, if this is the case, the mere acceptance of the administrator's own view conceals the bias, the ideology, implicit in that view. And, if that view limits the freedom and creativity of the individual, it should be subject to critique. At this point, the approach based on phenomenology would seem to be limited. Harmon's acceptance of an epistemology based on phenomenology would appear, in the end, to undercut his argument for a more critical perspective on administrative life. In order to achieve such a perspective, one must go a step further to investigate what has been called a critical theory of public organizations.

■ ■

CRITICAL SOCIAL THEORY: JURGEN HABERMAS

The critical perspective recognizes that a certain tension exists between our own strivings and the limitations imposed on us by social conditions, even those conditions of which we are only vaguely aware. The role of theory is to reveal these contradictions and thus permit us to pursue our own freedom. "Critical thinking . . . is motivated today by the effort really to transcend the tension and to abolish the opposition between the individual's purposefulness, spontaneity, and rationality and those work-process relationships on which society is built. Critical thought has a concept of man as in conflict with himself until this opposition is removed" (Horkheimer, 1972, p. 210). Since this revelation provides the opportunity for emancipation, it is inevitably connected to action in pursuit of the true needs and desires of the individual.

In contemporary times, the critical perspective has been elaborated by a number of major scholars, most prominently Jurgen Habermas, who has attempted the most comprehensive restatement of the critical position (see Habermas, 1970, 1974, 1975, 1979; also Bernstein, 1976, and McCarthy, 1978). Through the work of Habermas, supplemented by that of other theorists, we will consider several aspects of the critical approach of particular relevance to the study of public organizations. (A sampling of other works of relevance to the critical perspective is contained in Arato and Gebhardt [1978].) Specifically, we will examine (1) the critique of instrumental reason, (2) the scientization of political life and the reduction of the public sphere, and (3) the relationship between knowledge, effective communication and human interests.

Critique of Instrumental Reason

Members of the Frankfurt School, an institute created in the early 1920s for the investigation of a critical theory of society, sought to expose the roots of social domination in modern life, thus opening the way for the eventual realization of freedom through reason. But, in this task, they immediately encountered a challenge to reason itself, or, more precisely, a redefinition of the basis for social rationality (Jay, 1973). Max Horkheimer, the school's administrative and intellectual leader, discusses this issue by contrasting two modes of reasoning. Most of the great philosophical systems, he argues, assume reason to be a principle existing objectively in nature by which one can evaluate the reasonableness of one's actions. Reason, in this sense, guides social choice and speaks in the language of justice and freedom, violence and oppression. In contrast to this mode of rationality, Horkheimer (1974, p. 18) points to the rise of a more instrumental form concerned simply with the most favorable (meaning "efficient") means to attain a given end.

Herbert Marcuse (1968) points out the limitations of the modern interpretation of reason in a critique of Weber. Specifically, he argues that Weber's notion of rationality as concerned with the way in which means are developed to attain presupposed ends not only removes from discussion the various social interests being served by allegedly rational institutions but also elaborates patterns of technical control, "methodical, scientific, calculated, calculating control" (pp. 223–224). Since existing modes of technology imply domination, Weber's notion of rationalization becomes not critical but apologetic, in the sense that acts may be justified through their contribution to technically rational action (pp. 214–215). In place of reasoned contemplation and enlightened action, we are to be content with the limited task of finding technical solutions to the design problems of the existing social machinery.

Habermas extends Marcuse's critique of Weber by examining the alternatives one might propose to an extended rationalization of society. Both agree that Weber's dependence on a technical definition of rationality ultimately constitutes an ideological justification of the extension of domination, but they are even more concerned with Weber's description of this outcome as inevitable. They argue, to the contrary, that an alternative scenario may be developed, since human institutions are socially constructed and therefore may be reconstructed by conscious choice and effective action. Whereas Marcuse sees the possibility of altering the conditions of domination described by Weber in a new mode of science and technology, one offering a different relationship between man and nature, Habermas (1970, ch. 6) suggests instead that science and technique as defined in the modern world are inevitably associated with purposive-rational action. The effort proposed by Habermas involves restoring an alternative structure of action, that of symbolic or communicative interaction, to its proper status.

By "purposive-rational action," Habermas means the field of work seen in terms of instrumental action in pursuit of given goals. The preoccupation of purposive-rational action is technique, the solution of means-ends problems. By "interaction," on the other hand, Habermas (p. 92) describes the building of the normative structure of society, one "governed by binding consensual norms, ... which must be understood and recognized by ... interacting subjects." Social systems may therefore be distinguished according to whether purposive-rational action or interaction predominates.

Habermas argues that the translation from traditional to modern capitalist societies described by Weber's concept of rationalization is marked by a shift in the basis for social legitimation. In traditional societies, the field of purposive-rational action is so fully embedded in the normative structure of society that it rarely threatens the efficacy of cultural traditions. In emerging capitalist societies, however, for the first time, there is a guarantee of permanent economic growth, and, consequently, the field of purposive-rational action becomes self-sustaining. "In this way, traditional structures are increasingly subordinated to conditions of instrumental or strategic rationality: the organization of labor and trade, the network of transportation, information, and communication, the institutions of private law, and, starting with financial administration, the state bureaucracy" (Habermas, 1970, p. 98). The possibility then arises that the field of symbolic or communicative interaction will eventually become lost in the emerging field of purposive-rational action.

Reduction of the Public Sphere

Such a development would have important implications for the political system. In an early essay, Habermas (1974) describes the "public sphere" as that arena in which the various interests in society engage in discourse related to the establishment of the normative agenda for society (see also Pranger, 1968). In recent times, the public sphere has been considerably narrowed, to the point that the interests being voiced tend to be those of hierarchical superiors in business, labor, and the professions, mediated or administered by the mass media. Such a delimitation of the public sphere is consistent with a subjugation of political power to a purposive-rational intent. Under these conditions, the field of politics is no longer required to concern itself with the normative structure of society, with the relationship of society to the "good life," and so forth. These concerns are now subordinated to the new tasks of politics, which are to secure the private form of capital utilization, to facilitate the growth of the economy, and to bind the loyalty of the masses to their new condition. Politics, in this new interpretation, is oriented toward eliminating the risks and dysfunctions associated with capital production. "Government activity is restricted to administratively soluble technical questions, so that practical questions evaporate, so to speak" (Habermas, 1970, p. 103). (In this context, practical questions are those that guide social practice, not simply those that are pragmatic.)

Obviously, the increasing preoccupation of government with solving technical problems has special implications for notions of democratic citizenship, for public discussion is not required in order to solve technical questions; indeed, the involvement of the masses may be dysfunctional. Thus, the reduction of the public sphere results in a general depoliticization of the citizenry. Their role is no longer one of aiding in the choice of social directions but one of occasionally choosing between alternative sets of administrative personnel, whose function in turn is to deal effectively with those problems that impede the smooth operation of the social and economic system. All of this is explained, as Marcuse (1964) points out, by the logic of scientific and technical progress and is made more palatable by the promise of increasing goods and services for all. Most important, Habermas (1970, p. 105) comments, "it is the singular achievement of this ideology to detach society's self-understanding from the frame of reference of communicative action and from the concepts of symbolic interaction and replace it with a scientific model." The result is a new consciousness in which the world is viewed in terms of technique.

Restoring Undistorted Communication

In the critical view, however, the connection between theory and practice, once severed by traditional theory, is reestablished. Habermas (1970, pp. 274–300) illustrates this process through an examination of Freudian psychoanalysis as a critical discipline. Habermas interprets repression, the central concept in psychoanalysis, as the privatization of language, the withdrawal of certain symbols from public communication to a place where they are inaccessible to, but still influence, the ego. The resulting power struggle or internal disturbance affects the individual, but in ways of which he or she is unaware. The task of analysis is to reestablish effective intrapersonal communications by restoring a part of the patient's hidden life history. This result is achieved through a strictly personal process aimed at rediscovering one's self and confirmed as correct in its interpretation only by the patient. In this way, inquiry and autonomy become one: "In self-reflection, knowledge for the sake of knowledge attains congruence with the interest in autonomy and responsibility" (p. 314).

Whether speaking of the individual or the society, Habermas argues that the key is the restoration of undistorted communication. In his more recent work, Habermas (1979) has sought to specify a theory of communicative competence, or a "universal pragmatics"; he suggests that the very act of speech itself provides the basis for a reconstruction of autonomous existence (pp. 1–68). "The human interest in autonomy and responsibility is not mere fancy, for it can be apprehended a priori. What raises us out of nature is the only thing whose nature we can know: language. Through its structure, autonomy and responsibility are posited for us. Our first sentence expresses unequivocally the intention of universal and unconstrained consensus."

Truly rational action can only occur by removing restrictions on communication, including the restriction that most often distorts our attempts to arrive at consensus, domination. Where communication patterns are asymmetrical, that is, where one party to the communication has power over the other, inevitable distortions occur, in social life just as in the individual psyche. These distortions must be revealed prior to any process of emancipation. "Public, unrestricted discussion, free from domination, of the suitability and desirability of action-orienting principles and norms, . . . such communication at all levels of political and repoliticized decision-making processes is the only medium in which anything like 'rationalization' is possible" (1979, pp. 118-119). Through a process of generalized, critical self-reflection, we may restore the intimacy of theory and practice needed for enlightened human action, that is, praxis.

■   ■

TOWARD A CRITICAL ANALYSIS OF PUBLIC ORGANIZATIONS

Although few explicit attempts have been made to apply critical analysis to the study of public organizations (but see Dunn and Fozouni, 1976; Hummel, 1976), several questions raised in the literature of critical theory bear on such an effort (see, for example, Burrell and Morgan, 1979). Habermas, like Weber, illustrates the operation of technical rationality through reference to the public bureaucracy, for the sphere of state administration epitomizes the concern for technique and efficiency that is becoming increasingly more pervasive in society in general. At the same time, as critical theorists and others have noted, increasing amounts of social power and discretion are being concentrated in the public bureaucracy. The convergence of these trends—increasing power being placed at the disposal of basically technical interests—amounts to an implicit redefinition of the role of the public bureaucracy and thus raises important questions that might well be addressed from a critical perspective.

In a time when the intentions of bureaucrats are not clearly understood and are even held suspect by the public, there is ample reason to be concerned about the continued legitimacy of the public service. Today the very presence of public officials elicits distrust in some and outright hostility in others, a situation that implies at least a perceived lack of congruence between the interests of bureaucrats and those of the public. But perhaps the contradiction of interests that appears to exist is in fact based on systematically distorted communications between the various parties. Under these circumstances, the analysis of structural limitations in communicative practices called for by critical theory would seem a useful place to begin. Specifically, a critical theory of public organizations would examine the technical basis of bureaucratic domination and the ideological justifications for this condition, and would ask in what ways members and clients of public bureaucracies might better understand the resultant limitations placed on their actions and in turn develop new modes of administrative praxis.

Such an approach to public organization would first construct its understanding of the formulation and implementation of public policy on a value-critical basis, placing such questions in the larger historical and normative context in which they properly reside. It would seek to lay the foundations for greater autonomy and responsibility both within the bureaucracy and in its interactions with others. Moreover, a critical approach would insist on highlighting those aspects of bureaucratic theory and practice that serve to limit the individual's recognition of and contribution to the process of governing. In contrast to the current restrictive relationships within the bureaucracy and the excessively depersonalized treatment of those outside, a critical approach would see an essential connection between personal and societal self-reflection, on the one hand, and personal and societal development (including so-called organizational learning), on the other (see Argyris and Schon, 1978).

In contrast to the emphasis on order and regulation that we find in the mainstream literature in public administration, a critical approach would emphasize the conditions of power and dependence that characterize contemporary organizational life and the considerable potential for conflict and disorder that these conditions portend. Such an approach would enable us to rethink issues of organizational change in dialectical terms, as a consequence of competing forces operating in a linguistic context, and would thus permit a more dynamic understanding of organizational life. Moreover, such an approach would reveal certain contradictions inherent in hierarchical organizations. By specifying the ways in which current relationships of power and dependence result in alienation and estrangement, a critical theory of public organizations would suggest more direct attempts to improve the quality of organizational life (see Denhardt, 1981, ch. 6).

One avenue for accomplishing this analysis would be to focus on the flawed patterns of communication that now mark both internal and external relationships in public organizations. Hierarchical relationships between managers and subordinates and between bureaucrats and clients obviously restrict the possibility for entering into discussions in which the various parties to the communications are considered equals. To analyze and to reorder those linguistic patterns that now limit our interactions might permit the expression of values previously repressed.

For example, the critical approach might suggest an alternative style of management aimed not at control but rather at assisting individuals (members or clients) in discovering and pursuing their own developmental needs, even recognizing that these may sometimes be at odds with those of the dominant values of the bureaucracy. (If we assume that the bureaucracy and the society share the same dominant values, this approach might seem problematic; however, since bureaucracies take on a life and values of their own, we have reason to question the correspondence of organizational values with those of the society at large.) What Brian Fay (1977, p. 206) has referred to as an "educative" mode of inquiry assumes that "repressive and frustrating social conditions exist at least partly because people are systematically unclear about their needs and the nature of their social relationships." His educative approach seeks to assist people in determining their true needs as well as the social conditions that prevent fulfillment of those needs. Through self-reflection, persons may achieve new clarity about the distorted conditions under which they live, thus permitting them to act to alter those conditions. Similarly, an educative style of management would seek to assist individuals in discovering and then pursuing their own needs and interests, a situation that would open greater spaces for communication and normative dialogue among the organization's members.

These same considerations would apply with perhaps even more force to the relationships between bureaucrats and their clients. A dialectical understanding of these relationships would point out the way in which members of bureaucracies exercise power over clients, subject clients to rigid and depersonalized procedures, and limit, through cooptation and other devices, the contribution clients might make to the operation of the agency. (A critical view would, of course, recognize that such acts do not necessarily occur with malicious intent on the part of individual bureaucrats but occur rather as a consequence of structural deficiencies.) For citizens, such clients are both producers and consumers of government services.

To give priority to the developmental needs of all parties, both bureaucrats and clients, is to reaffirm a commitment to democratization of social relationships of all types and to focus on the distortions that have prevented the true needs of individuals from being expressed through organized social and political action. In an age when the public sphere has been transformed into a field of competition among group interests, the internal democratization of those groups, including the public bureaucracy, provides one possible way of maintaining a commitment to democratic processes. Moreover, democratized structures would represent the interests and values of a substantially greater proportion of the citizenry than are presently engaged in public dialogue, to some extent restoring a proper relationship between purposive-rational and communicative interaction. Under such conditions, the public bureaucracy might even become a primary vehicle for societal self-reflection and critique.

■ ———————————————————————————————— ■

REFERENCES

Arato, Andrew, and Gebhardt, Eike, eds. *The Essential Frankfurt School Reader.* New York: Urizen Books, 1978.

Argyris, Chris, and Schon, David A. *Organizational Learning: A Theory of Action Perspective.* Reading, Mass.: Addison-Wesley, 1978.

Berger, Peter L., and Luckmann, Thomas. *The Social Construction of Reality.* New York: Doubleday, 1966.

Bernstein, Richard. *The Restructuring of Social and Political Theory.* New York: Harcourt, Brace Jovanovich, 1976.

Burrell, Gibson, and Morgan, Gareth. *Sociological Paradigms and Organizational Analysis,* London: Heinemann, 1979.

Dahl, Robert A., and Lindblom, Charles E. *Politics, Economics, and Welfare.* Chicago: University of Chicago Press, 1976.

Denhardt, Robert B. *In the Shadow of Organization*. Lawrence: Regents Press of Kansas, 1981.

Dunn, William N., and Fozouni, Bahman. *Toward a Critical Administrative Theory*. Beverly Hills, Calif.: Sage, 1976.

Fay, Brian. "How People Change Themselves." In *Political Theory and Praxis*, edited by Terence Ball, pp. 200–233. Minneapolis: University of Minnesota Press, 1977.

Fay, Brian. *Social theory and Political Practice*. London: George Allen and Unwin, 1977.

Golembiewski, Robert T. *Public Administration as a Developing Discipline*. New York: Marcel-Dekker, 1977.

Habermas, Jurgen. *Knowledge and Human Interests*. Translated by Jeremy J. Shapiro. Boston: Beacon Press, 1970.

Habermas, Jurgen. *Theory and Practice*. Translated by John Viertel. Boston: Beacon Press, 1974a.

Habermas, Jurgen. "The Public Sphere." *New German Critique*, 1974b, *3*, pp. 49–55.

Habermas, Jurgen. *Legitimation Crisis*. Translated by Thomas J. McCarthy. Boston: Beacon Press, 1975.

Habermas, Jurgen. *Communication and the Evolution of Society*. Translated by Thomas J. McCarthy. Boston: Beacon Press, 1979.

Harmon, Michael M. *Action Theory for Public Administration*. New York: Longman, 1981.

Horkheimer, Max. "Traditional and Critical Theory." In *Critical Theory: Selected Essays*, translated by Matthew J. O'Connell, et al. pp. 188–243. New York: Seabury Press, 1972.

Horkheimer, Max. *Eclipse of Reason*. New York: Seabury Press, 1974.

Hummel, Ralph. *The Bureaucratic Experience*. New York: St. Martin's Press, 1976.

Jay, Martin. *The Dialectical Imagination: A History of the Frankfurt School and the Institute of Social Research, 1923–1950*. Boston: Little, Brown, 1973.

Jung, Hwa Yol. "The Political Relevance of Existential Phenomenology." *Review of Politics*, October 1971, *33*(4), pp. 538–563.

Kirkhart, Larry. "Toward a Theory of Public Administration." In *Toward a New Public Administration*, edited by Frank Marini, pp. 127–164. San Francisco: Chandler, 1971.

McCarthy, Thomas J. *The Critical Theory of Jurgen Habermas*. Cambridge, Mass.: M.I.T. Press, 1978.

Marcuse, Herbert. *One Dimensional Man*. Boston: Beacon Press, 1964.

Marcuse, Herbert. "Industrialization and Capitalism in the Work of Max Weber." In *Negations: Essays in Critical Theory*, translated by Jeremy J. Shapiro, pp. 201–226. Boston: Beacon Press, 1968.

Maslow, Abraham. *Toward a Psychology of Being*. New York: D. Van Nostrand, 1962.

Maslow, Abraham. *The Farther Reaches of Human Nature*. New York: Viking Press, 1971.

Natanson, Maurice. *Edmund Husserl: Philosopher of Infinite Tasks*. Evanston, Ill.: Northwestern University Press, 1967.

Ostrom, Vincent. *The Intellectual Crisis In American Public Administration*. University: University of Alabama Press, 1974.

Pranger, Robert J. *The Eclipse of Citizenship*. New York: Holt, Rinehart and Winston, 1968.

Ramos, Alberto Guerreiro. *The New Science of Organizations*. Toronto: University of Toronto Press, 1981.

Schutz, Alfred. *The Phenomenology of the Social World*. Translated by George Walsh and Frederick Lehnert. Evanston, Ill.: Northwestern University Press, 1967.

Scott, William G., and Hart, David K. *Organizational America*. Boston: Houghton Mifflin, 1979.

Silverman, David. *The Theory of Organisations*. New York: Basic Books, 1971.

Waldo, Dwight. "Organization Theory: An Elephantine Problem." *Public Administration Review,* Autumn 1961, *21*(4), pp. 210–225.

Waldo, Dwight. "Scope of the Theory of Public Administration." In *Theory and Practice of Public Administration: Scope, Objectives, and Methods,* edited by James C. Charlesworth, pp. 1–26. Philadelphia: American Academy of Political and Social Science, 1968.

White, Jay D. *"A Critique of Reason in Public Policy and Policy Analysis."* Unpublished dissertation, George Washington University, 1982.

Whyte, William H., Jr. *The Organization Man.* Simon & Schuster, 1956.

8

THE PRACTITIONER
AS THEORIST

Thus far, a number of important contributions to public administration theory have been reviewed, and, hopefully, the complexity of the issues faced by anyone involved with public organizations has been appreciated. Theory, of course, requires complexity; it demands that we examine all sides, that we seek explanation and understanding, that we look both to the past and to the future. But theory also requires simplicity, requires that we select those issues that are of greatest importance to us (and be clear about how we made our choices); that we bring together and synthesize those concerns; and that we find a satisfactory way of relating our theories to our actions. As we each build our own theory of public organization, we inevitably develop perspectives that are simultaneously complex and simple.

But how can we possibly hold perspectives that are both complex and simple? Even more to the point, how can we possibly bring together such apparent opposites as politics and administration, efficiency and responsiveness, fact and value, autonomy and responsibility, theory and practice? Certainly, the task is not easy. Indeed, the seemingly paradoxical nature of theory building is exactly why some students of public administration find theory so intractable. How nice it would be if we could find a carefully worked-out theory that would answer all our questions and provide a comfortable and secure basis for our actions. Students seek answers (and some theorists even encourage this by pretending they have answers), but, in the end, there are no permanent answers for those seeking guides to action. At best, there are only questions and directions—hopefully, the right questions and directions.

At this point, in many books on theory, the author, having pointed out the weaknesses of earlier works in the field, would attempt to provide a new answer, a new theory of public organization. I will not attempt to present such a theory. Instead, I would like to make a few comments about the process of theory building itself and share some concerns that have been and continue to be important to me as an administrator and a theorist in building my own theory of public organization. Perhaps there will be issues here that you, the reader, might also wish to pursue as you seek a satisfactory framework for your actions. At a minimum, we should identify the questions we both must answer.

THEORIES AND THEORY BUILDING

By reading this far, you have implicated yourself as one concerned with those issues that have traditionally occupied the attention of public administration theorists. As inevitably you must, you will build and rebuild your own theory of public organization many times. The way in which you do this, the choices you make and the relationships you develop, will guide your actions in your day-to-day work in public organizations. Your theories will provide a context and a direction for your actions. You will develop a perspective and, by developing a perspective, you will be able to think of your work as meaningful. The continuing process of constructing your own theory of public organization will be among the most important and possibly most subtle tasks of your career.

Importance of Theory For Practitioners

But, of course, the importance of theory, which I stress here, is something thoughtful practitioners have always recognized. While I was working on this book, for example, a number of prominent persons in the field of public administration visited our campus for discussions with our faculty and students. Among these were the regional director of the Office of Personnel Management, the city manager of San Antonio, Texas, the director of the Council of State Governments, and the budget director of the State of Missouri. In every case, without excessive prompting from the faculty, these practitioners emphasized the importance of theory for public administration education. They seemed to be saying that the basic techniques of administration are of only passing importance. What endures in their work is the context, the sense of meaning that theory provides. The difference between a good manager and an extraordinary manager lies not in one's technical skill but in one's sense of one's self and one's surroundings, a sense that can only be derived through thoughtful reflection, through theory.

Many faculty who have been involved in teaching both preservice and in-service students in master's programs in public administration have come to recognize the importance of theory to practitioners. They report, often somewhat to their surprise, that in-service students (practitioners) are much more interested in theory than preservice students. Although one might expect that students just out of undergraduate programs might be more academically inclined, and practitioners involved in the work of public agencies might be more interested in technique, exactly the opposite seems to be the case. My own explanation for this is that preservice students have the idea that administrative life revolves around technical or nuts-and-bolts skills. But in-service students recognize that such skills are only the beginning and that the really difficult concerns have to do with the context of administration.

From the standpoint of the practitioner, therefore, the problem is not whether or not to be concerned with theory but rather how to locate or construct theories that provide useful guides for action. Practitioners want guidance as to how they might carry out their work more effectively, and they want a context through which they can sustain their identity. They want to know how what they are doing fits into the larger picture. Yet many practitioners claim that existing theories are inadequate for this purpose. The works of the classical theorists do not seem to comprehend or to explain the experiences of practitioners.

As an administrator myself, I share that discomfort. I find few theories of public organization that are directly helpful on first reading. The experiences I have are not made immediately vivid or complete by my review of the classics of public administration. Yet I sense that the work of many theorists would enhance my own work if I could personally engage their theories and make them meaningful in terms of my own experience. This view suggests that the development of more effective approaches to theory building lies in the capacity of both practitioners and theorists for reflection and learning.

Again, this approach does not diminish the importance of theory itself, but it does suggest a problem in our past efforts to develop theories of public organizations. In the traditional or mainstream model of theory and practice, theories are developed independent of practice, then passed on to the practitioners, who seek to apply them in whatever ways seem appropriate. The practitioner is not a part of the process of theory building; the theorist is not a part of the work of the organization. Consequently, the match between theory and practice is at best imperfect, at worst totally unsuitable.

The problem in the past has been not a failure of theory but a failure of theory building.

Personal Learning and Theory Building

To develop more effective approaches to theory, we must make a clear statement of why existing efforts at theory building—the building of either formal or implicit theories—have failed to provide the guidance we require, and we must seek new approaches to theory building that will permit more cooperative and more relevant efforts by both practitioners and theorists. Surprisingly, the first task may be the more difficult of the two. Although practitioners (and, believe it or not, theorists) often complain about the irrelevance of existing theories, they are hard-pressed to specify exactly what is missing. (We should note that some of these complaints are simply complaints about excessive quantification or jargon in academic research. Although I am a theorist, I am critical of such tendencies myself—they belong neither in theory nor in practice, and, in any case, they are not the real issue.) Many feel a certain discontent but find it difficult to say exactly what went wrong in the theory-building process. To my mind, the corrective lies in a personal approach to building theories of action.

Let me again illustrate from my own experience. I do not sit around my house at night and wonder where my theory went wrong. I wonder about my practice. I wonder about my failure to understand the viewpoint of a particular department chair or my exasperation at the arbitrary decisions of an administrative committee. But, when I think about practice, when I think about the particular experiences of the day, I always view them retrospectively. Since my concern is with action in the future, such thoughts are necessarily confining. After all, I know that exactly the same situation will never be repeated in exactly the same way.

At the same time, I know that similar situations may, and likely will, occur. Consequently, if I can move from the immediate experience of the day to reflect and to generalize about the future, I will be more effectively served. If I can analyze my experience, if I can compare it with the experiences of others, if I can look to existing research (including existing theoretical research) for guidance, then I may be able to develop a perspective that will satisfactorily guide my actions in the future.

To put all that has been said thus far in more formal terms: theory and practice seem to be connected in the process of personal learning. As individuals live and work in public organizations, as they read and inquire about the work of others in such organizations, they build a body of experience that is extremely valuable for practice. However, until that body of material is analyzed, reflected on, and generalized into theory, it is really not useful for action. To build a theory is to learn a new way of viewing the world; indeed, it is to construct a new reality for our lives and our work. The process of theory building is a process of learning. Therefore, any approach to action in public organizations must encompass not only a theory of organization but a theory of learning as well.

In order to move beyond the limitations of these efforts, I would suggest that we redirect our thinking by conceiving of our effort as one of building theories of public organization, not theories of government administration, and by seeking theories of action that balance our concern for organizational questions with our concern for learning. Let us examine each of these issues in terms of our administrative experiences and in terms of new approaches to theory building that might inform those experiences.

■ _____ ■

TOWARD THEORIES OF PUBLIC ORGANIZATION

Let me again share with you some of my personal concerns as an administrator. When I consider my administrative role, a notion of democratic responsibility weighs heavily on my mind. Yet that notion is not the one prescribed by traditional theories of legislative accountability. Rather, it suggests the infinite ways in which I as an administrator can respond to the needs and wants of those with whom I work. The theory of democratic responsibility that I require far exceeds that offered by most public administration theorists in the past. I am not sure what the alternative might be—but I know it must recognize my role as one who reacts to, interprets, expresses, and even evokes the public interest. It recognizes that public organizations are a different breed because they express public, not private, values.

I also often wonder how change occurs, how I manage change, and whether I always even recognize change. I quickly lose confidence in theories that prescribe cures for administrative "problems," for I recognize that what are problems to administrators are prerogatives, even pleasures, to other people. For example, I have a problem with a certain director in our organization. But is that his problem or mine? In either case, I believe that the problem cannot be resolved simply through an exercise of control on my part; rather, in order to be durable and effective, my response must be communicative and consensus seeking. It must enable action.

Connecting Values and Actions

Both my concern for responsibility and my concern for change are influenced by my commitment to democratic processes and procedures. But this theoretical commitment cannot stand apart from the psychological considerations required to actualize it. To act in accord with democratic processes of equity and participation is very difficult for managers in our society. Especially in matters involving some interpersonal tension, a democratic approach to administration opens one and one's vulnerabilities to others. To do this, one must have a high degree of personal security as well as a firm understanding of where one stands and what one is about. One must have a very personal kind of theory.

To connect the value commitments we hold and the actions we take in public organizations suggests the need not only for greater precision but also for greater flexibility in the frameworks through which we act. This point returns us to the limiting assumptions (discussed in the first chapter) under which the study of public organizations has operated in the past— that public administration is government administration and that public administration is primarily concerned with large hierarchical structures. We noted that not only have these ideas limited the range of organizational designs studied by theorists of public organization, but they have also brought into question whether such a study can even aspire to any theoretical coherence.

This issue can be viewed in terms of both the political and intellectual heritage of public administration. In my view, public administration theory has been limited in its consideration of political issues by either an explicit or an implicit policy–administration dichotomy. The idea is that political decisions will guide the work of administrative agencies and that moral accountability should only be conceived in hierarchical terms, in terms of the responsiveness of agencies to elected public officials. Especially as they have been content to define public administration as government administration, theorists have retained remnants of the policy–administration dichotomy and the limited view of democratic governance that it implies.

But the problem is magnified when seen in terms of the intellectual heritage of public administration theory. Those in public organizations have a direct impact on the lives of individuals, not only as they execute orders given from above but also as they act on their own in pursuit of public purposes. Moreover, the growth of public organizations has meant that these organizations affect their members and clients simply by virtue of their size, complexity, and impersonality. The proper moral basis for public organization, therefore, is not contained in the hierarchical relationship between agencies and legislatures but is one that must be faced directly.

We have seen that political science as a discipline fails to comprehend the full range of concerns of those in public organizations and particularly fails to give full consideration to organizational and managerial issues. We have also noted that the field of organizational analysis is limited, failing to adequately comprehend the moral context of public organization. And some have argued that public administration is merely a profession that can never attain theoretical significance but must always borrow from other disciplines—which simply means that theories will never exactly correspond to practice.

Managing Change in Pursuit of Public Values

A discipline, both in the academic sense and in the practical sense, is formed by the possibility of theoretical coherence within a given field. It is now possible to develop such coherence in the study of public organizations by centering on those in public organizations as managing change in pursuit of publicly defined societal values. Such a definition suggests an integration of the perspectives provided by political science and organization analysis (as well as those of other disciplines that contribute to the study) by acknowledging the importance of change processes in organizational contexts and the responsibility of managers to deal effectively with such processes. At the same time, it suggests the important role of those in public organizations in influencing public life and their responsibility to manage such an impact in a way consistent with democratic standards.

To define our study in this way obviously permits us to embrace the traditional concerns of public administration theory but also to suggest that public administration be considered part of the larger study of public organization. The theories of public organization described in this book have been developed within the tradition of public administration theory in this country. Yet these works suggest implications for the more general organizational society in which we live. To the extent that large and complex organizations dominate the social and political landscape, it is appropriate to ask whether all such organizations should be so governed as to maintain our commitments to freedom, justice and equality. The question then becomes not, "How should we view the operations of government agencies?" but rather, "How might organizations of all kinds be made more public, more democratic, and better able to express the values of our society?"

Certainly, major aspects of public policy today are being decided or seriously affected by so-called private agencies. Many of these private organizations far exceed, in their size and complexity, governments in other places and previous governments in this country. Modern organizations— government or nongovernment—have an enormous impact on the personal lives of individuals in our society. As the nation-state has in many ways given way to the conglomerate, the relationship between state and citizen, organization and client, is becoming very close. This trend suggests that all organizations be evaluated by the degree of their publicness, the degree to which they express societal values defined publicly rather than privately. In such an effort, public administration theory, especially theories of democratic administration, might come to be a model for organization theory generally.

Such a viewpoint directly suggests what public administration theorists in the past have often resisted: that public organizations should be required by definition to act in accord with democratic procedures and to seek democratic outcomes. For we commit ourselves to the expression of publicly defined societal values if we can do no less. Therefore, a theory of democratic administration, a semineglected counterpoint in public administration theory, must now come to the forefront. The work of such theorists as Waldo, Golembiewski, Ostrom, Harmon, Denhardt, and the new public administrationists all point in this direction. Although this work has, from time to time, been pushed aside in the rush toward science and technique, it remains very important to the field of public organizations today, for it best expresses the moral commitment of our discipline. And it is the moral commitment that is implied in human action that practitioners cannot escape.

ORGANIZATION AND PERSONAL LEARNING

Administrators need extraordinary flexibility in the way they approach organizational questions; they need to be able to change, to adapt, to learn. Unfortunately, existing approaches to theory building tend to restrict an administrator's options rather than enhance them. For example, implicit in the positive science approach is the idea of a structured world behaving according to regular laws expressing functional imperatives. The mode of action suggested by this approach is hierarchical, structured, and authoritarian. (Please note that these are hardly the watchwords of democratic governance. Hopefully, public organizations are guided by theoretical inclinations toward understanding and consensus, communication and involvement.) If the range of responses is limited in this way, theory is constraining rather than enabling.

More important, existing approaches to theory building may inappropriately model the process of knowledge acquisition and thereby limit learning. By viewing the world as constituted independently of our participation in it, mainstream social science theory concentrates on explanations or understandings of existing phenomena. But the administrative world is constructed and reconstructed through the actions and interactions of individuals and groups. Consequently, those permanently "valid" explanations of mainstream science are only valid within the context of a particular construction of reality. They do not allow and certainly do not encourage the possibility of change, the possibility that we might alter existing realities. Yet, as we saw earlier, change is not only inevitable but necessary. The very necessity of change requires an approach to learning different from the one prescribed or modeled by mainstream social science.

Similarly, most approaches to theory building currently in use seem unable to handle the synthesis of opposites like those mentioned at the beginning of this chapter. By assuming that the social world, the world of administrative action, is ordered in such a way that causal relationships can be determined, theorists emphasize the resolution of such concerns. They seek the "right answer." By making a different assumption, however—that the social world is marked by conflict and change—we can accommodate opposites as being in a constant state of tension with one another. We come then to focus more on process issues, patterns and relationships constantly working themselves out in our lives and in the lives of others. To work with such issues, to accept their ebb and flow, to move with the currents of change, and to draw new lessons wherever we can is the essence of personal learning and, as such, the connection between theory and practice.

The figure below outlines the implications of various approaches to public organizations in terms of three central organizational processes: ways of knowing, ways of deciding, and ways of acting. Administrators must constantly seek information about the world, must make decisions based on their understanding of the world, and must take actions based on those decisions. To the extent that we direct our learning toward broad organizational processes such as these, our understanding of organizational life will be increased.

	Rational model	*Interpretive model*	*Critical model*
Ways of knowing	Positive social science ↓ control	Interpretive theory, phenomenology ↓ understanding	Critical social theory ↓ emancipation
Ways of deciding	Rational decision-making processes	Emotive-intuitive	Value-critical
Ways of acting	Instrumental action	Expressive action	Educative action (praxis)

Figure 8.1. Three models of administration viewed in terms of three organizational processes.

Although mainstream theory presents itself as the only available theory, many who have contributed to the intellectual and political heritage of public organizations have suggested alternative approaches. Completeness in the study of public organization requires that we be attentive to the full range of approaches available to us. In its approach to knowing, the rational model of administration employs the techniques of positive social science in seeking causal explanations based on the objective observation of human behavior. The interpretive model, on the other hand, seeks to provide an understanding of the meanings that individuals bring to organizational activities. This approach recognizes that the world of public organizations is socially constructed and focuses its attention on the way in which intersubjective meaning is constituted in that world. Finally, the critical model seeks to uncover those patterns of belief or ideology that inhibit our fullest development, either as individuals or groups in society. Whereas the rational model seeks knowledge in order to control, the interpretive model seeks understanding on which communication can be built, and the critical model seeks emancipation from the social constraints that limit our growth and development.

Each of these models implies a particular approach to decision making. The rational model places considerable emphasis on rational or cognitive processes. Decisions are made on the basis of an objective analysis of the data or information at hand. The interpretive model, however, recognizes that such objectivity is not fully descriptive of human action, nor should it be. Indeed, at times, decisions are made, and should be made, on the basis of human emotions or intuitions. The interpretive model therefore permits decision-making processes that employ different psychic approaches than the rational model. Finally, the critical model seeks an integration of these approaches through a rational analysis of one's circumstances that might provide one with the possibility of seeing the world as it really is. But our passions, our emotions, begin to move us toward more effective action. The critical model then provides a critique of the values that we hold and suggests ways in which we might more clearly establish and seek to obtain important human values, including, most prominently, the value of freedom.

Finally, each of the models implies a particular way of acting. The rational model suggests an emphasis on instrumental behaviors that contribute to meeting organizational objectives. Through the actions individuals take, control is extended. The interpretive model seeks expressive actions that permit us to reveal our normative commitments and to work with others to develop a greater sense of interpersonal understanding. Expressive actions allow us to enter into personal relationships accepting of others as they present themselves and cleansed of the tendency to objectify. Finally, the critical model suggests that individuals bring together autonomy and responsibility, communication and consensus, theory and practice, into a mode of enlightened action through which they will educate themselves and one another. The rational model suggests an educative approach to organizational life that would prove enabling rather than constricting to human action. It would provide for an enlightened approach to human action that might well be captured by the term *praxis*. In praxis, we find once again the connection between personal learning and the relationship between theory and practice. The notion of praxis implies that, as we acquire knowledge about our circumstances and as we view that knowledge in a critical manner, we are compelled to pursue more effective communication and consequently greater autonomy and responsibility. In my view, it is toward administrative praxis that practitioners as theorists must guide their theory building and their actions.

■   ■

A NEW ROLE FOR THEORISTS

I have emphasized the role of practitioners as theorists, in part because of my role as an administrator. But I also claim to be a theorist of sorts. How, then, do I see my role and the role of other theorists in building theories of organizations? Obviously, I do not feel that theorists should spend all their time and energy working out supposedly causal relationships that may or may not be of importance in the real world. Theorists need to direct their attention to actual problems, perhaps the most pressing of which is the problem of understanding how public organizations can work to the benefit of a democratic society.

Academic research has an important role to play in building a sound basis for the study of public organizations. Much of this research is frankly not directed toward practitioners, and need not be. Certain complicated and detailed questions must be examined, evidence must be gathered, and considerable discussion must take place before any impact is felt on the world of practice. This role is an appropriate one for academics, even for theorists, a role that practitioners need neither fear nor disparage. Practitioners should not, and largely do not, want theorists to be exactly like them, to see the world just as they see it. They want theorists to have a broader view, or at least to see the world from another viewpoint.

As mentioned earlier, public organizations now face a crisis of legitimacy. Citizens are questioning the efficacy of our institutions and the intentions of those who occupy them. They feel that the views of public officials are inconsistent with their own expectations. Government cutbacks, massive government deficits, and frequent intimations of scandal highlight this crisis. These conditions demand a theoretical as well as a practical response.

Many practitioners today are experiencing discouragement, frustration, and exhaustion, part of which is due to the lack of theoretical development. As Freud taught, individuals act on hidden assumptions that may be to some degree inappropriate to the world as it is encountered. Symptoms or discomforts result that the therapist may use as clues to recovering a portion of the individual's life history, thereby enabling him or her to live a fuller, more congruent life. Similarly, Marx argued that societies adopt false patterns of belief, ideologies that disguise the actual oppression under which people live. For example, although members of bureaucratic organizations may live under conditions of alienation, they may only vaguely recognize what is happening to them. They may experience their alienation as a vague sense of discomfort that is symptomatic of a misdirected framework for action.

Individuals or social groups may come to recognize the insufficiency of the theories on which they base their actions by carefully working out an understanding of the larger picture to which these symptoms or discomforts provide a clue. People require a context in which to see things as they really are, to see things in terms of the larger picture—and therefore to see things differently. In psychoanalysis, to assist in this effort is the role of the therapist. In critical social theory, to assist is the role of the theorist. The role of the theorist of public organizations is to help the actor build a theory on which new and hopefully liberating, enabling, and communicative action (praxis) can be based.

Finally our mutual concern, whether as administrators or as theorists, is to develop approaches to our work that will both allow us to see practice as it is and to see practice in perspective. Theory does not simply reflect life; it also projects life. Good theory does not merely analyze but it synthesizes a variety of elements and looks toward the future. In anticipating the future we must consider both facts and values. The future demands that we make choices, that we constantly change and adapt to new circumstances. The future demands that we learn.

From Waldo and Barnard, we learned that intelligence and compassion are required in public organizations; now, having finished our study, we can appreciate their recommendations more completely. Waldo, the proponent of intelligence, devoted his life's work to the pursuit of a theory of democratic administration; Barnard, the proponent of compassion, argued for an understanding of change not merely in terms of control but also in terms of communication and consensus. Democratic administration, Waldo's dream, seems, if anything, further away now than ever before. Today the language of productivity and efficiency seems to prevail over the language of democracy and concern. But, as we now know, the long-run viability of public institutions—indeed, the very survival of democracy itself—requires a theory of democratic governance that includes democratic administration. At the same time, the hope for a "sense of the organization," Barnard's plea, also seems outdistanced. Hierarchy, structure, and command are strong—perhaps especially strong because we take them for granted and often fail to recognize them for what they are.

Waldo and Barnard sought to resolve this dilemma by seeking to enhance the moral integrity of a few influential managers. But perhaps a broader lesson can be drawn—that public organizations exist only in a state of tension, in a state of development and, therefore, individuals must constantly be learning in order to remain up-to-date. Such an effort, in which theory and practice would be as closely integrated as learning and action, would require not only that practitioners think as theorists and vice versa but also, more important, that all recognize their mutual responsibility for the fullest and best expression of our democratic values.

■ APPENDIX ■

■ THE ADMINISTRATIVE JOURNAL ■

One of the greatest difficulties facing students and practitioners wishing to broaden their understanding of public organizations is the apparent gap between theory and practice in the field. What seems to make sense in principle does not always seem to work in practice; theories generated by academicians often bear little resemblance to the real world of the public administrator. The Administrative Journal is a practical device to aid the reader in making the connection between theory and practice in public organizations. Through careful use of the Administrative Journal, the reader should be able to bring together theories of the individual and the organization, on the one hand, and the way he or she thinks, feels, and acts in administrative situations, on the other.

The Administrative Journal is based on an approach to learning that suggests that the most significant learning about administration is grounded in, though not limited to, the experience of the individual. Whether we are students or practitioners, we all have a variety of experiences that, if used constructively, can contribute to our understanding of organizational life. We act in administrative capacities, we read and discuss theories of organizational dynamics, we study and analyze case studies, we engage in simulations and other training activities, and we come up with new ideas, even fantasies, about the possibilities for effective public action. By actively reflecting on our experiences and by drawing generalizations from them, we can learn important lessons about the way organizations work and about the way individuals act in organizational settings.

The Administrative Journal asks that we focus our attention not on the immediate tasks in which we are engaged (although these are important and provide the base for learning) but rather on the basic human processes that underlie action. We speak of the things being done as *tasks* and of the ways they are being done as *processes*. For example, to speak of the monitoring of welfare applications is to describe an organizational process. Similarly, to speak of a person engaged in learning is to describe a task; to speak of that learning as active or passive is to describe a personal process. Importantly, these process issues are the ones that administrators find most lasting. Although the tasks in which we engage change from day to day, we still find ourselves confronted with the same concerns—for communication, power and authority, and so on. The most important lessons we can learn, therefore, are those that relate to organizational processes common to many different situations.

For example, one writer has indicated six basic organizational processes that underlie the actions of individuals and organizations: communication, leadership and authority, members' roles and functions, group norms and group growth, intergroup dynamics, and decision making. Another characterization of human processes focuses on ways of knowing (how we acquire knowledge), ways of deciding (how we make choices based on the knowledge we have), and ways of acting (what specific steps or behaviors we employ to execute our choices). In any case, the Administrative Journal takes the position that our understanding of the dynamics of organizational activity will be best comprehended through attention to organizational processes.

If we suggest that learning is enhanced as we begin to generalize from our immediate experience and move from a consideration of tasks to a concern for *processes,* we can see the kind of learning pattern that results. Most of us begin with what we are doing on a day-to-day basis; we are occupied with our immediate task-related experience. But substantial learning can occur as we move toward the realm of process generalization. Here connections can be made between the data generated by our experience and theories or generalizations that can help explain that experience. Thereafter, as we approach future tasks, we do so in a more informed way; our experience has been enlightened by both our reflection and our generalization, thus enabling us to act more effectively.

Of course, in public organizations, people often get so caught up in the pressure of immediate events that their concentration remains fixed in the task-experience sector. They are concerned with meeting deadlines, with attending conferences, with negotiating various positions, and so forth, and have little time to engage in reflection and in the kind of informed learning that reflection may bring. Some learning, of course, occurs in these situations; however, the Administrative Journal suggests that much more effective use is made of our experience if we take the time to explicitly explore the underlying processes of our day-to-day experiences.

Similarly, we need to fully involve ourselves as whole personalities in the process of learning from our experiences. Since, in a real sense, we are what we learn, we must connect our learning to the innermost depths of our personalities, dealing with issues of the heart as well as the head. We must be concerned not only with what we think but with what we feel, not only with what we do but with who we are. For this reason, the Administrative Journal encourages us to consider all aspects of ourselves as we approach the learning process; it suggests that our understanding of organizational life is guided just as much by our inner experience as by our outer experience.

■ ─── ■

THE JOURNAL FORMAT

The Administrative Journal provides a practical way of transcending the immediate situation and engaging in more extensive learning by enabling us to see each experience from four different perspectives. Our approach to working in the journal is to bring ourselves to a relaxed state and then enter the journal at whatever section seems most appropriate to our experience. We first write down our thoughts as they are guided by the interests of that particular section, then move to another section and comment on the same idea or event from the standpoint of that section, and so on. As we continue to work back and forth in the various sections, we begin to establish connections between the meanings we hold and the actions we undertake. And, as we become aware of the flow of our activities, new ways to enhance our learning present themselves, and we can explore the possibilities that they hold for our lives.

The journal consists of four main sections and an Appendix, which are briefly described below. Several examples of entries appear at the end of this discussion.

I. Outer Experience

The first section of the Administrative Journal is used to record our everyday experiences as they relate to public organizations. These may include ongoing administrative work in which we are engaged, case studies, simulations or other training activities, or simply our own impressions. In this section, we briefly record a particular experience so that it can provide a basis for later reflection and generalization. The description of the experience need not be long or detailed; we need only enter enough information to enable us to recall the incident when we return to this section later. It is, however, important that we try to be as objective as possible in recording exactly what happened and that we resist the temptation to immediately evaluate our experience. One way to proceed is to assume a third-party perspective, that is, to take the position of someone outside the experience writing about the experience from that position, uninvolved and nonjudg- mental. The key to our work in this section of the Journal is to be clear, concise, and nonevaluative.

Questions that can be answered in this section include the following: What were the circumstances surrounding the experience? Who were the people involved? What was the time period? What actions did I take in this situation? What did others reveal about themselves? Am I being fully honest and completely factual in my account of what happened?

II. Reflections and Generalizations (Outer Experience)

Following both the outer experience and inner experience sections is a section for reflections and generalizations. Although the content of these sections differ, they approach the journal material in similar ways. In either case, the primary effort is to move beneath the surface of the experience in order to eventually move beyond it. In this section, we will seek a deeper understanding of the dynamics of the situation we have described, looking for clues to understanding at the individual, group, and organizational levels. As we reflect on the experience, we may be led to connections between this experience and other experiences, and we may find that we can begin to generalize our immediate experiences in terms of larger lessons. Similarly, we may find that we are aware of important theoretical material that would help our understanding of the experience. In any case, having reflected on the experience, we seek to draw out the larger, more enduring lessons for which this experience provides a ground.

Questions relevant to this section include the following: What human processes were operating in this situation? What did the experience have to do with the six dimensions of organizational process or with ways of knowing, deciding, and acting? What commentary does the experience provide concerning any of these? Based on this experience, what general advice could I give concerning the workings of organizational processes? What theoretical material have I encountered recently that would help explain this situation? Where could I look for further explanation? What persons might serve as resources for my continued learning about this type of event?

III. Inner Experience

In the outer experience section, we adopted a third-party standpoint in order to provide an objective account of our experience; in this section, we will assume a first-person stance and seek a fully subjective account. We will ask how the experience affected us—emotionally, physically, intellectually, and spiritually. Aspects of our inner life activated by the experience should be recorded here. We may, for example, have felt pleasure or pain, a sudden surge of energy or some depression, or we may have become aware of some new insight or rejected an earlier lesson.

Questions we may wish to answer here include the following: How do I feel about what is happening? What are my strongest emotions? What is my physical condition at this moment? Have there been any changes during the experience? Do I feel stress or a sense of release? Am I tense or relaxed? Do I feel intellectually alive and active, or am I more passively taking things in? What is the aesthetic sense of this moment? Does this experience in any way transcend the ordinary flow of events and take on a spiritual quality?

IV. Reflections and Generalizations (Inner Experience)

This section of reflections and generalizations again permits us to move more deeply into our experience and to establish the connections between the immediate experience and a larger view. Here we might want to answer the following questions: How does my inner experience at this moment compare with that of previous moments? What is the significance of the emotions I am now experiencing? How do these emotions compare with those I have experienced in other similar situations? Similarly, what can I understand of my present physical, intellectual, or spiritual experience at this moment? How does this relate to similar experiences? What portion of my inner experience is most prominent? Is this portion often most prevalent, or am I focusing on a part of my experience that I usually neglect? What outside sources can help me understand my inner experience at this moment? What poetry, music, or literature provides insight? What are the implications of my experience for the future?

V. The Appendix (Period of Growth)

Although most of our daily or weekly work will involve the four major sections of the journal described thus far, at some points, we will want to step back and take a broader view of the development of our learning about administration. The Appendix provides a place to record this view. One way to begin work in the Appendix is to describe the particular period of personal and professional development in which we find ourselves at present. This period may be as long as several years, as in the case of someone who has moved to a new job and has been learning about the new organization; or the period may be as short as a few days or even a few hours, as in a training session. In any case, let the period define itself. Think of an event that begins the period (for example, enrolling in an M.P.A. program) and an event that concludes it (for example, completing the program). Record that period in the Appendix and then elaborate using the following questions as a guide: What is the phase of my life and my work in which I now find myself? What is the current circumstance of my learning? What are the events that mark the beginning and may mark the end of this period? What have been the basic patterns of my experience during the period thus far? (If you have already been working in the journal for some time, the four main journal sections will provide important data to help in answering this and other questions.) What have I been doing? What have I been learning? What are my plans and expectations for the rest of the period? In what ways have they affected my learning? How do I feel about my own work during this period? In terms of my own personal development, what do I want most out of this period?

■   ■

WORKING IN THE ADMINISTRATIVE JOURNAL

In order to work most effectively in the Administrative Journal, we should find a time and place in which we are not likely to be disturbed. We begin our work by sitting quietly and letting our thoughts run freely through the events of the day. At first, in keeping with the hectic pace of administrative life, we are likely to find our minds racing from one event to another in frantic fashion. However, as we begin to relax and still our minds, thoughts will flow at a more natural pace. We will feel more comfortable with our thoughts and will be better able to sense the deeper processes of our experiences. Soon we will begin to focus on a single event or idea that we would like to use as a starting point for our work in the Administrative Journal. We turn to the appropriate section of the journal and begin to write down our thoughts, not seeking literary style but simply writing down whatever comes to mind.

Of course, many sources will provide us with beginning points for our work in the journal. Obviously, most relevant to our understanding of public organizations will be the concrete experiences we have had as members or clients of such groups. However, experiences occurring outside organizations yet involving human processes that occur in organizations (communication, decision making, etc.) may be equally important. Finally, case studies, simulations, and even imaginary situations may provide avenues into the journal. In each of these cases, it would probably be most appropriate to begin our work in the outer experiences section and then move through the other three sections in order.

This procedure, however, is by no means the only way to work in the journal. After reading a particular article or having a particular discussion about theories of organization, we might make notes in one of the sections on reflections and generalizations. After noting the theoretical material, we could then move to the experience sections, asking in each case how the theory comments on past experiences that we have had or future experiences that we project. Similarly, we might be compelled by a very emotional experience to begin with an entry in the inner experiences section of the journal that could then be elaborated in each of the other sections. In any case, movement back and forth from one section of the journal to another is essential for discovering the pattern of our work. We should therefore label each entry to provide cross-reference to entries in other sections.

The objective of the Administrative Journal is to provide a basis for making connections among the events and reflections that are part of our learning and our personal development. For this reason, we will find that the sections of the journal are by no means discrete. Considerable overlapping will occur, and the "proper" location for a particular entry may not be at all clear. Similarly, we may at first think that the individual entries themselves reveal very little about our learning, and we may feel discouraged about our work. In either case, however, we should remember that the most important results of our journal activity will appear as we begin to develop enough information to establish a sense of the continuity of our development. After we work in the journal for a period of time, we can read back through the various entries and discover recurring problems or themes, which may in turn be used as beginning entries for further journal work.

The purpose of the Administrative Journal is to aid in connecting theory and practice in our understanding of public organizations. The main sections of the journal require that we view experiences from different vantage points, thereby seeing them not only more completely but also in a way that allows us to integrate them into our own learning. By working through the various sections of the journal on a continuing basis, we will discover that our learning about organizations has a pattern of its own and that we can indeed affect the course of our own learning. And, as we become more effective in our learning, we will find rewards both in the work we do and in the pleasure we receive from that work.

Examples of Journal Entries

The following are two entries in the journal of an M.P.A. student enrolled in a class in organization theory and behavior. Note that "entry one" refers to all comments on one particular experience, and "entry two" refers to comments on a second experience. In an actual journal, all outer experience entries would be grouped together, all reflections and generalizations on the outer experience would be grouped together, and so on.

Outer experience (entry one). In one of my courses, a midterm examination was given and the class was informed that it would receive the graded paper back the next class session. During the interim one of the class members had a personal conference with the professor, in which the professor told the student his grade on the exam. The professor also volunteered that every member of the M.P.A. program taking the exam had received an A with the exception of one person. The student who had the interview mentioned this to several people, and rumors and speculation immediately started as to who might be the unfortunate person who missed the A.

Hearing the information directly from the student who had had the conference, I also spread the word. Everyone, myself included, was worried that they were the one with the B.

Reflections and observations on outer experience (entry one). The experience of anxiety produced in the class by the revelation that one student had not received an A involved many levels of the administrative process, the most important being communication and group norms. The professor was at fault for violating the norm of revealing all the class grades at the same time. However, revealing one individual's grade would not have been so bad if he had not also revealed that all members of our program except one had received As. The student was also partially to blame, as he could have kept the information to himself and should have perceived the negative impact that the revelation would have. The aforementioned factors— of the violation of norms by the professor and communications involved— are very important, as similar situations arise in any organization. The importance of the administrator analyzing the implications of his actions or communications must be stressed. The professor in this case may have been making a personal gesture of trust and friendship to the student and may have expected the student to maintain confidentiality. This gesture, however, was not perceived by the student, who used poor judgment in telling the class.

This incident also relates to Maslow's theories on motivation. For example, what initially motivated the professor to do what he did? And what motivated the student to react the way he did? Maslow states that people have certain basic needs and that unsatisfied needs motivate behavior. The professor was most probably fulfilling "social needs," which include friendship and affiliation. The student was probably fulfilling "ego needs" by letting the class know that the professor confided in him and no one else; thus, he hoped to raise his prestige and status. The class was motivated to speculate and worry because of shaken "security" and "self-actualization" needs. Again, the awareness of the potential effect of one's actions and communications should be taken into consideration. Also, it should be noted that the reaction of the class reflects the instability of an organization (i.e., the M.P.A. program) that puts undue pressure on its members to perform at unreasonably high standards. It causes instability, insecurity, and dissatisfaction with the organization.

Inner experience (entry one). I personally felt quite upset that the student told me about the grades. Like everyone else that he told, I assumed that I might be the one with the B. This caused me great anxiety. I was angry at the teacher for telling the student his grade when I didn't know my own, and I was also angry at his confiding in the student the overall M.P.A. grades. In retrospect, I was ashamed of myself for taking part in the rumor spreading; if I had it to do over again, I would not have taken part. The nervousness about the grade (which I would have to wait four days to verify) made me feel very tense emotionally, and my muscles were also tense until I was able to discover whether or not I was the unlucky person.

Reflections and observations on inner experience (entry one). I very often become tense at times of uncertainty. The insecurity of not knowing how I have done on a test, even when the odds are in my favor, is quite distressing. I also often react with feelings of anger to what I feel is bad judgment or incompetence on the part of other individuals. I am trying to make a conscious effort to be more tolerant of human errors in judgment. Intellectually, I have been quite aware of the importance of clear communication for many years. I attempt to make clear any deep or hidden meaning that I feel is important and is not being perceived. The studies of Maslow and Jung in psychology would be helpful in understanding why and how individuals are motivated to act the way they do, and the importance of clarifying deep or hidden meanings. The importance for an administrator of being aware of the aforementioned factors cannot be overstressed.

Outer experience (entry two). During the course of the last few weeks before final examinations, I was literally swamped with papers. In order to keep up with my other class work I hired a typist to type my papers for me. The typist was a personal friend and worked for very little pay yet was unreliable as far as having the work ready on the date specified. After two instances in which a paper was not ready when I needed it, I switched to a professional typist who charged twice the fee but had my papers when I wanted them.

Reflections and observations on outer experience (entry two). The experience with the typist brought home to me the importance of continual evaluation of service on many levels. The administrator must not only be concerned with quality and quantity of service but also with reliability and time deadlines. These aforementioned levels of evaluation involve the very important process of decision making. Simon, in his rational action model, notes a three-step process of decision making that includes: looking at the known alternatives available, examining the possible consequences of the alternatives, and choosing the best alternative. The personal action model stresses that the decision-making process should not be concerned with just coming up with an answer to the problem but should be creative and think of the problem in many different ways—for example, by asking, "What are we not doing that we could be doing?" By examining the problem from many angles, one does not limit oneself to the preexisting alternatives. In the case of my typist, I looked at all the alternatives available and weighed the price against the lack of reliability and subsequent aggravation. The lack of reliability and the tension and aggravation lost out, and I decided that it was worth paying more money for the comfort of knowing that I would have my papers when I needed them. In the field of administration, an analogy could be drawn to a hospital administrator who contracts with a laundry service, although its prices may be very reasonable, its sporadic reliability and quality may cause the hospital's accreditation to come into question. Therefore, the administrator should consider paying a little more for the comfort of reliability.

Inner experience (entry two). I had become extremely nervous about the unreliability of my typist friend. I usually try to have my papers finished a few days in advance of the due date, and she was barely getting them to me an hour before the class sessions were to meet. I was emotionally shaken and physically tense because of the aggravation. My father had taught me an old adage: "Fool me once, shame on you! Fool me twice, shame on me!" I had experienced the reliability problem with this typist many times in the past and decided to draw the line. After making the decision to pay more money for a more reliable typist, I felt a tremendous sense of relief, as if a weight had been lifted from my shoulders. My muscle tension dissipated, and my mind was at ease, for a change. I felt that I had taken back control of a situation that had gotten out of hand. I felt intellectually active during the decision-making process and liked that feeling much more than the feeling of passively letting things happen to me. The moment of decision took on a spiritual quality in that I felt at peace with myself.

Reflections and observations on inner experience (entry two). In the past, I have had to make similar decisions involving the weighing of one factor against another. My interest in law has probably led me to employ this balancing act in decision making more often than many people. I often weigh such factors as quality, quantity, price, time, and aggravation in making decisions. The feeling of frustration and physical and mental tension caused by a lack of control is a reoccuring theme in my life. My approach to a solution to the problem is quite often an attempt to regain control. The regaining of control alleviates almost all of my symptoms of tension and frustration. Many rock-and-roll songs deal with losing control or with being out of control and the frustration and mental anxiety that result. I often relate personally to these songs, as I strongly feel this drive for control over my life. Psychology, especially behavioristic and humanistic psychology, also delves into the human needs of security and control. Some people may like to be passive travelers on the road of life and may feel a sense of security at being led. As the Fire Sign Theater says, "We're all bozos on this bus." Personally, I would prefer to be the bus driver.

Credits

NAME INDEX

Allison, Graham T., 83–84
Anderson, James E., 139
Appleby, Paul H., 15, 48, 51, 121–122, 124
Argyris, Chris, 92, 97–101, 102

Bailey, Stephen K., 124
Bardach, Eugene, 135
Barnard, Chester, 1, 15, 93–94, 187
Berger, Peter L., 162, 164
Bernstein, Richard J., 155
Blake, Robert, 96–97

Caldwell, Lynton, 42
Cleveland, Frederick A., 50, 51
Crenson, Matthew A., 109
Cyert, Richard, 84

Dahl, Robert A., 72, 73–75, 138–139, 153
Denhardt, Robert B., 17, 154
Dickson, William, 94
Dimock, Marshall, 49, 63
Downs, Anthony, 136
Dror, Yehezkel, 119–120, 140
Dye, Thomas, 120

Easton, David, 12, 120
Edwards, George C., 137

Fay, Brian, 172–173
Finer, Herman, 125, 127
Follett, Mary Parker, 66
Frankfurt School, 167
Fredrickson, H. George, 110–111, 112
Freud, Sigmund, 21, 32–36, 38, 186
Friedrich, Carl J., 125

Gaus, John, 125
Giddens, Anthony, 28–29
Golembiewski, Robert T., 92, 101–107, 146–147
Goodnow, Frank, 45–46, 48–49, 134
Gulick, Luther, 47, 59–61, 62, 63, 64

Habermas, Jurgen, 167–171
Hamilton, Alexander, 41–42
Harmon, Michael, 163–167
Hart, David K., 112, 154
Harvard University, 94–95
Hegel, G. W. F., 21–22
Horkheimer, Max, 77, 167, 168
Husserl, Edmund, 159

Jefferson, Thomas, 41–42
Jung, Hwa Yol, 160

Kaufman, Herbert, 87–88

SUBJECT INDEX

Accountability, 125, 164–165, 166
Acting, ways of, 184–185
Actions, *see* Behavior
Action theory, 159–163, 166–167
Active social paradigm, 163–167
Activism, *see* Citizen participation
Administration (*see also* Democratic
   administration; Management;
   Organizations; Politics-administration
   dichotomy; Public administration):
   equating public and government, 15–16
   generic approach to, 13, 71
   proverbs of, 72–75
Administrative branch, 46–47, 49–50
Administrative Journal, the, 188–197
"Administrative man," the, 78–79, 80–81, 139,
   143
Administrators (*see also* Bureaucrats;
   Managers):
   authority, 59
   character, 123–124
   personal responsibility, 165–166
   significance in policy action, 48
   world view, 166–167
Affirmative action programs, 128
Alienation, 23, 24–25, 186
Alternative epistemology, 164

Antitheses, 22
Appearances, reality and, 39
Authority, 29–30, 31–32, 59, 78, 79 (*see also*
   Hierarchical structures):
   in theory of democratic administration,
   144–145
Authority-obedience approach, 96–97
Autocracy, 61–62
Autonomy, individuals':
   cultural constraints and, 35–36
   language and, 170–171
   organizational rationality at cost of, 79

Behavior, theories about, 3, 4–7, 25–26,
   32–33, 37–38, 70–81, 91–116, 158
Beliefs, limitations of, 38
Bourgeoisie, 23
Bureaucracy:
   analysis of ideal-type, 29–30
   expansion of, 30–32
   organizations defined in terms of large, 15
   policy process and, 48, 119, 120–122 (*see also*
      Policy)
   representative, 127–128 (*see also* Democratic
      administration)
Bureaucrats:
   alienation of, 186